LOVING

HIM

WELL

ALSO BY GARY THOMAS

LOVING

HIM

WELL

PRACTICAL ADVICE ON INFLUENCING YOUR HUSBAND

GARY THOMAS

Previously published as *Sacred Influence*

ZONDERVAN

Loving Him Well
Copyright © 2006, 2018 by Gary L. Thomas

Previously published as *Sacred Influence*

Requests for information should be addressed to:
Zondervan, *3900 Sparks Dr. SE, Grand Rapids, Michigan 49546*

ISBN 978-0-310-34190-1 (ebook)

Library of Congress Cataloging-in-Publication Data

Names: Thomas, Gary (Gary Lee), author.
Title: Loving him well : practical advice on influencing your husband / Gary Thomas.
Other titles: Sacred influence
Description: Grand Rapids, Michigan : Zondervan, [2017] | Previously published in 2006
    as Sacred Influence. | Includes bibliographical references.
Identifiers: LCCN 2017029419 | ISBN 9780310341888 (softcover)
Subjects: LCSH: Wives—Religious life. | Influence (Psychology)—Religious aspects—
    Christianity. | Husbands—Psychology. | Marriage—Religious aspects—Christianity.
Classification: LCC BV4528.15 .T56 2017 | DDC 248.8/435—dc23 LC record available
    at https://lccn.loc.gov/2017029419

Published in association with Yates & Yates, www.yates2.com.

Cover photo: Daniel Grizelj / Getty Images
Interior design: Kait Lamphere

First printing December 2017 / Printed in the United States of America

23 24 25 26 27 LBC 21 20 19 18 17

To Drs. Steve and Rebecca Wilke—

The pleasantness of a friend
springs from their heartfelt advice.

Proverbs 27:9

CONTENTS

PREFACE TO NEW EDITION

Loving Him Well is a new edition of what was originally published in 2006 as *Sacred Influence*. It has been given a new title because it has been completely rewritten, with chapters added and some older chapters deleted. An additional decade in marriage ministry, along with seven years of living in the fourth largest city in the United States, has opened my eyes to a broader understanding of the issues wives face as they live with their husbands. If you've read *Sacred Influence*, you will notice some familiar stories and chapters, but even here, the lessons and teachings have been clarified, making *Loving Him Well* essentially a new book.

FOREWORD

By Lisa Thomas

Dear Readers,

Thanks for picking up my husband's book! I hope and pray that you will choose to read it. If you're like me, you have a pile of really good and helpful books waiting to be read, and sometimes it's hard to prioritize them. I truly believe that Gary has something worthwhile to say in this book; I know your marriage will be blessed if you do read it.

Gary wrote this book partly in response to the many emails and questions received from women who had heard him speak or who had read his other books. He heard their frustration, pain, and sometimes anger at husbands who just didn't seem to be getting it. Because of this, he deals with real-life stuff, addressing issues that women like you and me are dealing with. He doesn't offer "five easy steps" that are guaranteed to transform your situation, but he tries to help women gain a better understanding of how men tick and catch a glimpse of the spiritual dynamics at work within their marriages. I hope you'll see his brotherly love as he walks you through the process of your own marital journey.

I'm often asked if Gary really lives what he writes, and my answer is always a resounding yes! Because he is a man of integrity, I can wholeheartedly recommend his books. And just in case you're wondering, yes, he did ask my permission to use every story involving me. It is our hope and prayer that our vulnerability will be used by God to bless others. Like any couple, we don't have a perfect marriage, but it's a marriage I thank God for every day. I can't imagine another life, and if our journey can in any way inspire your own, I'm pleased to share it with you. May you be encouraged.

Enjoy!
Lisa Thomas

GOD HEARS AND SEES

He just doesn't get it.

I was counseling a young engaged couple, and it became clear that the future wife was making some very significant concessions in order to marry this man. I kept calling the young man to an equal response: she was willing to give up this; would he work harder at that?

It became painfully apparent that this young man just didn't understand the incredible gift this young woman was offering him—the gift of herself.

Performing weddings is one of the most awe-inspiring things I do. I can't get over the commitment, the vulnerability, the joining of two lives into one, and how each partner agrees to live out an uncertain future together, to give all that they are and have to each other—to in a very real sense make their happiness vulnerable to the other's character and concern.

There really is nothing like marriage; it gives two people the power to bless, encourage, and build, but also to tear down, discourage, and destroy.

A good marriage can be so, so good, totally worth fighting for. A disappointing marriage can color every day with a grey hue.

As I began writing this book, I spent some time in prayer to get a sense of God's heart for what I believe he wants to do in these pages—to encourage women who are in good marriages that could get even better; and to offer hope and a new path forward to those women who feel invisible or marginalized in their marriage.

I realized that if I could truly understand God's heart for his daughters, if I could but glimpse the passion he feels for you and the tears he cries when you cry—how he feels each slight you feel and how he hates the very things you often hate about the way wives sometimes get treated in marriage—then I might begin to realize why God would care about a book like this and why he might put it in my mind to write it. He doesn't want to leave you alone in relationships that bring you less than what he designed.

In fact, God sees and hears everything taking place in your life and relationships. He knows the many wives who suffer in loveless marriages. He knows how men sometimes look down on women and act condescendingly toward their wives. He knows that men can provide great strength, nurture, comfort, and security, but also that they can be frustrating, terrifying, demanding, and selfish. He sees the women who feel trapped in difficult marriages, as well as those who enjoy relatively good marriages with men who still occasionally act selfish, thoughtless, or distant.

But he also knows the holy ways in which a woman can profoundly move a man. He is eager to empower a wife-and-husband team to come together to shape and transform this world. When a marriage becomes a true partnership of influencing not just each other but also the world, well, there really is nothing else like it.

With more than twenty years in marriage ministry behind us, my wife and I have heard enough heartbreaking stories to know there is no guarantee; some husbands will resist change no matter how earnestly their wives pursue them or how brilliantly their wives confront them. But we've also interacted with couples who have learned to value and honor each other, who inspire each other to be who God made them to be, who share a rich friendship, a mutual respect, a fulfilling physical relationship, and a close partnership. I'm thinking of one husband who worked two jobs so that his wife could pursue her dream to become a photographer without her having to worry (initially) about earning any income.

Some of you may be asking, "That's what *I* want, but I'm not sure it's what *he* wants. How do I get from where we are to there?"

I'll be up-front with you: you can't *change* a man. But you *can* influence him or move him—a far subtler art. And that's what we're going to discuss in this book.

HOPE FOR THE HURTING

I believe God has heard your prayers, and I *know* he sees your pain. I further believe that, since he designed marriage, you should look first to him about how you can best encourage, inspire, challenge, and appropriately influence the man you married. God wants you to feel loved, to be noticed, and to be cherished. He didn't create you and cast you adrift on a sea of happenstance or circumstance.

But even more than this book is about your husband, it's about *you*. While you may be able to influence your husband, you're not "raising" him. This is a book for wives, not for mothers, and by that I mean you are not your husband's mother. It is not your responsibility to discipline him or help him behave or get over an addiction. Frankly, if your husband is addicted and wants to become free, he is going to have to be convicted by God and motivated to do this himself, not to please or even to keep his wife. I say this at the start to set you free from ever valuing yourself or your marriage by your husband's reactions or obedience.

Some Old Testament prophets, clearly called by God, urged their people to repent, and the people did. Others, like Jeremiah, lived pious, faith-filled lives, spoke God's truth courageously, and watched their hearers ignore God's truth as they marched to their own ruin.

Your husband is his own man. You can do everything right, and he may still do everything wrong. That's not on you. It will never be on you, and it will never define you. My friend Dr. Melody Rhode describes the sacred challenge of marriage as "the challenge to learn to give ourselves in marriage, whether to an appreciative recipient, a giving partner, or a black hole."

What if your husband never gets it? Marriage as God designed it would result in a husband loving you like Christ loves the church. This pictures a husband who blesses you and serves you and cherishes you as you heal and grow and serve. You matter to God. He adores you, and in his perfect design, this is the kind of marriage and relationship you would enjoy. Because of the fall, however, too many marriages get turned upside down, where wives are asked to become godlike figures to their husbands, trying to rescue their men from ruin and destruction. What God wants to bless you with thus becomes one of your biggest burdens.

I will not put this burden on you. You are your husband's wife, not his god, not his mother, and not his rescuer. You have your own needs and many other demands, perhaps as a mother, a sister, a daughter, a friend, a business owner, an employee, and certainly a servant in God's kingdom with your own call and purpose.

The journey of marriage can result in a stronger you. Learning to love a fallen husband can help you rely more on God's love, affirmation, acceptance, mercy, and strength. Developing new skills and practicing them on your spouse may not change your spouse, but it will certainly change you—and you are so important to God and loved by God that a changed you is still a very beautiful gift to give to the world.

Whatever happens in your marriage, know that you're not alone. You have a divine Friend who cares for your husband even more than you do, but who also adores you as you seek to be a positive influence in your husband's life.

The words spoken to Daniel at the end of the book that bears his name are a soothing balm to every wife. After "the man clothed in linen" gives Daniel the truth and tells him what to say, Daniel asks, "My lord, what will the outcome of all this be?" (12:8). Daniel wanted to know if all his warnings would bear fruit. Would the words God had given him be heeded? Would the nations listen?

The response is honest: "Many will be purified, made spotless and refined, but the wicked will continue to be wicked. None of the wicked will understand, but those who are wise will understand" (Daniel 12:10). He then adds, "As for you, go your way till the end. You will rest, and then at the end of the days you will rise to receive your allotted inheritance" (12:13).

This is such a word of hope. Some, when hearing the truth, will be refined, but some wicked people will continue to be wicked. So Daniel should speak the truth and know that at the end of his days, he will rise to receive his inheritance from God. If the wicked continue to be wicked, that's on the wicked; it's not on Daniel.

This is a compelling call to wives to focus on their relationship with God over any "success" at influencing their husbands. Do what you do in marriage out of love for God, being inspired and empowered by God. If your husband is influenced, you will be blessed as a wife and he will have been richly blessed to be married to you. If he is not influenced, you will still be blessed as God's daughter who has been faithful to her Lord and who will be rewarded by her God, even if she is never appreciated by her husband.

As you make your way through these pages, I long for you to see God's care and concern between every line. He truly loves you. He really is intimately familiar with your situation. One day in the not-too-distant future, I pray that you'll wake up in bed, look at the man lying next to you, and finally experience *hope*. A woman who commits herself to God and who learns to act with his wisdom is a fully empowered woman who is embarking on an exciting and life-changing journey. I trust in the reality of God's presence in our lives. It may sound like a cliché, but it's still a biblical truth: *With God, all things are possible.*

ONE WORD OF CAUTION

Please allow me to express one caveat up front: what is good advice for many marriages can be really bad advice for other marriages. The advice in this book is not geared for—and sometimes wouldn't be appropriate for—women in destructive and abusive marriages. There is a chapter in which abusive marriages are addressed, but the spiritual principles contained in this work are designed for women who want to and are able to work on their marriages, not for women who need to be saved from their marriages. It is impossible to write a book that is suitable for everyone. Some marriages are beautiful; some are generally healthy but could be enhanced even further. Some are difficult and disconnected, but they can be resurrected. Some are destructive and abusive, and this last category deserves an entirely different approach from what we'll be talking about here. If you wonder if you are in a destructive or abusive marriage, I recommend Leslie Vernick's *The Emotionally Destructive Marriage*.[1]

For instance, when I talk about dealing with your husband's anger, "normal" anger is something very different in a healthy man than it is in an abusive man. In the same way, however, chapter 3, where I talk about "functional fixedness," might seem unduly confrontational if you are married to a genuinely good man. One wife told me her greatest frustration with her husband is that he leaves little piles wherever he goes, emptying out his pockets and such. I asked her how she dealt with it, and she said, "Gary, he's such a good man in so many ways—he loves the Lord; he treats me so well; he even cleans the toilets. So I just pick up the piles and thank God he's in my life." If you're married to a husband like that, trying to address a rather minor issue isn't a wise thing to do.

I'm writing as a Christian brother who has been involved in marriage ministry for more than two decades. There are other books written by trained therapists with specialized knowledge about handling abuse and other issues. This book is designed for

Christian wives who want to be a positive influence on their husband in marriages that are hurting but can become healthy, that are healthy but could be better, or that are suffering from apathy and normal doldrums and need a boost. God has used the previous edition of this book to rescue many deeply struggling marriages as well, but no one book can address all the challenges presented by modern marriages.

Having said that, let's get started.

PART 1

YOUR MARRIAGE MAKEOVER BEGINS WITH *YOU*

CHAPTER 1

THE GLORY OF GOD IN A WOMAN

Understanding Who You Are in Christ

Historically, neurologically, socially, and even biblically, one can make the case that women tend to be more invested in their relationships and marriages than are men. Not all women and not all husbands—of course. But as Dr. Melody Rhode, a psychologist and marriage and family therapist, puts it, "Women are bent to their husbands; we just are." This reality has its roots in the very first family.

Back in Genesis 3, after the fall, God tells Eve, "Your desire will be for your husband" (verse 16). The word *desire* has been rendered as something so strong it is "bordering on disease."[1] It comes from a root word connoting a "violent craving" for something.

Some women exhibit more of this than others. I once heard a woman describe how her husband had carried on a secret affair for more than four years. The husband had acted cruelly on many fronts. He had introduced his mistress to his wife, for example, and in his wife's absence he had brought the mistress home. In fact, he even took his mistress into his wife's bed. The illicit relationship ended only when the mistress died.

But do you know what surprised me the most? The wife seemed more concerned about losing this man than she did about facing a life with a serial cheater! Even though he had disrespected her as deeply as possible, trampled on their marital intimacy, and offended their marriage bed, she felt more afraid of waking up without him than of waking up next to him. In fact, she really wanted to find out more about the mistress! What did she look like? What kind of personality did she have? What did her husband see in her?

Contrast this with a question-and-answer article in *Sports Illustrated* in which a number of professional male athletes were asked if they would ever take back a "runaway bride," a woman who left them at the altar and embarrassed them in front of their family and friends. *Not a single athlete said he would.* One of the men responded so colorfully that I couldn't print his answer in this book.

Why the discrepancy? In some cases, it may indeed be that women are more spiritually and emotionally mature, willing to forgive for the sake of the family and larger considerations. But in other cases, it may be less noble than that. Some women never rise above a propensity to define themselves according to their likability—or acceptance—by men. Unfortunately, some men seem to have an ultrasensitive spiritual radar that picks up on this. They somehow intuit a woman's spiritual neediness and will exploit it for their own ends.

Because of Christ's work and the conquering power of the Holy Spirit, however, Christian women can be set free from such psychological dependency and destruction. Consider these words from 1 Corinthians 7, as rendered by Eugene Peterson in *The Message*: "And don't be wishing you were someplace else or with someone else. Where you are right now is God's place for you. Live and obey and love and believe right there. God, not your marital status, defines your life" (verse 17).

Did you catch that last line? *God, not your marital status, defines your life.*

Is this true of you? The more it is, the more success you will have in influencing your husband, because weak women usually forfeit their influence.

If you don't respect someone, you probably won't care much about what he or she thinks of you. They're never going to *influence* you. When their opinion doesn't matter to you, they could go out of their way to communicate clearly, honestly, and practically, but you're still not going to listen to them. In the same way, if your husband doesn't respect you, neither your tears nor your insights will influence him. His deafness might be fed by his own sinfulness, but you can guard yourself, in part, by refusing to value his acceptance of you over your identity as a daughter of God.

We will only be free when God, not our marital status (whether single, widowed, happily married, or frustrated in our marriage) defines who we are. To make the most influence in our marriage, we must rise above our marriage.

Now let's put a positive spin on this. If someone you really respect, greatly admire, and enjoy spending time with comes to you with a concern, aren't you going to give their words extra thought? Aren't you at least going to consider that they may have a point and that you need to pay attention?

This explains why the type of woman who moves her husband is a woman who also *impresses* her husband. I heard one man gush about his wife's business acumen, while another raved about his wife's intelligence. Yet a third man went on and on about his wife's spiritual maturity and her ability to understand the Bible. A reserved, introverted husband spoke with great admiration about his wife's ability to make friends, while another man described in detail his wife's most recent athletic accomplishment.

You may not have realized this, but most husbands like to brag about their wives. They may not say it to you, but they notice your strengths and take pride in them. Far more important than your business savvy or social skills is your spiritual core. This is what will give you the strength and respect that are so necessary for being a godly change agent in your marriage. And it will bless your husband immensely. According to 1 Timothy 3:11, a man's qualification for spiritual office includes being married to a woman "worthy of respect."

The first step toward influencing a man is becoming such a woman—the unique person God created you to be, in all your glory.

What do I mean by *glory*? I mean someone who radiates the presence of God, whose mind is filled with his wisdom, whose courage is strengthened by God's affirmation, whose boldness is supported by the security she derives from him, and whose spirit is marked with the perfectly balanced gentle/courageous character of Christ. It takes time to grow into this. God loves you plenty, just as you are, but he has a vision for you that encompasses all these strengths.

Truly understanding the radical and liberating nature of Jesus' message concerning women will help you become such a person. I'd like to move those of you who define yourself based on the fall— "I'm worthy because men like me"—to defining yourself based on your relationship to God: "I matter because I'm made in the image of God, am loved by God, and am regularly empowered by God to make a difference in this world."

WORLD SHAPERS

The Bible affirms women in a way that was quite radical for the time in which it was written. The Old Testament stepped outside its cultural milieu to insist that women mirror God's own character and image just as fully as do their male counterparts: "So God created mankind in his own image, in the image of God he created them; male and female he created them" (Genesis 1:27). Right from the start, we learn that women and men *together* mirror the image of God. Males, by themselves, are not up to the task; since God is above gender, males alone (or females alone) fail to adequately represent his character and image.

While the apostle Paul does ascribe a certain significance to the fact that God created man first, if you look at the line of creation, females are the *culmination*. Everything keeps getting more sophisticated, more intricate, until finally a woman appears—and only then does God rest.

Just as tellingly, the admonition to act on this world, shape this world, and even to rule over this world is given to women just as much as it is to men: "God blessed *them* [the man *and* the woman] and said to *them*, 'Be fruitful and increase in number; fill the earth and subdue it. Rule over the fish in the sea and the birds in the sky and over every living creature that moves on the ground'" (Genesis 1:28, emphasis added).

Women are not told to sit passively on the sidelines and cheer for their husbands as the men run the show. On the contrary, from the very beginning, women share God's command for humans to rule, subdue, and manage this earth. They are co-regents.

Some ancient theologians tried to amend this somewhat by blaming Eve for the fall, thus implying that women are spiritually weaker, but the Bible itself is far fairer to women. While it acknowledges Eve's complicity in the fall, it also trumpets Eve's redemptive role in the future. The Genesis account doesn't end with Eve (and Adam) eating the fruit. God prophesies that though the serpent "won" this round, his certain and annihilating defeat would come *through the woman.*

And while the times of the Old Testament culturally favored men, there is, for an ancient book, an astonishing number of heroic women, including Rahab, Deborah, Jael (Judges 4:17–22), Esther, and Ruth, who is said to be "better . . . than seven sons" (Ruth 4:15).

JESUS, FRIEND OF WOMEN

This strong, affirming view of women continues into the first book of the New Testament, with the inclusion of women in the genealogy of the Messiah (a literary act that breaks with the tradition of the first century). Yes, there is Abraham and David and Joseph—but there is also Rahab, Ruth, Mary, and Bathsheba. Who would expect such a thing from a patriarchal and even misogynistic culture? It took *both* men and women to set up the human events that led to the birth of the Messiah. God chose women of diverse personality and status to build the human line that ushered in the Savior of the world.

Just as significantly, Jesus came into this world through a woman. Not a single male had anything to do with the immediate conception or birth of our Lord. Instead, God chose a woman to accomplish the miracle of the incarnation. Think about this: Mary, a woman, is the only human who contributed to Jesus' DNA. Jesus is, biologically, really and truly Mary's descendant, while he is only "spiritually" Joseph's descendant.

While the notion that we have to tear down men to lift up women is destructive and unhelpful, it is nevertheless amazing to realize how often the men who surrounded Jesus simply didn't get it, while the women did—and how honest the New Testament is about this. One time, a Pharisee was having dinner with Jesus when a prostitute came in and washed our Lord's feet with her tears, drying them with her hair (Luke 7:36–50). This act appalled the Pharisee, but Jesus said, in essence, "You just don't get it! She understands who I am, while you, even with all your learning, remain blinded to my place and glory."

In addition to the clueless Pharisees, the male disciples of Jesus also occasionally revealed slow thinking. One time, a woman poured costly perfume all over Jesus' head (Mark 14:3–9). Some of the disciples said to themselves, "What a waste!" while Jesus thought, *Finally, here's someone who really gets who I am.* In fact, Jesus declared that this woman's action would be remembered wherever his gospel would be preached. Not one person out of a hundred can name all twelve disciples, but most people have heard of this bold woman. The disciple named Thaddaeus spent three years with Jesus, and there's not a single written record of any particular act of devotion on his part; this woman spent one hour with Jesus, and she is remembered around the world.

Jesus also elevated women in his teaching. In Mark 10:11, Jesus astonishes his disciples when he tells them, "Anyone who divorces his wife and marries another woman commits adultery against her." Why was this astonishing? According to rabbinic law, a man could commit adultery against another married *man* by sleeping with that man's wife, and a wife could commit adultery against *her husband* by sleeping with another man, but no provision stipulated how a husband could commit adultery against his wife. Jesus "is expressing a reaction against the frequently low esteem of women, even in Judaism . . . This sharp intensifying of the concept of adultery had the effect of elevating the status of the wife to the same dignity as her husband."[2] Jesus was telling those first-century men, "Your wife has equal value in God's sight. It is possible for you to sin against her every bit as much as it is possible for her to sin against you."

And let's look at Jesus' death. While one male disciple betrayed our Lord and ten others cowered behind locked doors, some very courageous women dared to watch Jesus' final minutes on this earth. Mark goes out of his way to emphasize the scene at the foot of the cross: "Some women were watching from a distance. Among them were Mary Magdalene, Mary the mother of James the younger and of Joseph, and Salome. In Galilee these women had followed him and cared for his needs. *Many other women who had come up with him to Jerusalem were also there*" (Mark 15:40–41, emphasis added). In Jesus' most trying moments, he was supported by many women. Modern readers might read right over this narrative fact—but in the early history of the church, this was a startling truth and a challenge to any false view of male superiority.

But perhaps the boldest statement came after Jesus died and was raised from the dead. According to ancient Pharisaic law, a woman's testimony was inadmissible in a tribunal as too untrustworthy. Only men could give witness. So when Jesus rose from the dead—the most important event that has ever occurred or ever will occur—who was present to give witness and testimony? Women! Jesus pointedly uses women, whose testimony could not then be heard in contemporary courts of law, to proclaim his glorious resurrection.

This elevation of women at all points in theological pronouncements, historical accounts, and practical teaching should astonish us, given the male-oriented culture in which the Bible took shape. Let the words of the Bible wash away any mistaken cultural notions you may hold that inaccurately depict God's view of women.

The Bible presents a woman as a strong image bearer of God, able to stand against the world, powerfully influencing men and culture (witness Deborah in the Bible or Teresa of Avila in history) as she lives the life God created her to live. Despite the negative messages you may have received—whether from your family, church, or culture—you need to:

- understand the glory of being a woman made in God's image
- experience the strength you have as the recipient of his Holy Spirit
- find refuge in the worth and purpose you have as his daughter

Through this mighty spiritual core, you can influence the world—including your husband. *God, not your marital status or the condition of your marriage, defines your life.*

I believe you owe it to the God who created you—and to yourself, to the husband who married you, and to any kids you've given birth to—to become the woman God designed you to be, in all your glory, power, strength, and wisdom.

WHEN MARRIAGE BECOMES IDOLATRY

Let's apply some simple theology here. Who does the Bible say is your refuge—God, or your husband? Deuteronomy 33:27 provides the answer: "The eternal God is your refuge, and underneath are the everlasting arms."

In whom does your hope lie? Your husband's continuing affection? First Peter 1:21 says, "Your faith and hope are in God."

Where will you find your security? In you and your husband's ability to earn a living and your husband's commitment to stay married to you? Philippians 4:19 answers, "My God will meet all your needs according to the riches of his glory in Christ Jesus."

Where will you find supreme acceptance that will never fade or falter for all the days of your life? "As a bridegroom rejoices over his bride," replies Isaiah 62:5, "so will your God rejoice over you."

If you're trying to find your primary refuge in your husband, if you've centered your hope on him, if your security depends on his approval, and if you will do almost anything to gain his acceptance, then you've just given to a man what rightfully belongs to God alone.

And that means you've turned marriage into idol worship.

When you do that, both you and your husband lose. You can't love a false idol long term. You just can't. You may worship it for a while, but eventually that idol's limitations will show, and you'll become bitter and resentful. Just as surely as a block of wood can't speak wisdom, so a human man can't love you as God created you to be loved. And what happens when an idol disappoints you? Bitterness, sadness, and sometimes even despair.

In addition, how will you ever find the courage to confront someone whose acceptance so determines your sense of well-being that you believe you can't exist without him? How will you ever take the risk to say what needs to be said if you think your future depends on your husband's favor toward you?

Your future depends on God, not on a fallen man. Your security rests with your caring Creator's providence, not with your husband's paycheck. Your acceptance as a person became secure when God adopted you, not when your husband proposed to you. If you truly want to love, motivate, and influence your husband, your first step must be to stay connected with God. Find your refuge, security, comfort, strength, and hope in him.

ANDREA'S STORY

Andrea freely admits, "I was the wife who longed to be accepted by and praised by my husband. I would diligently cook new recipes to gain his approval, only to be let down by his disapproval and harsh remarks about how it could have been better. I would share business ideas and thoughts the Lord laid on my heart that day or week, only for my husband to tell me why they wouldn't work, without even really trying them."

Perhaps the time that stung the most was when their son was driving with Andrea and prayed to invite the Lord into his heart. With great excitement, Andrea called her husband to tell him the good news, only to be met with an angry demand of why they couldn't have waited until he got home.

"I was crushed," Andrea remembers. "And things like this would occur almost every day. I can hardly describe how much I hoped and desired to be approved of and praised by my husband. All that did was make me live in a constant state of discouragement."

This went on for a decade until one day, as Andrea was about to give up hope of ever having the life she had dreamed about, a friend challenged her: "You're waiting for your Christian husband to join you when he's clearly not going to. You're wasting away your value and purpose by waiting for somebody else. You can begin living in the Lord now and see if that wakes up your husband."

Andrea began seeking God as she never had before. She got alone with him, carving out time every day to pray and read the

Bible and write in her journal. She started listening for God to speak, and in her words, "I started to fall more in love with Jesus instead of falling more in love with my husband."

It's not that she stopped loving her husband or even loved him less; it's that she woke up to the reality that she had to stop living for her husband's approval, which she wasn't getting at all, and start pursuing God's love, which is freely given.

"God made it clear to me that he alone was enough to quench my every longing and thirst for favor and approval."

About a year after changing her focus and approach, Andrea finally began to see a change in her husband. It hasn't been dramatic, but it's not insignificant either. "He has become softer and more open to listen to what I have to say. I've also seen him start to spend more time with the Lord on his own. It seems that the more he's seen me fall in love with the Lord, the more he pursues God."

While Andrea is grateful for this change, she also admits it's not like the problems have been "solved." "I'm still growing; I'm not completely on the other side yet. And honestly, I don't know that our relationship is different as much as *I'm* different. I cling to Exodus 14:14: 'The LORD will fight for you; you need only to be still.'"

What's changed the most for her, then, if not her husband?

"Exodus 14:14 means I take my request to God instead of to my husband. I accept that God is in control, and I have more peace."

I appreciate the honesty of Andrea's story. Her spiritual focus hasn't changed everything, but it's made it better. She has positively influenced her husband at least a bit in the right direction, but their marriage is still a work in progress. What sustains her, however, is that she is a different person, with more peace and the joy of knowing she is accepted, loved, and adored by her heavenly Father. So even if this approach doesn't change your husband, it will be worth it for how it might change you and your perspective.

I encourage you to reevaluate and affirm your biblical standing as a woman. More often than not, this will be a process—perhaps you'll have to pray over the Bible verses in this chapter until they become real to you. But you *must not* accept any identity that gives you less than the Bible offers you. Before you run the race, you have to train. Before you can influence someone, you must become spiritually strong.

QUESTIONS FOR DISCUSSION AND REFLECTION

1. What is the difference between trying to *change* a man and trying to *influence* him?

2. Do you think it's true that women tend to be more invested in their marriages than men? If so, why do you think this may be the case? What are the challenges of such a reality?

3. If you "caught" your husband bragging about you, what do you think he would be saying? What would you like to hear him say in the future? Identify some things you can start doing to build on this.

4. On a scale of one to ten, one being "I feel best about myself when men like me and pay attention to me," and ten being "I believe I'm worthy because I'm made in the image of God and am loved by God," where would you fall? What can women do—for themselves and to encourage other women—to move up that scale?

5. How does your image of yourself as a woman compare with the Scriptures Gary shared in this chapter? What was compatible? What was different?

6. What are the marks of a woman who has turned her marriage into idolatry? How would doing this undercut a woman's power to positively influence her husband in a godly way?

CHAPTER 2

"BE WORTHY OF ME"

How God Uses the Weaknesses
of Others to Help Us Grow

Bestselling author and historian David McCullough stumbled across a startling letter by John Adams, written to his wife, Abigail, in the heat of the Revolutionary War: "We can't guarantee success in this war, but we can do something better. We can deserve it."

Later, McCullough read another letter, this one by George Washington, that uses the exact same line. He traced the words to a play called *Cato*. This line summarizes the spirit behind the birth of our country, and it can help modern women reform their marriages. McCullough explains, "That line in the Adams letter is saying that how the war turns out is in the hands of God. We can't control that, but we can control how we behave. We can deserve success."[1]

The same principle is true for you in your marriage. You can't guarantee how everything will turn out; you definitely can't control another human being. But you *can* "deserve" success. You can act in such a way that transformation is more likely.

This is not to put all the responsibility for your marriage on you.

It is possible that a woman can do everything right, and a hard-hearted husband may still not respond. That doesn't mean *you* failed; it means *your husband* failed. This is really more about giving your husband the best chance to respond in a positive way to God and to you, but he will always be ultimately accountable for his response.

As it pertains to you, however, I want you to think about something: What if your husband's faults are God's tools to shape you? What if the very thing that most bugs you about your spouse constitutes God's plan to teach you something new? Of course, I am not talking about violence or emotional terrorizing—but what if God is giving you the opportunity to become a stronger believer and a better-rounded person by daily rubbing shoulders with a very imperfect man? If you believe you have room to grow and you want to grow, your marriage can become a "spiritual gym" to make you spiritually and relationally stronger, fitter, and healthier.

For instance, what if God is teaching you to have the courage to speak the truth in love, to stop enabling destructive behavior to continue, or to learn how to see your value and worth in who *he* says you are and not who your husband says you are? God's work in your difficult marriage may not be limited to making you more forbearing, loving, gracious, or forgiving; it might also be about building in you the gutsy elements of mature spirituality, like overcoming evil with good, refusing to keep destructive secrets, figuring out how to avoid colluding with sin, standing up for righteousness, etc. It shouldn't surprise you when I ask here, as I have before, "What if God designed marriage to make us holy more than to make us happy?"*

"BE WORTHY OF ME"

Napoleon Bonaparte's astounding military success found a rival only in his raging ego. In one letter, he chastised his wife, "I insist

---

* This is the subtitle of my book *Sacred Marriage* (Grand Rapids: Zondervan, 2000, 2015).

you have more strength. I am told you are always crying. For shame, that is very bad! . . . Be worthy of me and develop a stronger character. Make a proper show in Paris . . . If you are always weeping I shall think you have no courage or character. I do not like cowards. An empress should have heart."[2]

While Napoleon's condescension both nauseates and offends us, I think he stumbles onto an interesting turn of phrase: "Be worthy of me." This should be the goal of every husband and wife—a man aspiring to be worthy of his wife, and a wife aspiring to be worthy of her husband.

In our self-esteem-obsessed culture, telling someone he or she needs to become worthy sounds anathema, but there's biblical precedence for this. Jesus says that anyone who fails to take up his cross is not worthy of him (Matthew 10:38). Paul urges the Ephesians to "live a life worthy of the calling you have received" (4:1). Saints are urged to be worthy, or commended for being worthy, in Philippians 1:27; Colossians 1:10; 1 Thessalonians 2:12; 2 Thessalonians 1:11; 3 John 6; and Revelation 3:4.

These passages aren't about earning salvation, just as your actions toward your husband aren't about "earning" your marriage. You're already saved, and you're already married. These verses address the ongoing commitment to live up to what you already are. As God's daughter with a high calling, fill your mind with Scripture, surrender your heart to the empowering work of the Holy Spirit, and be committed to love others deeply, from the heart. And in marriage, take up the call to be a wife in the best sense of the term. Don't take it for granted or grow weary of the responsibilities of a wife. Be just as eager now as you were on the day you got married. Let your husband be blessed with your understanding, your courage, your grace, your support.

Napoleon refers to his wife as an "empress," but the Bible refers to you as a queen. Genesis 1 tells us that God blessed both the man and the woman and told them to rule (verse 28). In the New

Testament, you are called "a chosen people, a royal priesthood, a holy nation, God's special possession, that you may declare the praises of him who called you out of darkness into his wonderful light" (1 Peter 2:9). The book of Revelation speaks of those Jesus died to save: "You have made them to be a kingdom and priests to serve our God, and they will reign on the earth" (5:10) and later adds that God's followers "will reign for ever and ever" (22:5).

Of course, all of us reign as vice-regents under the King of kings, called by Jesus to seek first the kingdom of God, not our own, but it's clear that God didn't create women to be passive victims waiting to be saved by men. Any such notion is cultural, not biblical. In Christ, you are filled with the Holy Spirit! You can take charge as the ruling regent God created you to be. You thus don't have to wait for something to happen; *God can empower you and then use you to make something happen.*

Instead of resting on what already is ("I'm a believer, so growth doesn't really matter"; "he's already married to me, so it doesn't matter whether I develop as a wife"), resolve to become the maturing, influential servant of God and wife to your husband that God wants you to be. Staying engaged in your marriage like this can reinforce your resolve to stay engaged in your faith. With Christ in us and the Holy Spirit transforming us, we have no excuse for persisting in immaturity. The apostle Paul charged Timothy to fully develop the gifts God gave him, and then he wrote, "Be diligent in these matters; give yourself wholly to them, so that everyone may see your progress" (1 Timothy 4:15). Paul wants Timothy to know, "You're not perfect, but people should see *progress* in your life. In five years you should be wiser, stronger, and more mature in character than you are now."

My wife married a very immature twenty-two-year-old. I sincerely hope that her husband is now more mature, more loving, and less selfish than he was back then. And I pray fervently that in another ten years, her husband will have become that much more mature, that much more loving, that much kinder and wiser and more selfless.

This growth won't happen by accident, of course. It won't occur unless I am—to use Paul's words—"diligent in these matters," unless I "watch [my] life and doctrine closely" (1 Timothy 4:16) and "persevere" in them. If I won't grow, my wife may well grow past me. I can't give Lisa a perfect husband, but I certainly don't want to give her a spiritually lazy one. I want to become "worthy" of her. I may never fully get there, but it won't be for lack of trying. I'll never be as thin as I once was, and I'll never have the hair I did back then, but I can become a man whose character far outshines that of the twenty-two-year-old she married.

As this relates to your marriage, when you grow in character, when you sink your spiritual roots deep, when you learn to hear God's voice and build your mind with his wisdom, when you allow his Holy Spirit to transform your character and reshape your heart— then you can make your husband fall in love with you over and over again (assuming, of course, that he values godliness), and he'll be all the more motivated to maintain your respect and affection. My wife is now more than fifty years old, but when I see her faith in action, she grows even dearer to me by the day. Nothing compares to being married to a godly woman—nothing. And nothing gets more tiresome more quickly than living with a narcissist or a weak wife or a fearful one.

If you married a good man, your husband chose you as you were and accepts you as you are, but you can bless him with the woman you want to become. Will you do that? Will you honor his faith in you by becoming a woman he could only dream about?

The other key is leaving an example for your children. If you can't give your children two godly parents, at least give them one. Let your children see the difference God makes in a life. While it would be ideal for them to see both a mother and a father pursuing God, it may be that you can only offer a contrast between one parent who is deeply in love with God and one parent who is marginally interested in God, or who pretends to be godly but is an impostor. Surrender to God fully so they can see firsthand the difference God makes.

PAINFUL (BUT PURPOSEFUL) PERSEVERANCE

Another reason it's important for us to concentrate on our own growth is so that we can more successfully struggle against the sin of pride, which constantly tempts us to focus on changing our spouses while neglecting our own weaknesses. Jesus warned against this with startlingly strong words: "Why do you look at the speck of sawdust in your brother's eye and pay no attention to the plank in your own eye? How can you say to your brother, 'Brother, let me take the speck out of your eye,' when you yourself fail to see the plank in your own eye? You hypocrite, first take the plank out of your eye, and then you will see clearly to remove the speck from your brother's eye" (Luke 6:41–42).

Making over your marriage *begins with you*. I'm not saying it's wrong to desire more from your husband. I'm not denying that you might enjoy your marriage more if your husband dropped some bad habits and paid more attention to you (which is why we're going to discuss strategies in later chapters to do just this). I *am* saying that if you use this book to focus on changing your husband in such a way that you neglect to grow yourself, all I've done is inspire another Pharisee, not the godly woman God seeks.

Keep this perspective in mind throughout the book.

How is God using the reality of living with an imperfect man to teach you how to grow in patience and understanding? Here's one example. Mary Ann's husband, Patrick, fell from a truck when he was younger and landed on the concrete, sustaining a closed head injury. He survived, but doctors had to remove a major portion of the right frontal lobe of his brain and the tip of his left frontal lobe as well. Patrick learned to walk and talk again, but he lost his short-term memory. He lives with a maximum two-minute retention. He can learn things, but they must be rehearsed over and over until those actions become a part of his long-term memory.

Patrick does the mail run at Second Baptist Church in Houston, Texas. He began by counting steps and recording doorways, occasionally having to call Mary Ann (who also works at Second) so she could help him find his way back. Now, after twenty-five years, he no longer needs notes and can even direct guests, often even taking them to where they need to go (but he has to write on his hand where he leaves the mail cart so he can find it afterward).

Mary Ann met Patrick in choir. Music is the one thing that sticks with Patrick the first time he hears it. He can hear a song once and sing all the words from that point on. "The mind is an amazingly mysterious thing," Mary Ann marvels.

Wives are often understandably upset at their husband's memory when it comes to birthdates, appointments, errands, you name it—imagine the challenges of a husband who can't remember past two minutes! Yet Mary Ann focuses on the blessings.

"The Lord has taught me so many wonderful things as Patrick's wife," Mary Ann says. "Most people think that having this memory thing is so stressful on a marriage, and thus they assume it's a negative thing. It certainly has some drawbacks, but the Lord has revealed several huge lessons to me through Patrick's affliction. I have always heard that when we confess our sin to the Lord, he is faithful to hear us and forgive us, and we repent and walk on in his grace. He is not waiting for us to mess up again so he can remind us we repeated a sin. I have always had that head knowledge, but I have a personality that wants to please. It is not easy for me to forgive myself or let go of guilt. With Patrick, if we have a disagreement or some hiccup in our relationship, we need to immediately solve it, or Patrick will forget about it and we'll never be able to work through it.

"When I would hold on to something past Patrick's memory,

he would see my hurt and ask me, 'Did I do something wrong or has someone hurt you?' I would tell him I was feeling bad because I had been impatient with him or spoken harshly to him. He asks, 'Did we talk it through?'

"'Yes, we did, and you forgave me, but I'm still feeling bad that it ever happened.' Then he tells me, 'Mary Ann, if we talked and we confessed our wrong and got it right, I certainly don't even remember it—so I don't want you to waste another moment of joy you could have over something I do not even recall.'"

Here's what's so amazing and powerful: Mary Ann has finally realized that in his short-term memory, Patrick is exactly how God is when it comes to our sins. When we repent and are forgiven but hold on to the guilt and let it sap our joy, we're holding on to something God has already forgotten. Mary Ann says, "The Lord smiles and says, 'Child, you are forgiven; go and sin no more and live in the abundance of joy I desire for you.' It is through Patrick that I finally realized that the Lord does forgive me when I confess and repent, and he doesn't want me to waste precious time with guilt or the fear that I may repeat the sin, but he wants to see me joyfully move on in his grace."

Mary Ann laughs in an endearing way when she talks about Patrick's special ministry among the church staff. When he sees someone who is clearly having a bad day, he's happy to listen to them and let them blow off steam, reminding them, "You can tell me anything and get it off your chest. I won't tell anyone because I won't remember it two minutes from now. But if it makes you feel better for saying it out loud and it helps you move on, I'm here for you. And you'll never have to look at me with guilt because I won't even remember the conversation."

Mary Ann says, "I can't tell you how many times a gal or guy has called me to say, 'Patrick just blessed me today by listening, and I wanted you to know so you can tell him he was a blessing to me.'" She adds, "I may have to deal with reminding Patrick three times to put out the trash—that's just part of what we have to do—but I will take that because I am a particularly blessed woman who will never have a sin or character flaw be resented, held over my head, or brought up again. It never returns as a zinger in a fight or discussion. Reminding Patrick to put out the trash pales in comparison to that."

I fully understand there's a difference between showing compassion and understanding to a husband whose limitations arise from an accident rather than from deliberate willfulness. Some men are best served by extra patience for their weakness, while others may be best served when their wives stop covering up for irresponsible behavior or laziness.

In either case, you protect your own heart from resentment by refusing to focus only on the frustrations and challenges and moving also to recognizing the opportunities for you to gain greater spiritual understanding and strength. Just as an elite athlete can be thankful for a grueling workout, so you, as an "elite wife" can be thankful for an opportunity to become stronger in love and character.

The challenge of marriage is that when you're married to a defective man (and all men are defective in some way), it's not limited to learning how to handle something once or twice; it's about learning to live with that defect perhaps for the rest of your life. That calls for perseverance.

God could, of course, speak the word, and your problem would be solved—voilà! But that's not how God usually works. He allows us to face issues that make us feel completely inadequate. He may even walk us through our deepest fears, so that we can grow in him.

The Bible is adamant about this. Spiritual growth takes place by persevering through difficult times:

- "We also glory in our sufferings, because we know that suffering produces perseverance; perseverance, character; and character, hope. And hope does not put us to shame" (Romans 5:3–5).

- "Consider it pure joy, my brothers and sisters, whenever you face trials of many kinds, because you know that the testing of your faith produces perseverance. Let perseverance finish its work so that you may be mature and complete, not lacking anything" (James 1:2–4).
- "These [trials] have come so that the proven genuineness of your faith—of greater worth than gold, which perishes even though refined by fire—may result in praise, glory and honor when Jesus Christ is revealed" (1 Peter 1:7).

Most of us will never confront the physical persecution these verses directly address (and they shouldn't be misused to keep women trapped in a persecuting marriage), but we do face spiritual and relational trials with the same effect. God can use your marriage to make you a stronger, wiser, and more complete woman—provided you don't run from the challenges that being married to your husband represent.

THE EQUATION OF CHANGE

Your marriage isn't just a number on a scale of 1 to 10; it's a mathematical equation: $a+b = c$. Your husband may be the a—a number you absolutely can't change. But if you change the b (that's you), you influence the overall result of your marriage: $a+2b = d$. That's at once both the beauty (change is always possible, even if only unilaterally) and the frustration (the nature of that change is limited and not guaranteed) of human relationships. It's also why this book focuses on how a woman can *influence*—or best love—a man, not on how a woman can *change* a man.

It is entirely natural and healthy to dream big things for your husband, but that's very different from selfishly *demanding* those things.[3] When you dream something in a positive way, you offer yourself to God as an instrument of love, change, and spiritual transformation. When you demand that someone change for your sake, you're literally trying to bend the world around your comfort, your needs, and your happiness. That's pride, arrogance, and self-centeredness—and God will never bless *that*.

So let's lay out our expectations right at the outset. What do you dream for your husband? Maybe you want him to drink less, to pay more attention to the kids, to pray with you, or to read with you. Or perhaps you want him to stop giving free rein to his temper, to quit looking at pornography, or to be more of a spiritual leader. Chances are pretty good you want your husband to be more relationally aware and involved.

These are good dreams. Any man would get a tremendous blessing if just one of them were to come to pass. The good news is that you and God are in this together. He knew, even before he created you, who you'd marry. And he will continue to give you the tools you need to become the person he has called you to be and to do the work he has created you to do within your current relationship. God would *never* leave you alone in any situation: "He will never leave you nor forsake you" (Deuteronomy 31:6). Even if you married a non-Christian, God's grace is sufficient for you. You cannot dig a hole so deep that it cuts you off from God's provision, care, and life-giving strength. Yes, our choices may result in unpleasant consequences, but even then, God helps us to endure or to muster the courage to confront.

That's the message I want to communicate: You and God are in this together, and he's beginning your marriage makeover with you. Let him transform you as you seek to move your husband. While you may never achieve the results you have in mind, you can change the equation of your marriage by remodeling yourself. It begins with understanding the glory of being a godly woman and acting with the strength and toughness of a woman who understands she was created in the image of God, forgiven of her sins through the work of Jesus Christ, and gifted and empowered by God's Holy Spirit to live the life God has called her to live.

You may have picked up this book simply to find out how you can motivate or even transform your husband. I'm here to tell you that as noble as this cause may be, it's too small for you. God made you to remake *the world*. By courageously facing up to the challenges that every marriage faces, and by letting God change *you* in the process, something wonderful takes place—the formation of a new woman, fully alive to God, who can take the lessons she learns at home and apply them everywhere else.

"We can't guarantee success in this war, but we can do something better. We can deserve it."

LEARNING HOW TO RECEIVE LOVE

I've been writing in this chapter about how God can use your marriage to teach you how to love, but I want to end it with a twist: marriage to an imperfect man is one of the ways God can help you learn to *receive* his divine love. In other words, marriage isn't primarily fueled by the love you give your husband; it's primarily fueled by the love you receive from God.

First John 4:19 tells us, "We love because he first loved us." If you're like me, you may think about God's love as almost a "luxury" when things are going well—you just don't feel like you need as much—but when things are breaking down, God's love becomes a desperate necessity.

Whenever your husband breaks your heart, let God fill it. Before you try anything else, even before you seek resolution, learn to run into the amazing, affirming, understanding refuge that is God. Allow the puzzle of loving an imperfect man to push you into a fulfilling partnership with the God who loves you and who loves your husband and will work with you in any holy endeavor.

Maybe you're forced into God's arms not because of your husband's moral weakness, but rather because of a physical weakness.

Coppelia experienced this dynamic with her husband, Adam, whom she describes as "an incredibly strong man." In thirteen years of marriage, Adam has suffered two brain tumors. It's a scary situation, to be sure, but Coppelia believes being married to a man who has gone through this has strengthened her spiritually.

"I feel I have become stronger because I've had to rely on God to get us through," she remarks. "I've had to pray harder, both with him and alone in waiting rooms. I have had to be willing to ask for help and accept it from the people around us, which has been hard for me—an introverted, perfectionistic control freak—to do. And the moments when we realize we're not in control drive us to ask the tough questions and determine if we're building our house on the Rock, Jesus, or on the sand."

Practically all of us say we want to rely on Jesus, but medical emergencies with a spouse can make the ideal a necessity. No wife would likely choose this, but God can certainly use it to build mighty women of faith.

When you learn to receive God's love even in the face of disappointment, marriage will always be a spiritual benefit. As the third of four children, I felt a bit left out in my family of origin. But that feeling of not fitting in or being appreciated chased me into the arms of my heavenly Father. If I had felt more secure, would I have been as tight with Jesus? Only God knows. I certainly don't want to sound like only insecure people seek God. But this is certain: God used my insecurity as a tool. God can use frustration, abandonment, and disappointment as tools as well.

Whatever your situation may be, whenever marriage empties you, let it be a reminder to go back to God to be filled. My book *Sacred Pathways* focuses on this very need—helping believers find the best way for them to connect with God so they can be filled up to live in a needy, disappointing, and fallen world that becomes glorious when we live in it as God's beloved children.

QUESTIONS FOR DISCUSSION AND REFLECTION

1. If it's true that your husband's faults may be God's tools to transform you, what do you think God is trying to work on in your life today?

2. Why is it important for wives to maintain a healthy biblical attitude of "becoming worthy" while seeking to influence their husbands' growth?

3. How is God using your marriage—as it is right now—to teach you how to love?

4. How has being married to an imperfect man made you stronger and wiser?

5. What is the difference between dreaming things for your husband and demanding that he change?

6. How does the notion that God is with you in your marriage help you face your current marital frustrations and struggles?

7. In what ways will an active and courageous addressing of the issues in your marriage prepare you to influence and transform the world?

CHAPTER 3

THE BEAUTY OF GOD'S STRENGTH IN A WOMAN

Becoming Strong Enough to Address Your Husband's "Functional Fixedness"

Mark admits to controlling behavior. Jim has a hundred reasons for his chronic unemployment for more than a decade.

Their wives have been patient and have put up with this behavior for years. Most frustrating to each wife was the fact that while the husband knew how much his behavior was causing her great and ongoing pain, *the husband wouldn't change.* Both husbands listened to their wives' complaints, and they even acknowledged the truth of what their wives were asserting. They both *said* they'd try harder.

But they never changed.

What both of these wives needed to know is at the heart of "functional fixedness," which can be defined in the form of a question: What if your husband isn't motivated by *your* pain? What if he's only motivated by *his*?

Many wives live with great frustration because they keep telling their husbands that something they are doing (or not doing) is causing them great pain, but the husbands never change. This confuses the wife. She thinks, *If I knew I was doing something that was really hurting him, I'd stop it as soon as I found out. Why won't he?*

The answer, according to my friend Dr. Melody Rhode (a gifted marriage and family therapist), is this concept of "functional fixedness."[1] This phrase can be used to describe a man who will never be motivated by his wife's pain but is only motivated by his pain. For change to occur, he has to feel his own discomfort. He doesn't like hearing you tell him you're not happy; in fact, it probably irritates him. But if the pain necessary for him to change is greater than the pain of putting up with your occasional expressed frustration, he simply endures the verbal outbursts as "the cost of being married" and will put the entire episode out of his mind as soon as it's over.

Why?

Because it's painful for him to remember the conversation, and he wants to avoid pain at all costs.

So, functional fixedness is a motivational and spiritual disorder common among men (but also present in many women) that keeps them from actually pursuing change. They will listen to their wives' complaints. They will acknowledge that their wives have valid reasons to feel aggrieved. But they don't change. It shows a lack of empathy and spiritual maturity.

According to Dr. Rhode, men don't normally change if what they've been doing appears to work for them. For example, when a woman allows her husband to treat her with disrespect, he has no motivation to change. It's unlikely he ever will.

Dr. Rhode notes, "There's a simple question I ask wounded women who seek help to endure belittling or degrading treatment from their man: 'Why does your husband treat you badly? Answer: *because he can.*'" She goes on to say, "If what he's doing is working for him, why change? He needs a compelling reason to change, and it needs to be more compelling than your unhappiness or private misery with the situation." This is *not*, in any way, to blame a woman for the husband's bad behavior, but to develop a new understanding in order to map out a different future.

A God-fearing man *would* be motivated to change simply by understanding that his actions or inactions hurt you. But you may be married to a man who doesn't care if his actions hurt you, as long as he gets what he wants. Allowing the behavior while complaining about it won't change anything because the husband keeps getting his way. Remember, with such men it's not *your* pain that motivates him; it's *his* pain (this is, again, the idea behind functional fixedness). You must be willing to create an environment in which the status quo becomes more painful than positive change.

CHANGING THE STATUS QUO

At the risk of depressing you, I need to tell you that studies show that many frustrations and disagreements in marriage (in fact, more than half) will never change. At some point, you may have to learn how to live with these realities. I'm therefore not urging you to apply "functional fixedness" to lesser concerns. Marriage calls us to many acts of grace, mercy, and kindness. It would be demeaning and wrong for me to try to remake Lisa into the image of my "model wife." That's narcissism, not love.

Let me give you an example of "lesser concerns" from the marriage of a pastor who confided in me. He's on the staff of a very large church. Staff members are supposed to use satellite parking and take a shuttle to the church. He told me, "The challenge is that my wife has her own special relationship with time. Going to satellite parking and taking a shuttle require at least an extra ten minutes on Sunday morning, and Ashley always intends to be ready early but in fact almost never is.

"I'm not going to get into a fight with my wife every Sunday morning. She brings so much into my life and serves our church so well in so many unseen ways that I have just accepted we will park as far into the outer reaches of the church parking lot as we can, but we almost never will be able to use satellite parking or we'll be late. Since it also sets a bad example for a staff member to consistently walk in during the middle of the service, I've had to pick my poison."

This is an example of a lesser concern, and I applaud this man's decision to deal with what is rather than try to change his wife. When talking to other husbands, I'll remind them that spending a bit too much on clothes one month or on a shopping trip is different than accumulating thousands of dollars of debt on a credit card.

No one wants to be married to a spouse who is always trying to "fix" you merely to suit their own desires.

I'm addressing issues in this chapter that threaten your family's future. Let's go back to the two examples at the beginning of this chapter to look at how two different women confronted their husbands' functional fixedness (men motivated only by their own pain, not their wives').

One woman begged her husband (Jim) for more than a decade to get more serious about pursuing a job. He always had a fresh excuse about why he couldn't. She finally had enough and filed for divorce, and in his desperation to get her to change her mind, her husband landed a job *within thirty days.*

Is that a coincidence, or is it just evidence that he wasn't motivated by her frustration; he was motivated only by the pain he would feel over losing his wife?

Another wife had been complaining for more than a decade about a controlling husband (Mark). Her husband admits he was very controlling. She kept trying to tell him she couldn't breathe, but he didn't pay much attention until she met with a lawyer to file for divorce and rented an apartment.

Her husband met with me in a state of panic, admitting his faults and now eager to address them. When I met with them, I realized the wife needed a break and affirmed the idea of a separation.

Except for one thing. Looking at the husband, I said, "*You* need to be the one who lives in the apartment, not her. Your actions led to the need for this separation, so you should feel the pain the most."

He agreed. His wife told me over the ensuing months that he truly did change and became an entirely different husband—and this change has been sustained over the long term. She had expressed her frustration for well over a decade, but it wasn't until he experienced his own personal pain and loss that he was willing to change.

The danger I've seen working as a pastor with couples in these situations is when a wife waits too long to hold the husband accountable. She puts up with it, puts up with it, and puts up with it some more until she's at her wit's end and leaves; that's when the husband says he'll *start* to change, but the wife is at the end of the negotiations, not the beginning.

Dr. Rhode sees the threat of a husband losing his wife as perhaps the greatest possible motivator for a husband. Of course, we have to place this within the context of a covenantal, committed marriage. That's why, on occasion, separation can be a way of allowing a husband to feel the pain of his poor choices, calling him to repentance.

Separation can also give the wife an opportunity to clear her mind and get closer to God. The separation isn't just to let the husband feel the pain of his consequences, but also to help the wife get her spiritual sense restored and to give her an opportunity to step out of the chaos of defining her well-being and person by the behavior of her husband. It's not a sin to need a "vacation" if your marriage is driving you crazy.

If it sounds harsh to hold your husband accountable, just remember that the same Bible that prohibits most divorces also prohibits harsh treatment of wives (Colossians 3:19: "Husbands, love your wives and do not be harsh with them") and adultery, including pornography (Matthew 5:28). We shouldn't act like one command is more important than another. God's Word is clearly bent toward preserving marriages while also clearly challenging husbands not to make their marriages miserable through abusive talk and behavior or lustful unfaithfulness. You didn't write the Bible, so it's not on you that God asks men to behave in certain ways.

Confronting misbehavior, then, is simply a method of achieving the kind of marriage God says he wants us to have. Allowing a sick marriage to be perpetuated without challenge doesn't fully honor God.

I've seen God work in so many miraculous ways when a woman becomes strong. One man was unfaithful to his wife so many times that anyone would have told her it was within her rights biblically to get a divorce. But she began to see a brokenness and repentance she had never seen before and was willing to work on the marriage with this caveat: her husband had to go to a sexual addiction recovery center that required him to take a lie detector test as she asked him any question she wanted to. And he agreed to submit to the lie detector test every three months for the next several years. It was also understood that one more act of adultery would result in immediate divorce.

Their marriage eventually reached a new level of intimacy, but notice, it wasn't built on looking the other way. It was built on, "You did this; these are the consequences; and this is the necessary step forward. If you won't accept the consequences and do the work necessary to become a different kind of husband, you lose me."

Regarding Jim, the man who just wouldn't get a job, the Bible is clear that a man's chronic refusal to provide for his wife and children is a serious spiritual abandonment: "Anyone who does not provide for their relatives, and especially for their own household, has denied the faith and is worse than an unbeliever" (1 Timothy 5:8).

If a man is unemployed and earnestly looking for work, it would be cruel for a woman to divorce him or separate from him. But when a guy has spent a decade finding excuse after excuse for why he can't get a job when he's well educated and able-bodied, one might question the wife's patience more than her calling him to account. I'm not recommending divorce, but I wouldn't object to her financially separating herself from him and letting him face the consequences of his inaction.

God is against divorce in most cases, but he is equally against marriages that are sucking the lives out of women who are married to spiritually sick men. If a man has an addiction but refuses to work on recovery, if he is unfaithful to her or so entangled in porn while refusing to get help that their intimate life has all but been extinguished, then the fault in the marital breakdown lies with the offense against the wife, not with the wife admitting that the marital vows have been broken.

And one Christian therapist reminds me that a "writ of divorce" is not a divorce. It's a statement that things can't stay the same, that the "get out of jail free" card has been turned in and things need to change. You will need to work through your own beliefs about the biblical basis for divorce and separation before employing any of these strategies.

Dr. Rhode seeks to encourage women "who, because of so many currents in their upbringing, socialization, and culture, don't realize the power they have been given in Christ, in their own character and personhood, to move their husbands. They feel powerless because of their gender, and this has resulted in a lot of pent-up anger, frustration, and even desperation."

As your brother in Christ, I'm encouraging you to be bold, courageous, and strong. Use the natural and very real spiritual influence and role that God has designed for you to move the man in your life. Learn how to express your person and your voice while developing new strength. Develop your sense of purpose and selfhood. In other words, don't just focus on helping your husband overcome his negative qualities; seek to grow your own positive qualities as well.

And please, don't let your husband's lack of spiritual health co-opt your own. Jesus told us to "seek first [the Father's] kingdom"

(Matthew 6:33), that is, to keep focusing on God's work through us, not to seek first a healthy spouse. Sometimes a wife has to step outside codependency and just admit, "If he is going to bring negative consequences on himself, I'm not going to participate. I'm still going to focus primarily on seeking first God's kingdom. How does God want to use me today? Is there another ministry I've been blind to in my obsession to keep my husband together? Is rescuing him yet again really the best use of my time? Maybe I need to hold a friend's hand while she's going through cancer rather than try to track down my husband's latest act of misbehavior."

Separation is a risky (though sometimes necessary) strategy. Short of moving out, your goal could be to figure out how to let your husband feel the pain of his choices. If he's financially reckless, for example, perhaps you have to eliminate cable television or simply refuse to eat out with him. If he doesn't do his share of the housework, the house doesn't get clean.

The general idea is understanding that he's not motivated by your hurt, but rather only by his inconvenience. It's an important distinction: you're not punishing him, but you're allowing him to face the consequences of his actions, transferring the hurt back onto his shoulders instead of yours.

That's how you address it relationally; let's look at the spiritual solution.

A NEW WAY FORWARD

Dr. Rhode points out that functional fixedness in men is rooted in the fall—our selfishness and sin nature. Many men never connect their spiritual conversion with how they relate to their wives. Ideally, discipleship would address how surrendering to God and the work of the Holy Spirit makes us more sensitive toward our wives, more engaged with them, and perhaps more gentle. Sadly, too few men connect "spiritual conversion" with "marital conversion."

Let me put it this way: if there's something wrong with the way a guy is treating his wife, there's something wrong with his heart toward God; he has an immature spiritual relationship with his heavenly Father. Dr. Rhode likens functional fixedness to "what the Bible calls being stiff-necked people or darkened in their own thinking, even hard-hearted. Having eyes, they don't see the woman in front of them except in relation to their own feelings and needs. Having ears, they don't hear the woman they are married to except as it pertains to them: Is she nagging me or affirming me? Is she saying something I want to hear or something I want to shut out? The real problem here is that women can't change this. The problem lies with the man. It is his uncircumcised heart and unrenewed mind that sees his wife as a self-object and her pain as something to be avoided, silenced, ignored, or even harshly treated."

Do you understand what Dr. Rhode is saying? You're thinking, *How can I get my husband to be more sensitive?* while your husband is thinking, *How can I end this conversation that is causing me pain?* He doesn't want *your* pain to stop; he wants *his* pain to stop. This is because his heart hasn't been renewed. He is a stranger to *agapē* (selfless, Christlike) love. Putting someone else's needs above his own doesn't even occur to him because he does not have a sacrificial heart or mind-set.

If your husband is mired in functional fixedness, any appeal to empathy is futile. He is spiritually incapable of empathy.

When a man is close to Christ, when he has surrendered to the work of the Holy Spirit, one of the first evidences will be a new sensitivity toward his wife and empathy for her welfare. Callousness toward our wives is, in fact, callousness toward God, who adores our wives and wants us to love them sacrificially. The problem of marriage is the problem of spiritual immaturity—the same men who obey Christ only when it is convenient love their wives only when it is in their best interest to do so.

What can a woman do? Form prayer groups with other wives

and pray for revival among your husbands. Ask God to move in a deep way so that men are convicted to love their God more deeply, take their marriage vows more seriously, and be more engaged in parenting.

It's one thing for a wife to nag her husband; it's entirely more effective when God *convicts* a husband. Keep first things first. Instead of obsessing over the symptom, ask God to heal the disease. This means you need to adopt a long-term view of change that will be internal and spiritual before it is external and marital. More than simply praying for a change in the way your husband treats you, pray first for a change in your own heart for God, that God will ground you in his strength to face the challenge ahead. Next, pray for a change in your husband's heart toward God. In the end, that's the most effective way for him to change the way your husband treats you and looks at you. He's spiritually bent, and that will need to be your focus before God. Instead of trying to *fix* your marriage, ask God to overwhelm your husband's soul so that he falls in love with the Suffering Servant, Jesus.

Join with other women to plead with God to bring a revival among the men in your community. But while you're praying about your husband, please keep praying for each other. Ask God to reveal your own functional fixedness and entrenched sins. Then, as wives joined in Christ, encourage each other by praying Ephesians 1:17–23 over each other:

> I keep asking that the God of our Lord Jesus Christ, the glorious Father, may give you the Spirit of wisdom and revelation, so that you may know him better. I pray that the eyes of your heart may be enlightened in order that you may know the hope to which he has called you, the riches of his glorious inheritance in his holy people, and his incomparably great power for us who believe. That power is the same as the mighty strength he exerted when he raised Christ from the dead and seated him

at his right hand in the heavenly realms, far above all rule and authority, power and dominion, and every name that is invoked, not only in the present age but also in the one to come. And God placed all things under his feet and appointed him to be head over everything for the church, which is his body, the fullness of him who fills everything in every way.

And when you're done with that passage, encourage each other with this one from Ephesians 3:16–21:

I pray that out of his glorious riches he may strengthen you with power through his Spirit in your inner being, so that Christ may dwell in your hearts through faith. And I pray that you, being rooted and established in love, may have power, together with all the Lord's holy people, to grasp how wide and long and high and deep is the love of Christ, and to know this love that surpasses knowledge—that you may be filled to the measure of all the fullness of God.

Now to him who is able to do immeasurably more than all we ask or imagine, according to his power that is at work within us, to him be glory in the church and in Christ Jesus throughout all generations, for ever and ever! Amen.

In these passages lie your ultimate hope, your glorious inheritance as one of God's daughters. It's always better to end a prayer session focusing on the power of God than on the weakness of men.

GOD IS YOUR FRIEND

In a frustrating marriage, God may feel like your only friend, so I'm passionate about helping you stay connected with him. This means accepting some responsibility for the situation you are in. When you marry a man with a hard heart, it may take a long time for the heart to soften, but don't forget—*you chose this man*. Perhaps he was a charmer who duped you, or you were less worldly-wise than you are now, so I'm not saying you should beat yourself up over it. But you did make a commitment of your own free will. It won't serve you at all to accuse God for choosing this man for you. I've addressed this in other books and blog posts. You need God on your side as an encouragement; nothing will be gained by becoming his accuser.

You might be tempted to say, *Why didn't God stop me from marrying him?* But that's like a bank robber sitting in jail, blaming God by shouting, *Why didn't you stop me from trying to rob that bank?*

We need God to comfort us when we face the consequences of our actions; it does no good to blame God for the consequences of our actions. Instead, we should ask God to help us apply his grace and power to help us move forward.

When you make a promise to someone, regardless of your motivation behind that promise, it's still a promise. You have to own it. Passive disappointment and feeling sorry for yourself won't change anything. Enthusiastic reengagement, fueled by your own passion for God, and courageous action, fueled by your security in God, is the best platform from which you can influence your husband.

BE BOLD

The first thing so many women in the Bible had to be told was to stop being afraid and become bold. When Hagar was abandoned by her husband and exiled to what looked like her and her son's slow starvation and death, God's angel encouraged her: "Do not be afraid" (Genesis 21:17). When the women who had been faithful to Jesus were beside themselves with grief, wondering what had happened to the body of their precious Jesus, an angel admonished them, "Do not be afraid" (Matthew 28:5).

I know I may sound as though I'm encouraging you toward risky action, but the "safe" path is sometimes a slow drift toward destruction. One of my favorite Christian philosophers, Elton Trueblood, put it so well:

> The person who never goes out on a limb will never, it is true, have the limb cut off while he is on it, but neither will he reach the best fruit. The best fruit which human life offers seems to come only within the reach of those who face life boldly . . . with no excessive concern over possible failure and personal danger. The good life is always the gambler's choice, and comes to those who take sides. Neutrality is seldom a virtue.[2]

Fear gives birth to paralysis—and sometimes inaction is our greatest enemy. Marriages can slowly die from years of apathy. I've seen many relationships wilt from unhealthy patterns that one or both partners refused to address. The most damaging thing you can do in an unhealthy relationship is *nothing*. FedEx founder Frederick Smith observed, "Too many think inaction is the least risky path. Sometimes action is the most conservative and safest path. Not doing anything is exceedingly dangerous. Before Pearl Harbor, they put all the airplanes in the middle of the airfield thinking saboteurs were the biggest risk, not a carrier-borne attack. They were undone by cautiousness, not bravado."[3]

If you always play it safe in your marriage, you're going to end up in some ruts. What I believe will give you the most boldness and courage to address issues that need to change is, first, understanding who you are in Christ and, second, letting God, not your marital status, define your life. Armed with that acceptance, security, and empowerment, you become a mighty force for good. You can then claim the power of Moses' words in Deuteronomy 31:8: "The LORD himself goes before you and will be with you; he will never leave you nor forsake you. Do not be afraid; do not be discouraged."

Fear and discouragement create stagnancy and persistent

disappointment in marriage. If you've had your fill of those, why not try God's path of faith and boldness? When you begin taking initiative instead of simply feeling sorry for yourself, you become an active woman, and active women mirror the active God who made them.

ACTIVE GOD, ACTIVE WOMEN

Genesis 1 provides our initial glimpse of who God is. The first thing God wants us to know is that he is an extraordinarily *active* God. In Genesis 1, *thirty-eight* active verbs describe what God does: he creates, he speaks, he separates, he calls, he blesses, he gives, and much more—all in just one chapter.

Then—and this is key—he tells the woman and the man *to do the same*: "God blessed them [male and female] and said to them, 'Be fruitful and increase in number; fill the earth and subdue it. Rule over the fish in the sea and the birds in the sky and over every living creature that moves on the ground'" (Genesis 1:28).

God made you, as a woman, to rule in this world, to subdue it, to act according to his image. Sin often drags us back toward sluggishness, despair, and despondency—giving in to life as it is rather than remaking life as it could be with God's redeeming power unleashed. People give up on their marriages, give up on prayer, give up on their churches, give up on their kids, and eventually even give up on themselves. They say, "It's no use," and start to sulk instead of painstakingly remaking their marriage—simply because their first (or even tenth) attempt failed.

Initial romantic intensity is unearned; it seems to fall on us out of nowhere. But marriage has to be built stone by stone. We must make deliberate choices. We must be active and confront the weaknesses we see in ourselves and in each other.

The current challenges in your marriage may well be God's vehicle for you to become the strong woman he created you to be.

QUESTIONS FOR DISCUSSION AND REFLECTION

1. Have you ever encountered functional fixedness in your own marriage? What did it look like? What didn't work as you tried to address it? Based on what Gary shared, what might be a more effective approach in the future?

2. What is an appropriate way for a woman who is committed to a biblical view of marriage—"till death do us part"—to stand up and say, "If this doesn't change, our relationship *will* be affected"? What might be the dangers of such an exchange? What might be some of the benefits—for the wife as well as for the husband?

3. Do you agree with Gary that the most damaging thing you can do in an unhealthy relationship is nothing? What keeps some women from acting boldly? What will help them act more courageously?

4. Have you ever given up on an issue in your marriage? In what way? What have you done that doesn't work? What have you done that seems to work?

5. In what area of your marriage is it most difficult for you to be active and to show courage? How can women encourage each other to be less passive and more active in their marriages?

6. List the top two areas in your marriage that need positive, God-honoring influencing. Begin praying for God to show you appropriate, active, love-affirming responses.

PART 2

CREATING THE CLIMATE FOR CHANGE

CHAPTER 4

ACCEPTING A MAN WHERE HE IS

Understanding a Man's Deepest Thirst

In a land laid waste by famine, with no food anywhere, a mother looked at the remaining flour and oil and realized she had enough for one last meal.

This scene played out nearly three thousand years ago, long before supermarkets overflowed with food and before convenience stores and fast-food restaurants on every street corner promised quick remedies for growling stomachs. Back then, during a famine and drought, no food meant, literally, *no food*. Every apple had been picked; every potato had been dug up. Even the bark had been stripped off the trees. Anything that could possibly be consumed had been consumed, leaving death as the last certainty.

Imagine you are this widow, whose story is told in 1 Kings 17. You've endured the trauma of watching your husband die—and now you face the awful prospect of watching your son slowly waste away from starvation.

Just then, a strange man enters your life, claiming to be God's prophet. He asks you to make him a meal. When you reply that you're running out of flour and oil, with just enough to make one last meal for you and your son, he assures you that if you'll bake him the last loaf, your jar of flour will never run out and your jug of oil will never run dry.

What do you have to lose? So you do what he says and then watch in amazement as his words prove true. For months on end, that tiny pile of flour and that small jug of oil continue to replenish themselves. At first, you opened that jar and jug with great trepidation. You wanted to believe you were living a miracle, but your mind fought the idea all the way: *Maybe the flour was just stuck to the sides of the jar; maybe the oil just ran down the sides and gathered at the bottom.* Gradually, after a few days, you realize that only one explanation makes sense: God is miraculously providing for you through this prophet named Elijah. No natural phenomenon can explain what you're experiencing.

Over time, you're no longer surprised when you open the jar and the jug. In fact, though it goes against all reason, you would be more surprised if those receptacles were empty than full. The replenishing has happened so often that it no longer seems like a miracle. It's just the way things are.

But then tragedy strikes and shakes you out of your complacency. Your son becomes seriously ill from a disease that bears no connection to hunger. After a painful battle, he succumbs to the sickness and dies.

Now you are furious with the man of God who has kept you from starvation. What good did it do you to be spared an early death from hunger, only to watch your son die from disease? You confront Elijah and tell him exactly what you think of him and how you wish you had never laid eyes on him.

Elijah takes your son into a back room, out of your sight. A short while later, you can't believe your eyes—your once-dead son walks straight into your arms! You've never felt joy like this, and in a spontaneous gush of praise, you cry out, "Now I know that you are a man of God and that the word of the LORD from your mouth is the truth" (1 Kings 17:24).

Suddenly it gets very quiet. You realize you've just insulted the man who saved your son. *Now* you know that he is a man of God and that God speaks through him? Only *now* you believe him? What have you been eating for the last several months? Where do you think that flour kept coming from? Who told you, against all reason, that the oil would keep flowing? And yet, still, it takes *this* for you to believe his words?

What happened to the widow so long ago continues to happen in many marriages today. Elijah's miraculous provision for this woman became commonplace. What once seemed like an extraordinary occurrence—flour and oil that never ran out—soon became a common blessing, so expected that it ceased to be noticed, much less appreciated. After a week or so, it was just the way things were.

Sadly, many women view their husbands in this very way. Their spouses' strong points become so familiar that the women no longer see them, much less appreciate them. But when one weakness rears its ugly head, all else gets blotted from memory.

Husbands pick up on this. In one poll of a thousand men taken a number of years ago, just 10 percent of husbands—only one out of ten—believed their wives love them more than they love their wives.[1] We think we're much happier with you than you are with us.

BLINDED TO THE BLESSING

On the first anniversary of the 9/11 airplane terrorist attacks on New York City and the Pentagon, Lisa and I watched several interviews with women who were widowed as a result of those attacks. "What has changed most about your perspective in the past year?" the interviewer asked. The first widow to respond said, "The thing I can't stand is when I hear wives complain about their husbands."

Every woman nodded her head, and then another widow added, "It would make my day if I walked into the master bathroom and saw the toilet seat left up."

The little things we allow to annoy us seem trivial compared to the loss of blessings once taken for granted. In the face of their enormous loss, these women no longer cared about the little irritations; instead, they had to face the big black hole of all that their husbands had done for them suddenly sucked out of their lives forever.

Sarah lives on the East Coast. She attended one of my "Sacred Marriage" conferences and had gathered with several women in a small group between sessions. One wife started boasting about the beautiful backyard rock garden her husband had built over a three-day weekend. Sarah seemed unusually quiet until she finally held up her hand and said, "Please stop! My husband spent all last weekend on the couch watching a golf tournament. I don't need to hear about how your husband spent those days working in the yard!"

Later, I spoke with Sarah one-on-one, wanting to put the principle of this chapter into action.

I began by asking her a few simple questions.

"How large is your house?" I asked.

"A little over two thousand square feet," she said. "And it has a nice yard."

"Wow, that sounds great, especially with three small children. You must feel fortunate to be there."

"I guess so," she said.

"Where do you work?" I asked.

"Oh, I don't work," Sarah replied. "My husband makes enough for me to stay at home with the kids, as I've always wanted to do."

"That's fantastic!" I told her. "Do you realize that 65 percent of the women in your situation have to work outside the home, whether they want to or not? You're one in three as far as being able to choose to stay home. That's gotta feel good."

"I guess so," she said.

I steered the conversation to the Monday following her husband's lazy weekend. Unbeknownst to Sarah, I had spoken with her husband, so I knew what had taken place on Monday. Jeremy took their son out for a little batting practice; the young boy was preparing to start his first T-ball season and was eager to get some tips from his dad. Later that afternoon, Jeremy took their daughters to a movie. On the way home, he called Sarah and asked if he could get anything for her at the grocery store.

After Sarah recounted all this, I asked her, "Do you have any idea what a single mom would say if for just one day a man came over and took her son out for some guy time, teaching him how to hit a baseball, or if he gave her a break by taking her daughters out in the afternoon and then called to see if he could pick up anything for her at the store on the way home? She would feel so blessed. She'd go to bed praying, *Thank you, Lord, for one day when it wasn't all on my shoulders.*"

I watched as a light switched on in Sarah's face. She glided over to Jeremy and kissed him on the forehead.

"What was that for?" he asked.

"For being you," Sarah replied.

Sarah had forgotten Jeremy's "common blessings." Minutes before, she had been blind to what her husband did by focusing only on what he hadn't done on one weekend. Now, she saw him in a new light.

LOVING ACCEPTANCE

It is a sophisticated spiritual challenge to not compare your spouse's weakness with another spouse's strength.

I admit that if I were talking to Jeremy, I'd challenge him to consider whether spending most of the weekend watching golf is the best use of time for a young husband and father. Jeremy very likely overdid it on that one occasion. Even so, it wasn't fair of Sarah to look at Jeremy only in regard to this one lost weekend. Jeremy had provided a beautiful home. He earned enough money so Sarah could stay at home with her kids, as she wanted to. He was involved in his children's lives. Jeremy wasn't a perfect man, but there was plenty to be thankful for.

I say this not to be your husband's advocate, but *yours*. To move a man, you must learn to appreciate him for who he is, which comes wrapped up in all that he is not. James 3:2 has revolutionized the way I look at family life: "We all stumble in many ways." Notice the words *all* and *many*. No spouse avoids this reality. We *all*—including your husband—stumble in *many* ways. To live with any man is to live with someone who is certain to let you down—not just once or twice, but in many ways. That "Mr. Perfect Husband" you see graciously open the door for his wife every Sunday, who always seems kind and thoughtful and who provides a wonderful income? Somewhere, in some concrete expression, that man stumbles in many ways. If you were to divorce your husband and spend five years interviewing potential second husbands, if you gave them psychological tests and interviewed their closest friends and family members, if you found a man who seemed to match you emotionally and spiritually and recreationally—if you believe Scripture is true, you'd still end up with a husband who would stumble in *many* ways.

Think about the marvelous and honest view of marriage in traditional vows: "for better, for worse, for richer, for poorer, in sickness and in health." These vows tell us that marriage is about accepting the fact that all of us are weak. Marriage is a commitment to accept our spouses' fallibilities as well as their strengths. In a sense, we're all lemons, but you can do very good and creative things with lemons when you accept their benefits and their dangers. God can do divine things through our weaknesses. Because he is a master musician, he can play exquisitely beautiful music through dented instruments. Made in his image, that becomes our goal in marriage too: bringing the best music out of our "dented" spouse.

Since every wife is married to an imperfect man, every wife will have legitimate disappointments in her marriage. Are you going to define your husband by these disappointments, or will you pray that God will open your eyes to the common blessings that your husband provides and to which you often become blinded?

My wife and I once met a woman married to a marvelous handyman, the type of guy who can fix anything. If he builds a tree house for his children, it has working doors and windows. He keeps his wife's SUV in perfect running condition. Nothing in their house stays broken for longer than forty-eight hours. But he isn't particularly deep, in his wife's view. He doesn't favor long, soulful talks. He's a good listener, but you won't hear him sharing a lot of personal feelings. And he never cracks open a book.

My wife immediately liked the sound of this man, because she lives with the constant frustration of having a mechanical klutz for a husband. She has to endure toilets that keep running, doors that stick, and projects that get put off until we save up enough money to pay a professional to do them. When I try to fix something, the problem invariably gets worse, costing us even more to fix it in the long run.

And yet this other wife made it pretty clear that she wished her husband would be available to talk things out. She wondered aloud to my wife what it would be like to be married to a husband who deals with concepts and who regularly talks to people and who likes to discuss books with his wife. I'm pretty sure my wife may have felt tempted to wonder whether this woman had a much better thing going, particularly when Lisa had to get up in the middle of the night (for the umpteenth time) to jiggle the handle on the toilet to get the water to stop running!

No husband comes in a perfect package. No husband can do it all. Your job as a wife is to fight to stay sensitive to your husband's strengths. Resist the temptation to compare his weaknesses to another husband's strengths, while forgetting your husband's strengths and somebody else's husband's weaknesses. Don't resent your husband for being less than perfect; he can't be anything else.

DISAPPOINTMENT DETECTORS

Why is this perspective crucial if you are going to provide a sacred influence? Husbands detect disappointment with uncanny accuracy. And we tend to react like this: *If I can't please her by trying my hardest, then why should I try at all?* I'm not saying we *should* react this way; I'm just saying that's how we usually react.

If you want to move your husband in a positive direction, then you need to appreciate him from your heart.

In her book *Capture His Heart*, Lysa TerKeurst tells of boarding a shuttle bus at the airport, where she met a sixty-year-old man who said something very simple but astonishing. Lysa commented that people must love to see the shuttle bus pull up because it means they're going home. The driver laughed. "Yeah, everyone is excited to see me pull up to the curb. That's why I like my job so much. People get on the bus and smile so big. They've just been waiting for me, and when I finally arrive, they are happy I'm here. I've often wished I had a video camera to tape people as they get on my bus with the smiling faces and 'glad to see ya' comments. I'd love for my wife to see a tape like that. That's the way I've always wanted her to look when I come home from work."[2]

That's the way I've always wanted her to look when I come home from work.

I doubt there's a guy alive who doesn't feel this way. Whether we're a shuttle bus driver, a CEO, a world-class athlete, or an assistant manager at a grocery store, it does something to a man's heart when his wife and kids look happy to see him. I know, sometimes because of our surly moods and our air of entitlement, we can make it very difficult for you to feel happy to see us.

My friend Dave Deur, a pastor at Central Wesleyan Church in

Holland, Michigan, taught a class on marriage, during which he asked all the men to list five ways they love to be loved. Virtually *all* the lists included acts or words of appreciation—and many men listed affirmation several times, using different words. I was struck by how many men used at least two (or often even three) of their five answers to describe affirmation. In fact, one man's list of five things could all be summarized as affirmation!

Which means the shuttle driver who wanted his wife's face to light up when she saw him isn't unusual; he's typical. Rule number one for influencing your husband is this: *Stop taking your husband for granted.* He wants to feel noticed, special, and appreciated. That puts him in a "moldable" mood. When he feels he is being taken for granted, he becomes defensive and resentful at the mere suggestion of change. Change will not happen in the absence of *motivation.*

Leslie Vernick, author of *How to Act Right When Your Spouse Acts Wrong*, once asked a husband in a counseling situation what he would most like from his wife. He responded, "There was a guy at work who was clumsy and never did the job quite right. None of us guys thought much of him, but when his wife came in one day, she looked at him like he could do no wrong. All of us guys were jealous of him from then on, because we knew he wasn't perfect, but his wife treated him like he was. I would love for my wife to look at me like that."

SPIRITUAL ACCEPTANCE

If you notice a lot of tension in your home, a high level of frustration and anger in your husband's life, a discouragement leading to passivity (where he underachieves), or an "escapist" mentality (where he spends his free time playing video games or watching sports, escaping the home with excessive recreation), you could be looking at a man who doesn't feel loved, appreciated, and respected—a man who is *coping*, not truly living. And men who merely cope never change; they just pass time. They're medicating the pain rather than attacking the disease.

I'm not blaming you for his passivity; you may indeed be appreciating a man who is sinfully passive. I'm just trying to help you understand a possible platform from which to confront it.

Affirmation is more than a man's desire—much more. Acceptance and encouragement are biblical requirements:

- "Accept one another, then, just as Christ accepted you, in order to bring praise to God" (Romans 15:7).
- "Encourage one another and build each other up" (1 Thessalonians 5:11).
- "Encourage one another daily" (Hebrews 3:13).

Even if your husband never changes—even if every bad habit, neglected responsibility, or annoying character trait stays exactly the same—then, for your own spiritual health, you need to learn how to love this man *as he is*. Too many books and articles ignore this point. Your first step—the primary one—is to love, accept, and even honor your imperfect husband.

Affirmed

Following a recent conference I led on my book titled *Cherish*, an African-American woman with a Southern drawl spoke to my wife at the book table. She had heard the way I talked about Lisa and just wanted her to know, "He love you. He *cherish* you. You a cherished wife."

My wife smiled and said, "I know," but what that woman doesn't know is the thirty years' journey it took us to get where we are.

Lisa married a man with stunningly few skills. I couldn't measure up to her dad in terms of business acumen, financial acumen, Mr. Fixit acumen, and any other number of issues. Furthermore, she was a bit naive when she married me. Because I was a leader in our college ministry and given some respect for my role there, Lisa told a friend, "I thought Gary could do no wrong. If he thought something, it must be right because he seemed so close to God. And if he did something, it must be right. But then we got married, and I found out he *could* be wrong. And he *could* sin."

That was a disillusioning discovery, I'm sure. And then we went through two decades of "ministry pay," meaning money was always elusive and bills were always painful. Plus, since ministry requires so much time, I was around the house less often than many husbands would be. In contrast, her dad had been self-employed and was around the house more often than most husbands.

I felt Lisa's early disappointment keenly. Looking back, it was a terrible wound because I'm a people pleaser and the thought that I couldn't please my wife was doubly hurtful. I wish I could just go back and give that young couple a hug and say, "It's going to be all right."

What I enjoy so much now, however, is that I feel accepted. Lisa knows what I lack and what I bring to the table, and she is finally at peace with it. She puts up with my quirks, respects the areas God has refined, and seems delighted to be married to me. In the last couple years, I've heard her tell others (and occasionally me) many times, "Well, I just happened to marry the best husband in the world"—but I'm not sure she said that *once* in our first two decades of marriage. And I've probably changed more in the last decade than I did in the first two decades combined.

Accepting your husband is one of the best gifts you can give him, as well as providing the most fertile soil to bring about even more change. As I wrote in *Cherish*, I cherish my wife because I promised to do so and because God called me to do so, but she is making it easier every day to do that. For a rather insecure person who never felt like he quite measured up—for me to be treasured above men I know are more capable, attractive, and intelligent than I am makes me want to please her more and more.

This won't be true of every husband, but age, quite frankly, helps. The male brain gets a greater percentage of estrogen as we age, and we tend to value being loyal to our wives and thus pleasing them a bit more.

But consider the strategy Becky Allender used with Dan when he was a younger man, and she caught him acting his worst on a ski slope.

"You're a Good Man"

In his excellent book *How Children Raise Parents*, Dr. Dan Allender describes how his young son lost his nerve on a ski slope. Andrew asked his dad to carry him down, but Dan refused because he wanted the boy to confront his fears. Andrew had a temper tantrum, falling to the ground and kicking his feet in full view of everyone.

Dan has a PhD in counseling, and a little boy's tantrum wasn't going to cut it. Dan raised his voice in anger, so his wife, Becky, stepped in and suggested he go on ahead and let her handle it.

Dan skied just thirty or forty yards down the mountain and then stopped to watch. Andrew continued his tantrum in spite of Becky's gentle entreaties. That was the last straw for Dan. He went back up the slope, fuming all the while, and met Becky with the words, "Move. Your way didn't work. I'll get him down my way."[3]

You're about to witness the profound power a strong, godly woman represents. I'll let Dan take it from here:

> Becky stood her ground.
>
> My wife looked at me with kindness and strength. When I finally reached her, her head slowly turned from side to side, and she said, "No."
>
> There was a moment of silence, and she said, "I know you've been shamed by many men who meant the world to you. And I know that is not what you want to do to your son." It was all she had to say. A myriad faces flashed in my memory; and I

felt again the raw experience of being humiliated and shamed by men who really did matter to me. It silenced my anger and I began to cry. My wife put her hand on my heart and said, "You're a good man." She turned away and in one fluid, graceful movement, she skied down the steep, icy slope.[4]

Even while Dan was at his worst, his wife called him to his best, using affirmation. She stood up to him, but she also touched him in his anger and firmly but gently reminded him, "You're a good man," even though he wasn't acting like a good man.

When Dan reached his son, he was chastened and softened. That's the power women have—one magnanimous gesture and one aptly spoken phrase can work wonders. Since Dan's son had seen and heard everything, Dan opted for the direct approach.

"Andrew, you saw my face as I was coming up the slope, didn't you?"

He quivered. "Yes."

"And you saw how angry I was, didn't you?"

"Yesss."

"And you were afraid, weren't you?"

"Yes, yesss."

"And you knew I'd make you pay if Mommy had not been so strong and loving and stood in my way and protected you."

At this point his eyes were bristling with tears, and his cheeks were shivering with fear. I looked at him, put my hands on his cheeks, and said, "Andrew, I was wrong. Mommy loved me well and loved you well too. She invited me to see what I had become and what I did not want to be. Andrew, I'm sorry for being so angry. Please forgive me."

The gift my son gave is incalculable. He put his hand on my heart as he had seen my wife do and he said with tears, "Daddy, Mommy is right. You are a good man."[5]

This could have been a nightmare story, alienating husband from wife and father from son. Becky's ability to see and call out the good in her husband, even when he was acting his worst, turned it into a special moment of uncommon intimacy between a dad and his boy.

Can you see the good in your husband, even when he's at his worst? Can you pause long enough to see the hurt behind the heat, and call him to his best? If you can learn to do that, you will begin the sacred pathway of influencing a man toward you, God, and your family.

QUESTIONS FOR DISCUSSION AND REFLECTION

1. List the three main positive traits that first attracted you to your husband. When was the last time you complimented your husband for these traits?

2. If your husband were to die, apart from his companionship, what two or three things would you miss most? How can you affirm these qualities now?

3. Does James 3:2 ("we all stumble in many ways") help you look at your husband—and your marriage—in a new light? How so?

4. What kind of expression is usually on your face when your husband returns home (or when you return home)? How can you greet him in a nurturing and affirming way?

5. How would your husband's friends describe the way you look at your husband? Does this need to change? How so?

6. Where is your man most likely to fail with regard to character? How can you—following Becky Allender's example—call your husband to his best with affirmation while still saying no to sin?

CHAPTER 5

ASKING GOD FOR FRESH EYES

How You Can Know Love with an Imperfect Man

When Bobby Kennedy became the United States attorney general, the leaders of the civil rights movement despaired. Bobby was, according to one leader at the time, "famously not interested in the civil rights movement. We knew we were in deep trouble. We were crestfallen, in despair, talking to Martin [Luther King Jr.], moaning and groaning about the turn of events, when Dr. King slammed his hand down and ordered us to stop the [complaining]. 'Enough of this,' he said. 'Is there nobody here who's got something good to say about Bobby Kennedy?' We said, 'Martin, that's what we're telling ya! There is no one. There is nothing good to say about him . . . he's bad news.'"[1]

Maybe you've felt this way at times about your husband. You see so many negatives, so many challenges and prejudices and bad habits to overcome, that you honestly can't think of one good thing to say about him. As long as you stay in this place, you'll never move him. You'll never influence him.

Martin Luther King Jr. understood this profoundly. He looked at his fellow leaders and said, "Well, then, let's call this meeting to a close. We will [reconvene] when somebody has found one thing redeeming to say about Bobby Kennedy, *because that, my friends, is the door through which our movement will pass.*"[2]

In his view, there was no way they could move this man toward their position until they found one redeeming thing to say about him. That one thing would be the door of redemption, the door of influence, the door of change.

King's plan worked. They discovered that Bobby was close to his bishop, and they worked through this bishop so effectively that, according to the same leader who once could not find a single positive thing to say about Kennedy, "there was no greater friend to the civil rights movement [than Bobby Kennedy]. There was no one we owed more of our progress to than that man."[3]

Their greatest nightmare turned into their greatest dream.

This incredible triumph was built on the power of recognizing one or two strengths, building on them, and finding the road for their movement through that. You'll move your husband in the same way. When you find yourself in despair, overcome by negativity toward the man you married, remember the words of Martin Luther King Jr.: "We will [reconvene] when somebody has found one thing redeeming to say about Bobby Kennedy, because that, my friends, is the door through which our movement will pass."

You need to know that men tend to be hypersensitive to criticism and judgment, especially from people we value. The dorsal premammillary nucleus (located in the hypothalamus), described as the "defend your turf" area of the brain, "contains the circuitry for a male's instinctive one-upmanship, territorial defense, fear, and aggression. It's larger in males than in females."[4] If we feel attacked, we often focus more on the fact that we're being attacked than on the content or substance of what someone is challenging us about. That rarely leads to a productive conversation. I'm not saying we *should* be this way. It's immature, and we can learn to deal with this natural reflex. Living in the real world, though, it's something wives need to be aware of with their husbands.

YOU'RE NOT ALONE

When I urge you to affirm your husband's strengths, I'm not minimizing his many weaknesses; I'm simply encouraging you to make the daily spiritual choice of focusing on qualities for which you feel thankful. The time will come when you can address the weaknesses—after you've established a firm foundation of love and encouragement. For now, you must make a conscious choice to give thanks for his strengths.

I have found Philippians 4:8 as relevant for marriage as it is for life: "Whatever is true, whatever is noble, whatever is right, whatever is pure, whatever is lovely, whatever is admirable—if anything is excellent or praiseworthy—think about such things."

Obsessing over your husband's weaknesses won't make them go away. You may have done that for years—and if so, what has it gotten you, besides more of the same? Leslie Vernick warns that regularly thinking negatively about your husband *increases* your dissatisfaction with him and your marriage. Affirming your husband's strengths, however, will likely reinforce and build up those areas you cherish and motivate him to pursue excellence of character in others.

Guys rise to praise. When someone compliments us, we want to keep that person's positive opinion intact. We love how it feels when our wives respect us; we get a rush like nothing else when we hear her praise us or see that look of awe in her eyes—and we will all but travel to the ends of the earth to keep it coming.

Isn't this approach, based in God's Word, at least worth a try?

To make this realistic, you must keep in mind that no man is ever "on" all the time. This explains why your husband can be so thoughtful, caring, and attentive one day and so aloof, harsh, and critical the next. You have to give your husband room to be a less-than-perfect human, to have bad days, "off" days, and average days. The spiritual challenge comes from the fact that you are more likely to define your husband by his bad days than you are to accept the good days as the norm. Hold on to the good; begin to define him by the good; thank him (and God) for the good—and thereby reinforce the good.

The rest of this chapter will provide practical spiritual exercises to help you learn how to appreciate an imperfect man. In one sense, marriage is about learning to live with another person's brokenness and weaknesses. My prayer is that it will guide you away from taking your husband for granted and toward becoming intensely and consistently grateful for the man God has given you as a companion in the journey of life.

I fully understand it can feel very difficult—it can even be a monumental spiritual challenge—to learn how to appreciate a man who disappoints you in many ways. But here are a few tried and true spiritual practices to point you in the right direction.

Adopt a Nurturing Heart

In my boyhood days, our family had a dog that loved to chase cars. One fateful afternoon, she finally caught one and was seriously injured. My dad ran out to the road to retrieve her, and our family pet became a monster. Frenzied with fear and pain, that dog kept biting my dad as he gathered her into his arms. He had rushed to help her and bring her healing, but the pain so overwhelmed her that she could only bite the very hands trying to nurture her.

Your husband can be like that. Even if he had extraordinary parents, he most likely still brings some woundedness into your marriage. Maybe his siblings teased him. Maybe a former girlfriend broke his heart. Maybe he had a cold and calculating mother or father. The possibilities are endless, except that he comes to you as a hurting man. Maybe you even married a *deeply* wounded man.

Unfortunately, hurting men bite; sometimes, like our dog, they bite the very hands that try to bring healing.

I am not talking about accepting or condoning abusive behavior or a pattern of him threatening you. As stated up front, this advice is not meant for those who need to "escape" their marriages because their marriage has become unsafe; it is meant for those who need to help their husbands learn to be more gentle and understanding and learn how to process their frustration, anger, and shame in more mature ways.

Perhaps you could view such a man's actions through this lens: "What if he is a deeply wounded man acting out of shame and pain?" Before a dating relationship morphs into a permanent commitment, many women see a hurting man and think, *I want to help him.* But something about marriage often turns that around and makes the same woman ask, *Why does he have to be that way?* The man's needs once elicited feelings of nurture and compassion; now these same hurts tempt his wife toward bitterness and regret.

Before you get married is the time to make a character-based judgment ("Do I really want to live with this man's wounds?"). Once the ceremony is over, God challenges you to maintain an attitude of concern and nurture instead of one of resentment and frustration.

I realize marriage reveals more clearly a man's heart. And men sometimes change after they get married. Having children, getting fired from a job, or losing a parent can all be triggers that release the negative, buried propensities in a man, so, once again, I am not chastising you for a choice you made in the past. But you did make a choice. In light of that choice, can you maintain a soft heart over his past hurts, patiently praying for long-term change? Or will you freeze him in his incapacities with judgment, resentment, condemnation, and criticism? Can you maintain a *nurturing* attitude instead of a judgmental one? It really does help if you look at your husband's faults through the prism of his hurt—not to excuse him, but to plot a strategy for healing and then positive change.

Look at it this way: How would you want your daughter-in-law to treat your wounded son? That's likely how your husband's heavenly Father wants you to treat his wounded son.

Give Your Husband the Benefit of the Doubt

Some wives can literally stew in their disappointment about their husbands' relational shortcomings: "Why won't he help me?" "Why won't he talk to me about this?" "Why doesn't he seem to care?" They fail to realize that their husbands may not know what to do. Many women accuse their husbands of being uncaring or unloving when, in fact, they may just be clueless. It's possible that he's not trying to be stubborn, uncaring, or unfeeling; he just honestly doesn't know what you need or what he's supposed to do. And there are few things most guys hate more than not knowing what to do.

This is a key insight: it's easier and less painful for us to ignore the problem than to admit incompetence.

One mature wife said to the younger wives in small group for married couples, "Women often feel that if their husbands loved them, the men would know what they are thinking and what they need. This simply isn't true. As wives, we need to learn to speak our husbands' language; we need to be direct in our communication and tell them what we want them to do. When we want them to listen to us and not give advice, we need to tell them so. When we want their help on something, we need to ask them directly."[5]

My brother once frustrated his wife even while trying to please her. The kids had run out of toothpaste, so he went to the store and purchased something he thought his kids would love: Star Wars toothpaste gel. His daughters squealed with delight, but his wife hated it. "Have you ever tried to clean up that blue gunk?" she pointed out. "It sticks everywhere!" But she understood this as a case of good intentions gone bad.

Sadly, far too many wives assume the husband doesn't care or worse, that he's trying to make their lives more burdensome, when the reality may be that he just doesn't have a clue. My sister-in-law could choose one of two ways to look at the toothpaste fiasco: either my brother cared enough to make the trip to buy the toothpaste, or he intentionally made his wife's life more difficult by purchasing a brand that creates a cleaning nightmare.

Another wife told me that when she and her husband first began traveling together, she would ask him, "Are you hungry yet?" He'd say no, and she'd sit and stew because obviously he didn't care about her. When she learned to say "hey, I'm hungry; let's stop for lunch," her husband was always accommodating. She eventually realized that her husband wasn't trying to be thoughtless; he just wasn't catching the hint.

May I slay a very destructive myth? Perhaps you think the more your husband loves you, the better he'll become at reading your mind. That's a romantic but *highly* unrealistic and even destructive notion. It can create havoc in a marriage and hinder mature communication by keeping you from being direct, while at the same time tempting you toward resentment when your husband proves utterly incapable of telepathy.

Here's a healthier strategy. Instead of resenting your husband's occasional insensitivity, try to address him in a straightforward manner. Be direct instead of hoping he'll guess what you need. His seeming reluctance to help may well result from his having no idea what you want. Donna, a wife I interviewed for this book, told me that early on in her marriage, she said to her husband, "Honey, the lightbulb is out"—and her husband thought she was making an observation, while she thought she was asking him to change it.

Respect the Position Even When You Disagree with the Person

Coppelia's first son was born the day before her and Adam's second wedding anniversary. They had recently moved to California for Coppelia's job. While Adam was busy looking for work, he couldn't find a steady enough or sufficiently high-paying job by the time the baby came. He worked, but it wasn't nearly enough for him to provide the main income, and he had no medical benefits.

Adam felt humbled. Before the move, he had earned twice what Coppelia did and thought that relocating wouldn't keep him from finding a similar position. They kept expecting a door to open, but after Coppelia required a C-section and the doctors informed them that the baby would need surgery within a year, they realized the only option was for Adam to stay home with the baby while Coppelia went back to work. Coppelia felt heartbroken to leave her baby at eight weeks. She said, "We were both pretty miserable, wanting our roles to reverse, but as hard as we tried, it just wasn't working out that way."

These are the times that can test the mettle of a marriage, but it only strengthened Coppelia's.

"I suppose I could have been upset about many things, but it came back to what we felt God wanted us to do. We both prayed hard about the decision for Adam to quit his well-paying job, and for me to accept the one that relocated us to California. We both had peace about that decision. We also knew from the beginning that our family budget would be one. I didn't see my paycheck as *my* money; it was always *our* money. We made the decisions together, as hard as they were. My husband's position as the head of our home never changed, regardless of his income. God placed him there, and my respect for him and his leadership did not change. And at the end of the day, it made us stronger to weather those storms. We saw God provide for us, guide us on the way, and strengthen our marriage and our family."

One of the reasons Coppelia's marriage thrived during this time is that she wouldn't let disappointment undercut her respect for her husband. Coppelia reminds us that the Bible calls wives to respect their husbands: "The wife must respect her husband" (Ephesians 5:33). It doesn't say wives should respect *perfect* husbands or even *godly* husbands. It says that husbands—no qualifier—should be respected.

Of course, respect isn't an unqualified acquiescence of an unhealthy situation or relationship. Respect doesn't mean hiding or covering up destructive behavior. It *does* influence how you address destructive or disappointing behavior.

Biblically, there is a certain sense in which respect comes with the *position*, not with the *person*. The apostle Paul insulted a man by using bold language ("you whitewashed wall!") but then apologized after he learned he had been speaking to a high priest: "Brothers, I did not realize that he was the high priest; for it is written: 'Do not speak evil about the ruler of your people'" (Acts 23:3–5).

Your husband, *because he is a husband*, not to mention God's image bearer, deserves respect. You may disagree with his judgment, object to the way he handles things, be disappointed that he hasn't succeeded, and thus legitimately confront him, but according to the Bible, his position alone calls you to give him a certain amount of respect. If you withhold this respect, your husband may very well stop hearing you.

Share a Slice of the Grace That God Gives You

Elyse Fitzpatrick, a counselor, once told her small group about how God had moved her from a legalistic, works-oriented faith to a "grace-filled, peaceful existence with my merciful heavenly Father."

"The pressure is off me," she told them. "Don't get me wrong; it's not that I'm not pursuing holiness. It's just that I know that my Father will get me where He wants me to be and that even my failures serve, in some way, to glorify Him. My relationship with God is growing to be all about His grace, His mercy, His power."[6]

Then Elyse's friend astounded her by responding, "That must be such a blessing for your husband, Elyse. To be walking in that kind of grace must enable you to be so patient and so grace-filled with Phil. To know that God is working in him just as He's working in you must make your marriage so sweet and your husband so pleased. It must be great for him to know that the pressure is off for him too."

The reason this friend astounded Elyse is that Elyse didn't initially make the connection her friend made. "I scarcely ever extended to Phil the grace I enjoyed with the Lord. Instead, I was frequently more like the man in Jesus' parable who, after he was forgiven a great debt, went out and beat his fellow slave because he owed him some paltry sum."[7]

There was a gap in Elyse's mind about receiving grace and giving grace. To her credit, she responded to the truth as it was presented, and her marriage was blessed accordingly. It takes great spiritual maturity to love mercy, to offer grace, and to give someone the same spiritual benefits we have received from our heavenly Father. Get in touch with how much God has done for you—how he has seen every wicked act you've ever committed, heard every syllable of gossip, noticed every malicious, ugly, and hateful thought, and still loves you. Even more, he adores you. And he has forgiven you and given you new life in him.

Now comes the hard part. Will you give your husband at least a slice of what God has given you?

Form Your Heart through Prayer

Practice praying positive prayers for your husband. Find the five or six things he does really well—or even just one or two—and try to wear God out by thanking him for giving you a husband with these qualities. Follow up your prayers with comments or even greeting cards that thank your husband personally for who he is.

I've practiced this with my wife with amazing results. One morning, I awoke early and immediately sensed my frustration from the previous evening. We had an issue in our relationship that we had talked to death over the previous two decades. Lisa acknowledged her need to grow in this area, but events of the previous weeks had convinced me that nothing had changed.

I felt resentful, and when I'm in a resentful mood, I can slip into what I call "brain suck." I start building my case. Like a lawyer,

I recall every slight and every conversation, and I prove to my imaginary jury how wrong my wife is and how right I am.

Suddenly, I remembered the widow of Zarephath—the one rescued from starvation through the prayers of Elijah (1 Kings 17:7–24). I decided to apply the truth from this passage, so I mentioned something about Lisa's personality for which I felt very thankful. That reminded me of something else, which reminded me of something else, which reminded me of yet another quality. After about fifteen minutes, I literally started laughing. I saw so much to be thankful for that it seemed preposterous that I should waste time fretting over this single issue.

Prayers of thankfulness literally form our soul. They very effectively groom our affections. Leslie Vernick explains this from a counseling perspective: "Cognitive therapists know that what we think about directly affects our emotions. If we think about negative things, nursing bad attitudes or critical spirits, our emotions take a downward spiral. Conversely, if we think about things that are good, true, right—things we are thankful for—then our emotions can be uplifted."

Make liberal use of this powerful tool. We have to give it time. One session of thankfulness will not fully soften a rock-hard heart. But over time, thankfulness makes a steady and persistent friend of affection.

Drop Unrealistic Expectations

Patricia married a determined and ambitious husband. She says she knew, even before marrying Luis, that her husband intended to zealously fulfill God's call to reach the lost: "God wants everyone to be saved (1 Timothy 2:4), and there have been times when I thought my husband was determined to do his best to reach the last four billion lost souls for Jesus Christ." Because of Luis's call, Patricia faced certain difficulties that would drive some women crazy: "extensive travel, lengthy separations, and mothering four boys alone at least a third of the time." Add to this an uncertain income and living in three countries during the first few years of their marriage, and later a long bout with cancer, and you might expect to find a resentful, bitter wife. Not if you talk to Patricia. "We expected things to be different from the norm," she says. "We also knew up front that we couldn't meet each other's needs 100 percent. That realization protected us from disappointments that result from unrealistic expectations."[8]

Your husband will not meet 100 percent of your needs. He probably won't even meet 80 percent. If you expect him to, you're going to become frustrated, bitter, resentful, and angry. God didn't set up marriage to meet 100 percent of your needs. If your expectations are out of control, your beef may not be with your husband; it may be with the One who created marriage. When you ask more of your marriage than God designed it to give, you're going to live with deep and pervasive disappointment.

You may be tempted to reply, "But *my* expectations are legitimate, and he's not meeting those!" That's the challenge, isn't it? Some expectations *are* legitimate. If your husband never wants to be physically intimate with you, refuses to get a job and help support the family, spends more time with video games than with you and the kids, or creates an environment where you don't feel safe around him, you're not being unreasonable, and the fault isn't with your expectations but with your husband's behavior.

This is why it's helpful to a marriage to have a mature friend with whom you can discuss the state of your heart regarding your spouse. I have a few men who will tell me the truth, regardless of what they think I want to hear. They are as likely to challenge me as to agree with me, and they've been a source of rich counsel in my own marriage.

One of the first things Saul did after being crowned as the first king of Israel was to surround himself with "valiant men whose hearts God had touched" (1 Samuel 10:26). As you seek to live out your calling as a queen in your home, you may find it helpful, as I have, to find bold friends who are sensitive to God's wisdom and voice and who will valiantly speak that truth to you.

Go to the Cross

Some desires are never going to be fulfilled and need to be "crucified." In fact, various studies have suggested that more than 50 percent of marital issues will never be resolved. This requires the brilliant but severe remedy of the cross. We need to constantly remember that our lives aren't defined by our marital happiness, but by seeking first God's kingdom and righteousness. That pursuit will, in the end, produce happiness, but we have to keep first things first.

So here's the spiritual trick. Transform the focus of your expectations from what you expect of your husband to what your God expects of you. We can't make any one person do what we think they should do, but we can surrender to what God would have us do in light of that.

Patricia discovered that accepting the role of the cross in her life helps her check her own desires. Listen once more to this wise woman:

> Perhaps some things are improved by a lack of inward focus. Instead of focusing on our marriage or our desires, Luis and I have focused on the call of God on our lives. We have lived for a cause that's bigger than both of us. And after forty years, we like each other, get along well, and have fulfilled one another as much as is possible.
>
> Our fulfillment is doing the will of God. Our heart prayer is, *Not my will, Lord, but Yours.* This focus kept me from saying "I deserve more help than this" when Luis has been gone for two weeks, leaving me with four little boys. I didn't think, *I can't believe Luis has to leave again so soon,* two or three weeks after his last trip. For me, the Lord's command to "take up your cross and follow Me" has meant letting Luis go while I take care of things

at home. No, it isn't "fair," but it brings life—eternal life—to others. And I gain peace, contentment, and satisfaction.[9]

Patricia's attitude works just as well for wives married to construction workers as it does for wives married to evangelists or pastors. Patricia surrendered to *God's will*, whatever it was. Raising children, supporting a husband, staying involved in one's church—all of these activities can constitute a call "bigger than both of us," even if such a call will never get celebrated in a history book.

Feel free to say, "This stinks!" but then add, "And Lord, how would you like me to respond in the face of its stench?"

Regardless of your situation, the Christian life does require a cross. Your cross may look different from Patricia's, but you *will* have a cross to bear. Resentment and bitterness will make each splinter of that cross feel like a sharp, ragged nail. A yielding, surrendered attitude may not make the cross soft, but it will make it sweeter, and at the end of your life, it may even seem precious.

When Patricia as a mature woman married for more than four decades testifies that she has gained "peace, contentment, and satisfaction," she means she has found what virtually every woman wants and yet very few find. Why? Because so many women look at the cross as their enemy instead of as their truest friend. Peace? Contentment? Satisfaction? From a woman who raised four boys with an often absent husband and who endured *two years* of chemotherapy? How can this be? Patricia understands something the world mocks: "In the end, nothing makes us 'feel' as good as does obedience to Him."[10]

If you don't die to unrealistic expectations and if you refuse the cross, you'll find yourself at constant war with your husband instead of at peace. You'll feel frustrated instead of contented, and disappointed instead of satisfied. Why? We often forget that both partners in a marriage have their expectations, and sometimes these expectations conflict.

Martie found this to be true in her own marriage:

> When Joe and I became engaged, I had a set of assumptions about how our married life would be. One of those was that Joe would be home most evenings and we'd spend hours together talking, sharing activities, and dreaming together, just like we did when we were dating. But those expectations didn't materialize. After we were married, Joe juggled seminary, a part-time job, and a ministry assignment in addition to his commitment to me as his wife. He often came home late and I would be upset about having to spend the evening without him after working hard all day at my frustrating job. I felt Joe was breaking some unspoken promise about spending time with me. But you see, that was the problem: I never spoke with him about my expectations. In my mind he was breaking a promise, but in his mind he was simply fulfilling his responsibilities.[11]

Eventually, Martie talked to Joe about her desires, and the two of them worked out an arrangement to spend some evenings together. Because of his vocation, Joe is not home every night, as Martie once dreamed he'd be. But he is home more evenings than he probably envisioned as a single man. Neither received all they wanted, but both bowed to something bigger than themselves. That's why I say that harmony, joy, and peace will never grace a home ruled by expectations instead of by the cross.

In her book *It's My Turn*, Ruth Bell Graham gets pretty blunt in this regard: "I pity the married couple who expect too much from one another. It is a foolish woman who expects her husband to be to her what only Jesus Christ can be: always ready to forgive, totally understanding, unendingly patient, invariably tender and loving, unfailing in every area, anticipating every need, and making more than adequate provision. Such expectations put a man under an impossible strain."[12]

Remember That Your Husband Isn't a Church

This fallen world will unfailingly disappoint us; that's why we need each other. You have a natural desire to know and to be known, to love and to be loved, to care and to be cared for. That's why God doesn't only call us into marriage; he also calls us into community. Your husband may be a wonderful, godly man, *but he's not a church*!

Your husband cannot possibly be all things to you. You are responsible to get certain things you need for your own personal development and emotional and spiritual health outside the marriage. If you've blown off your support system—your female friends, your hobbies, your recreation, your spiritual friendships—hoping your husband could replace all of these while also meeting all your relational needs, then you're setting up yourself (and your marriage) for disappointment and failure. No husband, by himself, is enough; you still need others, and it's *your* responsibility to cultivate those other relationships.

Could someone else help fill some of that aching void of disappointment you feel with your husband? For instance, maybe you wish your husband would pray with you about your family more often. While you're working on that, why not find another woman and pray with her about your families? If your husband feels too tired or simply doesn't want to go to a weekly Bible study with you, ask a female friend. Maybe your husband is more of a couch potato than a running partner, so try to find a woman who will run a few miles with you.

If you get some of these understandable and natural desires met outside your marriage, you will become less likely to resent your husband for what he doesn't do and more likely to recognize what he does do. Keep reminding yourself, *My husband is a man, not a church, and it's not fair to ask him to be all things to me.*

Ask God to Change You

As soon as you begin offering prayers of thankfulness for your husband, be sure of this: the enemy of your soul and the would-be destroyer of your marriage will remind you of where your husband falls short. You may find yourself growing resentful: "Why should I thank God that my husband works hard during the day, but when he comes home he won't even talk to me at night?" "Why should I thank God that my husband has always been faithful to me—when he doesn't earn enough money for us to buy a house and I have to work overtime more than I want to?"

You need to respond to this temptation with a healthy spiritual exercise: as soon as you recall your husband's weaknesses, the very second those poor qualities come to mind, start asking God to help *you* with your own specific weaknesses. That's right—as backward as it may sound, respond to temptations to judge your husband by praying for God to change *you*. Go into prayer armed with two lists: your husband's strengths and your weaknesses.

Lest you think I'm blaming women for everything, let me say that I do the same thing. I go into prayer armed with my wife's strengths and my weaknesses. I think *both* husbands and wives should do this, but since this book is directed at wives, I'm emphasizing your response, not your husband's.

Let me be brutally honest here. A husband married to a disappointed wife loses most of his motivation to improve his bad habits. Why do you think your husband worked so hard before you got married? Because he loved the way you adored him. He wanted to catch your attention, to impress you. And when he saw that you *did* notice and *did* appreciate him, it made him want to please you even more. *He felt motivated to move by the way you adored him.*

The relational cancer of blatant disappointment will eat away any motivation for further change. Before you try to influence your husband, sit back and enjoy him, appreciate him, and thank God for him. Before you begin to think about what he needs to change, make an exhaustive inventory about what you want to stay the same. Then thank God for that—and thank your husband too.

Get Fresh Eyes

Greg is now known as a gifted and financially successful man, but in the early days of starting his business, despite working as hard as he could, money was scarce and his young marriage was filled with tension. Greg's wife, Anne, was shocked at how incompetent Greg seemed in comparison to her own father when it came to practical things. They had a young baby, so Anne expected more and more of Greg; yet he needed to spend many evenings trying to get the new business off the ground.

Greg gained considerable esteem from his work outside the home. Many people praised him, thanked him, and affirmed him. He was a nice guy in a business with more than a few cutthroat jerks. He was also seen as a creative thinker, applying new strategies to get a new business off the ground. Yet at home, he always felt like the husband who didn't earn enough money or couldn't fix things or was always too tired.

Do you see the diabolical trap being laid?

Greg now freely acknowledges he was a less-than-stellar husband during that season. He was still in his twenties and self-centered, and he hadn't learned how to love or appreciate a woman. In hindsight, he completely understands how his wife became so frustrated with him.

Greg began working closely with a woman in his business. Initially, he wasn't physically attracted to her, so he let down his guard about the long hours they were working together. But after a few months, Greg went over the line emotionally. Scared of his thoughts, he foolishly went to the woman, explaining in a roundabout way that the two of them shouldn't spend any more time together.

The woman wasn't stupid. When Greg talked about how important his family was to him and how he didn't want to endanger that, she could read between the lines.

"So, you mean—," she said, not finishing her statement, but both of them knew full well what she meant.

"I can't believe this," she said. "You're just so perfect—"

Those four words—"you're just so perfect"—felt like the most potent drug Greg had ever known. Feeling unappreciated, disrespected, and taken for granted at home, and then hearing someone utter something so enthrallingly uplifting—*he was perfect!*—sent him soaring.

The relationship soon became an emotionally entangled mess. Greg decided he could work through the attraction on his own, but of course he couldn't. The relationship never became physical, but the emotional infidelity caused tremendous hurt. If not for the strong advice and correction of some godly men at Greg's church, as well as some noble choices made by the other woman, God only knows what might have happened.

Without a doubt, Greg blundered badly. His wife's perceived neglect did not drive him to this failure, nor does he blame the other woman. Greg freely admits his fault.

I tell his story in the hope that its painful lesson might encourage other wives. You see, the *same Greg* disappointed one woman and enthralled another. One woman saw him with tired eyes—seeing only what he wasn't providing—while the other saw him with fresh eyes. One looked at him through frustrated expectations; one saw him with unlimited possibilities.

With what set of eyes are you gazing at your husband? *Keep in mind, you're not the only one looking at him.* That's not a threat; it's just a statement of reality. This is a world filled with a lot of jerks. If your husband is a relatively decent man, he's probably going to draw some interest in his workplace.

Let me put it another way. Maybe your husband is "just" an assistant manager or a vice principal. While this might not seem like much to you, others still look up to your husband with respect and even affection—those your husband has hired or trained, as well as customers or church members who have come to rely on his leadership and skills. When a husband feels more respected and appreciated at work than he does at home, a precarious situation erupts. Eventually, his heart may gravitate to the place where he feels most cherished.

Working wives may face this temptation even more than stay-at-home moms, in large part because you may be among the almost 30 percent of women who earn more than their husbands (when both spouses work; the percentage of higher-earning women in marriage overall is about 38 percent).[13] Ginny Graves writes wisely, "Many women are angry and exhausted after spending long days at the office, then doing the bulk of the 'women's work' at home. And if they have children, they often yearn for more free time and less stress—and wish their partners would take on more of the financial burden, a desire that often goes unfulfilled because many men can't find higher-paying work."[14]

In the midst of living with this kind of frustration, it can be easy when you are looking at your husband through tired eyes to forget the things that first drew you to your husband: his sense of humor, his thoughtfulness, his spiritual depth, or any number of other strengths. Though you may become blind to these qualities, that doesn't mean everyone else will. Respect is a spiritual obligation and discipline. Give your husband his due!

Linda Dillow is married to an esteemed academic. One time, she spoke on the college campus where her husband worked. After the introduction, an eighteen-year-old said, "Oh, are you Jody Dillow's wife? I think he's wonderful!" Linda writes, "The last sentence was said with a sort of swoon. She went on to talk about my husband as if he were Tarzan, Albert Einstein, and Billy Graham all in one. I barely made it through my message that afternoon. All the way home I thought about the way this girl saw my husband. It jolted me to look at him through another woman's eyes!"[15]

How can you begin to appreciate an imperfect man? Ask God for fresh eyes.

IMMEASURABLE WORTH

In the twelfth century, the vast wealth of Weinsberg Castle in Germany made it a jewel just waiting to be taken. Enemy forces besieged the stone fortress and threatened the riches within. The inhabitants stood no chance of defending themselves against such a great horde, and the opposing marauders demanded a complete surrender. If the occupants would agree to give up their wealth and the men would give up their lives, the women and children would be spared.

After consultation, the women of Weinsberg Castle asked for one provision: to leave with as many possessions as they could carry. If the opposing forces would agree to this one request, the men inside would lay down their arms and hand over the castle's riches. Fully aware of the wealth of riches loaded within the castle, the enemy forces agreed. After all, how much could these women take?

Finally, the castle gates opened, and the sight that emerged elicited tears from even the most calloused soldiers. *Every woman carried her husband on her back.*[16]

How many of those rescued men were perfect? Not one. But every one of those imperfect men meant more to their wives than anything they owned.

Where is *your* greatest wealth?

QUESTIONS FOR DISCUSSION AND REFLECTION

1. Name at least one redeeming quality about your husband that provides a possible avenue for sacred influence.

2. What practical things can wives do to apply Philippians 4:8 to the way they think about their husbands? "Whatever is true, whatever is noble, whatever is right, whatever is pure,

whatever is lovely, whatever is admirable—if anything is excellent or praiseworthy—think about such things."

3. Do you define your husband more by his bad days than by his good ones? How can women develop realistic expectations—accepting the fact that their husbands will have off days while still working toward positively influencing their husbands?

4. What wounds did your husband bring into your marriage? How would you rate your current attitude toward these wounds—redemptively nurturing, or critically judgmental? How can a woman grow in this area?

5. Do you ever assume that your husband somehow just intuitively knows what you want? In what area will you be more direct in asking for his help or support?

6. Take some time to consider the grace that God has shown to you. Think of all the impure thoughts, ugly attitudes, and immoral acts for which God has forgiven you. Then ask yourself, *How can I offer the same grace to my husband that God has shown to me?*

7. Do you think you have been asking of marriage more than God designed it to provide, or do you think you are settling for less than you should?

8. Which relational and spiritual needs aren't being met in your marriage that might be met by cultivating other friendships? Do you see this as a compromise, settling for second best, or as a healthy benefit of Christian community? In addition to making sure these are same-gender friendships, what are some basic guidelines for forming these relationships?

9. Where does your husband get affirmation and validation? Where do you get affirmation and validation? What are some ways you can be in environments that offer you more affirmation and validation? What are ways you can make your home be an affirming environment for your husband and for yourself?

CHAPTER 6

THE HELPER

Embracing the High Call of Marriage

When Grant Fishbook decided to leave his position at a church, a few people didn't like his reasons, so they created their own and started slandering him. They called into question Grant's character and integrity, which only added to the misery he already felt. Grant began working at an eight-dollar-an-hour job, crawling under houses and trying to figure out how to pay his mortgage and feed his family while still listening to God's voice for the future.

Grant still believed God had called him to ministry, so the disappointment of recent events, the frustration of working at a less-than-satisfying job, the uncertainty of the future, and the sudden financial crisis all threatened to bury him with discouragement.

But Grant has a godly and strong wife who stepped up. Laurel saw the disappointment in her husband's face, but she never stopped believing in him. She never made things worse by asking how they could feed a family on eight dollars an hour, or what that meant for her in trying to make up the difference. In the midst of Grant's discouragement, Laurel became his protector rather than his accuser.

One day, Grant walked into the house and overheard Laurel talking on the telephone. Because Grant entered the room from behind her, Laurel wasn't aware of his arrival. But this is what Grant heard: "No, you *can't* talk to my husband. You don't get to him unless you go through me. And if you find a way to go around me, you'd better remember something: that's my husband, and I am his wife."

Grant realized from the tone of Laurel's voice that this wasn't the only time she had deflected calls like that. At those times when Grant felt most vulnerable, Laurel created a cushion to help him heal.

Today, Grant pastors the largest evangelical church in Whatcom County, Washington. And Grant would be the first to tell you that the reason he can do what he does is based in part on what Laurel did back then. At that time, he was a fragile man supported by a strong wife; but with Laurel's support, Grant has become a spiritual leader for an entire region.

This is exactly what God intended marriage to do—provide the supporting environment in which both husband and wife can become all that God created them to be. Since this is a book focusing on wives, however, let's focus on what it means for you to help your husband.

THE SPIRITUAL WEIGHT OF MARRIAGE

When God said, "It is not good for the man to be alone. I will make a helper suitable for him" (Genesis 2:18), he wasn't talking to himself; he was talking to *us*. He was letting us in on the Trinity's design for human marriage. God designed the wife to help her husband.

This doesn't diminish you as a woman, as if you were created only to be a sidekick to the male star. Genesis affirms the reality of women as image bearers of God. Christianity values women far beyond their traditional roles as wives or mothers. When a woman called out to Jesus in praise of Mary, "Blessed is the mother who gave you birth and nursed you," Jesus replied, "Blessed rather are those who hear the word of God and obey it" (Luke 11:27–28). Back then, a woman was valued primarily for what her children accomplished; Jesus directly refutes this as a woman's only value, saying he also exalts women who embrace his truth and go to work on behalf of his kingdom.

Paul even urges some widows in 1 Corinthians 7 to seriously consider staying unmarried, so they can more fully devote themselves to kingdom work. The unequivocal call of the New Testament is that a woman's highest call isn't to find a husband to help but rather a Savior to serve.

But once we choose to marry, our focus must include sacrificial devotion to and care for our spouse. In my book *Cherish*, I talk about how husbands are to showcase their wives as an extension of Ezekiel 16 and Ephesians 5. *This is not about gender politics; it's about the responsibility of marriage.* As soon as I get married, I'm no longer just a man; I'm a husband, with a certain responsibility to a particular woman. As soon as you get married, you're no longer just a woman; you're a wife, with a certain responsibility to a particular man.

And the Bible doesn't shy away from what may sound like painful truths:

> Submit to one another out of reverence for Christ.
>
> Wives, submit yourselves to your own husbands as you do to the Lord. For the husband is the head of the wife as Christ is the head of the church, his body, of which he is the Savior. Now as the church submits to Christ, so also wives should submit to their husbands in everything.
>
> Husbands, love your wives, just as Christ loved the church and gave himself up for her to make her holy, cleansing her by the washing with water through the word, and to present

her to himself as a radiant church, without stain or wrinkle or any other blemish, but holy and blameless. In this same way, husbands ought to love their wives as their own bodies. He who loves his wife loves himself.

Ephesians 5:21–28

If you take a job that involves answering email, you shouldn't say, "I don't want to answer their email! It's demeaning." That is part of the job you signed up for. What I'm about to say is not a reflection on your value as a person, either as an individual or as a member of a particular gender. It's part of the job of being married.

As a husband, out of reverence for Christ, I am to submit to my role of loving my wife as Christ loves the church. That's what I agreed to when I got married. Her spiritual health and vitality should be placed above my own desires and even my own physical welfare. Jesus endured torture and the cross for the spiritual benefit of the church. Paul is telling husbands that men must have this same attitude in marriage. As one pastor put it, "The best way for me to live this out is to keep asking myself, 'What is my love for my wife costing me?' If the answer is 'nothing,' then I'm not loving my wife as Christ loved the church."

This calls me to rise up on behalf of my wife and be proactive about her welfare, protective of her being and spiritual call, and quick to express love. This is how God wants your husband to love you, and it's what Ephesians 5 aims at. Unfortunately, the apostle Paul's words are often read as if the part toward men doesn't matter as much as the words written to women. I'll come back to this, but for now, I want you to see that in order to create a biblical marriage, *all* aspects of this passage need to function, not just verses 22–24.

It's not as if Ephesians 5 is the only passage where Paul calls women to rise up and be strong advocates for their husbands. In Titus, he assumes marital helping is a transferable, teachable skill. He urges a young pastor named Titus to ensure that older women properly train younger women how to love their husbands (see Titus 2:3–4). In Paul's mind, every Christian wife needs to receive training in and focus on how to love, support, and encourage her husband.

Since you're reading a book like this, you've already accepted the training part, at least for now. It's the application that can feel so painful. But since the issues of gender politics and the role of wives are such contentious ones these days, let's make a few things clear.

First, the Bible does *not* teach the subjugation of women to men. The Bible does not prohibit women from serving as government leaders or CEOs or from working outside of the home. The Bible addresses roles of a husband and wife and various roles within the church, not the relationships between neighbors or coworkers.

Second, biblical submission, properly defined, does not mean "inferiority." We are all one in Christ in such a way that you can say there exists complete sexual equality (see Galatians 3:28). God cherishes women every bit as much as he cherishes men. Women can be every bit as capable as men—if not more so.

Third, "helper" isn't an *exclusive* title for a wife. I am called to be a husband—a servant-martyr with regard to my wife—but that doesn't mean I don't have other roles God has called me to as well. I've sometimes heard biblical submission taught in such a way that it seems as though a woman's *only* role in life is to please and help her husband. Moses (traditionally regarded as the author of Genesis), Jesus, and the apostle Paul teach otherwise. "Helping" may be *a* defining role to which God calls married women, but it's not *the* defining role.

Finally, the context of submission is *mutual*. Right before Paul instructs wives to submit to their husbands (Ephesians 5:22), he tells all of us to "submit to one another out of reverence for Christ" (verse 21). The wife's submission to her husband gets placed in the context of a marriage in which a husband is called to be like Christ—laying down his life on her behalf, putting her first, serving her, caring for her, always loving her in the same sacrificial, lay-down-your-life manner in which Christ loves the church (verse 25).

Paul describes an idealistic view of a simultaneous commitment to the other's welfare. I don't mean to use *idealistic* in a negative way—certainly every marriage should strive for it. But I also think Paul would be the first to object if he heard women being urged to submit while condescending and dictatorial husbands heard no corresponding challenge to love in the manner of Christ. The church must not teach the submission of wives *apart from* the sacrificial love and servanthood required of husbands. This doesn't mean a husband's lack of sacrificial love *cancels* a wife's call to submission, but it does make applying this principle a little trickier.

When a man is condescending and dictatorial toward his wife, when he treats her like hired help, when he requires her to dole out sexual favors on demand, the last place he should look to justify his lifestyle is the Bible. His actions and attitudes offend God's revealed will and written Word. This is not marriage as God designed it, and it is not what Genesis, Proverbs, and Paul's writings teach about the roles of husband and wife.

What, then, are these roles?

SERVING TOGETHER AS COMPLEMENTS

The formal theological terms for the two primary views of gender roles within marriage are *egalitarian* and *complementarian*. The egalitarian view sees no such thing as gender roles in marriage. Thus every couple should make their own decisions about who does what best and then divide up the responsibilities on the basis of their individual strengths and weaknesses. In this view, marriage is primarily a collaboration that stresses mutual submission.

In the complementarian model, God has given the husband a role of loving servant leadership. The Bible describes the husband's role more as one of responsibility than as one of privilege, however.

While New Testament women ministered and even taught, the complementarian view stresses that Paul clearly expected men to lead the way at home and in church. This is what many believe the Bible teaches in Genesis 3:16; 1 Corinthians 11:3; Ephesians 5:21–32; Colossians 3:18–19; 1 Timothy 2:11–15; and 1 Peter 3:1–7, among other passages.

Younger believers seem to be moving toward a more egalitarian view of marriage, though some—admitting that the complementarian-oriented Scriptures are difficult to read any other way—are adopting a hybrid. Writing for *Today's Christian Woman*, Kelli Trujillo came up with "complegaltarian" to describe *her* view.[1]

When I'm working with premarital couples, I find that the vast majority describe an egalitarian marriage in theory, but then the future wife will often mention that she hopes her husband steps up to become a "spiritual leader" (which is more along the lines of the complementarian model). What I see happening is a younger generation rejecting a misapplication of a complementarian model perhaps even more than they are disputing the Scriptures used to advocate it.

There are plenty of places for you to pursue your search for biblical truth in this regard, and we don't have the space to do anything more than summarize much more nuanced views that can be found elsewhere. Just about everything taught in this book would work in both an egalitarian or a complementarian view of marriage.

In the complementarian view, if your husband senses you are not submitting and are trying to take over, he'll get defensive, not malleable. He'll fight for his turf without even trying to understand you. He won't hear you if he doesn't feel as though you support him. While this may feel a little demeaning, realize that this challenges women to grow in humility, which is the key foundational attitude for spiritual growth. The Christian classics call humility the "queen of the virtues" for good reason. By definition, without humility we won't grow because we won't think we need to grow.

It's worth pointing out that Jesus submitted ("was obedient," Luke 2:51) to his parents, not because they were somehow more worthy than him (since he never ceased being the Son of God), but because this is what his heavenly Father asked of him—to fulfill the legitimate roles of parent and child.

As a student of the Christian classics, I'm familiar with the spiritual tradition of "obedience" in monastic orders. Grown men and women who had taken vows of celibacy nevertheless found it essential to pledge to obey their superiors for the sake of their own spiritual health. Thomas à Kempis attacks the refusal to do this as evidence of sinful "self love": "Because you still love yourself too inordinately, you are afraid to resign yourself wholly to the will of others." He then uses Jesus as an example: "I became the most humble and the lowest of all men that you might overcome your pride with My humility."[2]

I want to honor you as a woman without dishonoring you as a Christian. Pride is a grave spiritual cancer. God designed marriage as a way to effectively cut through the pride of both men and women—when we define pride as putting ourselves first. I don't want to dilute that spiritual benefit by watering down something that seems like a hard application.

But let's also be fair to the egalitarian view. One of the strengths of this position is that when it comes to influence, the egalitarian view of marriage calls women to rise up to their responsibility and not just silently or passively allow their husbands to steer the family ship off course. This perspective reminds many of the industrious woman described in Proverbs 31.

In truth, a biblical view of complementarianism doesn't ask women to be passive, just as a biblical view of egalitarianism wouldn't deny the call to mutual submission. Egalitarians might emphasize the word *mutual* more than *submission*, but it doesn't help to create stereotypes or extreme straw men, only to tear them apart.

The fact remains that the Bible clearly calls wives to some act of submission, and every wife must wrestle with what that means if she seeks to honor God. In the words of Jenny Rae Armstrong, an egalitarian, "The question isn't 'should wives submit to their husbands?' Because, yes, they absolutely should, within godly limits." Then Jenny points to a difference between her egalitarian position and the complementarian view: "The egalitarian view is that men are to submit to their wives as well." She adds, "[Egalitarianism] isn't about *not* submitting"; it's about "the husband and the wife submitting to one another out of reverence for Christ, each one laying down their self-interest for the benefit of the other, instead of one of them setting the family's agenda and expecting the other one to get on board."[3]

And when the Bible talks about submission, we can assume that God knew full well that wives would have to watch their husbands fail and make mistakes. Thankfully, the apostle Paul qualifies submission as being "out of reverence for Christ," which means no husband or wife is ever obligated to do anything that would offend Christ.

In my own marriage, Lisa and I have leaned more toward the complementarian model, but that doesn't mean I concern myself with "men's work" while Lisa concerns herself with "women's work." On any given Sunday morning rush hour in our home, you're far more likely to find me ironing Lisa's clothes than Lisa ironing mine. Lisa handles all our financial transactions, tax returns, and the like because she's better at those things than I am.

The spiritual weight of fulfilling my role as a husband who sacrifices and serves and looks out for the good of his family matures me as a man in Christ. It confronts my laziness and self-centeredness. Lisa's calling as a helper keeps her from pride, self-centeredness, and frivolous living. Lisa was still a few weeks shy of turning twenty when we got married, and I was a very immature twenty-two-year-old—but the tasks of denying ourselves, learning to love, and creating a family together have resulted in an incredibly satisfying and soul-stretching journey. For both of us, marriage and family life have been essential components that move us further along toward spiritual maturity.

Regardless of which view you adopt on marital roles, Moses in Genesis and the apostle Paul in his writings are both quite explicit that the wife should embrace the spiritually powerful position of being her husband's helper.

SOMETHING TO GIVE

It's interesting to point out that far more often than calling the wife her husband's helper, the Bible calls God our helper.

- "My father's God was my helper" (Exodus 18:4).
- "He [the LORD] is your shield and helper" (Deuteronomy 33:29).
- "You [God] are the helper of the fatherless" (Psalm 10:14).
- "You [LORD] have been my helper" (Psalm 27:9).
- "The LORD is with me; he is my helper" (Psalm 118:7).

Genesis pictures a man created with an acute vulnerability. He is clearly not self-sufficient; he needs someone to come alongside him, to live this life with him.

If you have entered into God's invention called marriage, your role is to be your husband's helper. This does not diminish you any more than the Bible diminishes God by calling him our helper. In fact, being able to help assumes, in one sense, that you have something the person you are helping lacks. If you cease to think of yourself as your husband's helper, the marriage will suffer, because this role is the way God designed marriage to work.

You should not enter marriage and then entertain "single" thoughts. That is, you shouldn't become a wife and then act as though you're still single. The marriage vows of many of us included the line "forsaking all others." This goes beyond sexual fidelity to include "single" thinking. We agreed to forsake our me-first, single-oriented worldview and committed ourselves to building a *couple*. To be married to a man is to help him; that's the biblical model. Helping can take different forms, but it always serves the other person's good. In willingly assuming the role of wife, you pledge to spend a good deal of time and effort on the welfare of your *husband*.

I stress the word *husband* because contemporary life tempts women to focus everywhere else: your job, your home, and even your children.

To those of you who have children who have disabilities, let me stress that being your husband's helper first and foremost (family-wise) still applies to you. Living with a child who has permanent disabilities and requires extra help is one of the biggest challenges I've seen in contemporary marriages. Sadly, sometimes the husband fails to step up. He hears the initial diagnosis and expects the wife to deal with the consequences. This makes the wife feel she has to work double-time to make up for her husband's lack, and she may end up (perhaps passively) punishing him by pouring the vast majority of her time, effort, and care on the child, hoping (though it rarely works) that her husband will get the message and start doing his fair share.

Whenever this dynamic happens—the wife focused on the child as the husband continues to fail to do his share of nurturing—the marriage inevitably becomes miserable. The wife understandably grows bitter. The husband becomes resentful that his wife isn't there for him as much as she's there for the child. The wife thinks, *I could be there for you more if you'd help me more.* And of course she's right.

Even so, whenever the biblical model is superseded and a woman or man becomes a mom or dad first instead of a wife or husband first, the marriage suffers—very often irretrievably.

So what is a wife to do when child-rearing makes being her husband's helper so very difficult? Modern care (psychological and physical) has made it possible to spend a lot of money and almost all one's time treating a disability, and plenty of professionals will make moms feel guilty if they don't avail themselves of every possible treatment.

Maybe you don't need to do all that.

You don't neglect your child—of course not. But you also learn to not let life revolve around caring for the child. Don't let guilt drive your schedule; live your life according to biblical priorities. You have twenty-four hours in every day and a limited amount of resources. God won't judge you for not being able to spend what you don't have. Otherwise, the marriage may fail or at least lack any healthy affection, and your child with a disability ends up experiencing the effects not only of a broken body or mind, but of a broken home.

You may never be able to fix your child, but you *can* secure your child's home so that he or she grows up in a loving, emotionally close, and spiritually healthy environment. Isn't that as important as pursuing another expensive and time-consuming miracle cure?

To all of you wives, I ask, "How often do you give thought to this role of being your husband's helper? How often do you wake up and think, 'How can I help my husband today?' *only after* you've figured out how to first help every one of your children?" When you repeatedly ask this question about your husband, you're living in marriage as God designed it.

Lest you think I'm being unfair, please know that when I speak to men, I tell them we should entertain these daily thoughts: "How can I care for my wife today? How can I serve her? How can I lay down my life on her behalf, as Christ laid down his life for me?"

THE WAY MEN ARE

Laura Doyle shocked some of her feminist peers when she released *The Surrendered Wife*.[4] The title alone caused great controversy in New York publishing circles; when the book hit the "top ten" list, people really started talking.

In her book, Laura admitted to feeling unhappy with her marriage, so she started asking other husbands what they wanted from their wives. After listening to their comments, Laura concluded that her husband probably wanted the same things, so she tried to put them into practice. Laura stopped nagging her husband, cut out the complaints and criticisms, and then started letting him lead in important decisions. She did what she could to help him, and she even—this really raised a controversy—started having sex whenever he wanted it. Treated this way, Laura's man suddenly became a "fabulous" husband.

It doesn't always end this way but at the very least, Laura's journey shows that the typical man remains unmoved by power plays or criticism or by a wife who disrespects him. He's more likely to be moved by a wife who respects him and then helps him get where he wants to go.

This isn't merely cultural. Neuroscience has shown this is how men's brains are wired. For the most part, men are physiologically inclined toward certain attitudes at work and home. Wives, you can't make your husbands serve you or care for you, but you *can* focus on helping them, and that action alone may prompt them to serve and to care. Even if it doesn't, it will, in the words of one wife (whom you'll read about later), unleash a great spiritual adventure in your own life.

Here's a practical example. Unless I'm buying running gear, I hate shopping. On one occasion, I had been looking for a new watch for months. Lisa tore out an ad from a newspaper and asked me, "What do you think of this one?" I loved it, took it to the store, and gave the jewelry store clerk the picture. He ordered the watch, and a week later I picked it up. I didn't have to do a bit of looking around.

I *really* loved my wife that day.

Have you come across something on eBay that your husband has been looking for? Maybe you could simply take on a chore (getting the oil changed, ironing some shirts) that has felt like an anvil around his neck. Ask him this question tonight: "What frustrates you most about your job?" If you can find a way to help him work through that, you'll create a climate for profound positive influence. I think this is especially true of working wives. Your lack of time limits your ability to help, but if you can find one or two strategic ways to make your husband's life run more smoothly, you'll cement his affections. If you do that just once or twice a year, by the end of your third decade of marriage, you'll have laid down a lifetime of practical care, removing maybe fifty or sixty things that have frustrated him. In the process, you will have built up an enormous amount of gratitude and corresponding intimacy.

If you want to truly influence your husband, I urge you to begin by praying this prayer: *Lord, how can I help my husband today?*

TIRED HELPERS

Hannah works full-time while raising a preschooler and feels guilty about the waning romance in her marriage. "I wake up at six o'clock," she says, "and get my daughter ready, get myself to work, put in eight or nine hours, come home, spend time with my child, try to get us all something to eat, put the child to bed—and there's just not much energy left for physical intimacy."

Such weariness is legitimate. It's cruel to make wives feel guilty for not measuring up when their schedules overflow. The last thing I want to do when talking about helping husbands is to lecture working wives that they're not doing enough. I'm a realist, and real life involves compromises. A husband whose wife works outside the home must realize that other elements within the home will give way. If you're raising small children and working full-time (or even thirty hours a week), this is, in fact, essentially how you're helping your husband in this season of your life.

But occasional sacrifices can still speak volumes. Since I work full-time, I'll use myself as an example. I face the same struggles you do—trying to faithfully love my spouse while working well over fifty hours a week. One morning, I awoke and uttered a prayer that in "Sacred Marriage" seminars I encourage other couples to use: *Lord, please show me how to love my wife today like she's never been loved and never will be loved.*

It didn't take long to become convinced that I needed to take my daughter to a physical therapy session that afternoon. Normally, my wife carried out this four-hour task, but the more I listened to God, the more I became persuaded he wanted me to do this even though it would blow a hole in my work schedule.

When I mentioned my plans to Lisa, she responded with a tepid "Okay, whatever."

Frankly, I expected something a little heartier, like, "You know, I could search the world over and not find such a generous, loving man as you, one who is willing to give up his own work duties so I can have an afternoon off!" No such luck. But since I had already made the commitment, I was stuck.

As the morning wore on, Lisa began feeling ill. She took a nap right after lunch—something she almost never does. Then her sister called, informing us that she intended to visit. We had just moved into our house, and none of Lisa's siblings had seen it, so Lisa went on a tear to get the house ready for the next day.

When I prayed about loving Lisa, and God answered with a very practical suggestion, neither Lisa nor I knew she was going to feel ill, but God did. Neither Lisa nor I knew her sister would call to ask if she could pay an unexpected, last-minute visit, but God did. And he wanted to love my wife through me by removing a major time commitment from her day—at my expense.

On another occasion, I prayed that same prayer and sensed strongly that I needed to let Lisa sleep in while I got the kids up and made sure they ate breakfast and left for school with lunch bags in hand. As I thought about doing this, panic began to rise in my heart. I was due to give a keynote address the next day and still had to pull my notes together. Plus, I had to organize two workshops, and I am most productive during the early-morning hours. But God made it clear I was to put my wife's needs over the nine hundred people scheduled to hear me the next day. Lisa would essentially become a single mom the rest of the week in the absence of her husband, and her heavenly Father wanted her to get a little rest before that task descended on her.

Of course, I can't do this every day. I don't even do it most days. But I still think that, at times, God will ask us to let work suffer so that we can care for our spouse. I didn't arrive at that conference as prepared as I wanted to be, but my first and best commitment must be to Lisa, not to any employer.

In the same way, you should expect God to call you from time to time to make some vocational sacrifices so you can help your husband. My friend Melody Rhode has often impressed me in this regard. I'm convinced she has a groundbreaking book in her, but she has chosen to refrain from actively pursuing it right now because of family responsibilities. She works three days a week as a marriage and family therapist and believes that additional vocational effort would interfere with her ability to love and care for her family. She does, however, fully intend to pursue the writing of her book when her family commitments allow it.

As Melody and I discussed vocational and family responsibilities, she reminded me that life is about compromises. We shoot for the ideal, but we have to live in the real. Family, of course, always comes before personal ambition. Some couples may decide to drastically change their style of living so that the wife or husband doesn't have to work full-time or perhaps at all (assuming that's what the couple wants). Some of our friends made that choice and have achieved thrilling results. Of course, they had to learn how to do without certain things, but the intimacy that followed, combined with the sense of family togetherness that resulted, convinced them that the trade-off has been more than worth it.

Whatever choices you and your husband make, I pray that your decisions will draw the two of you together. Working two jobs to provide a home and food for your children can become a cooperative effort when you support each other, show interest in each other, and make those occasional sacrifices that show you care.

If in the midst of all this you can convince your husband that you're on his side, committed to his welfare and well-being, then you'll likely discover an intimacy and a loyalty that know no bounds. *How* you help your husband depends on your family's situation, but the call to help your husband never goes away.

QUESTIONS FOR DISCUSSION AND REFLECTION

1. Think of a time when your husband was feeling discouraged or vulnerable. How did you react? Was there something else you might have said or done? If so, what?

2. What are at least three things older women should teach younger women (according to Titus 2:3–4) about how to love and help their husbands?

3. Discuss Gary's comment, "He [your husband] won't hear you if he doesn't feel as though you support him." Have you found this to be true? How can wives be supportive of their husbands while also disagreeing with them?

4. List three things you can start doing that would really help your husband physically, emotionally, or spiritually.

5. How might helping your husband pave the way for you to influence your husband?

6. Describe two or three changes you can make in your life that will move you toward becoming a better helper.

CHAPTER 7

UNDERSTANDING THE MALE MIND

Learning to Make Your Husband's Masculinity Work for You instead of against You

Many marital problems arise not because of an issue between a specific couple—say, Jack and Jill or Larry and Shari—but because of a breakdown in understanding between a male and a female. In this chapter, I hope to give you an insider's view of the male mind so you'll learn how to better understand and communicate with your husband.

The last several decades of neuroscience have demonstrated that well before a baby comes into this world, while it remains safely tucked inside the mother's womb, the brain of a male baby gets bombarded with testosterone, while a female baby receives greater quantities of female hormones. Between the third and sixth month of that unborn baby's life, hormones begin to shape the tiny brain, influencing how that individual will interact with the world. Yes, males receive some female hormones, and females receive some testosterone, but the quantities of these hormones (males have up to *twenty times* more testosterone than females; females tend to have much more oxytocin than males) will stamp that child's brain by the sixth month of pregnancy—three months before any mother or father has a chance to "socialize" it.

Admittedly, there exist what neuroscientists call "bridge brain" males and "bridge brain" females. Our tendency toward masculine or feminine brains occurs on a continuum, resulting in various degrees of stamping. But even here, a "bridge brain" male will have more testosterone than a "bridge brain" female.

The male brain therefore functions much differently than the female brain. Dr. Louann Brizendine, who studied at UC Berkeley, Yale, and Harvard and is now on the faculty of UCSF Medical Center, states, "The vast new body of brain science together with the work I've done with my male patients has convinced me that through every phase of life, the unique brain structures and hormones of boys and men create a male reality that is fundamentally different from the female one and all too frequently oversimplified and misunderstood."[1]

Medical tests such as PET scans, MRI scans, and SPECT scans have exploded the quaint and false notion that gender difference is determined mostly by nurture rather than by nature. While our brains are more "plastic" (that is, moldable) than we used to think and therefore susceptible to socialization, according to Dr. Brizendine, "male and female brains are different from the moment of conception."[2] Since brains develop by degrees, stereotyping can lead us astray, but certain things tend to be true. For example, male brains usually have less serotonin than female brains. Since serotonin calms people down, men are more likely to act explosively and compulsively. Surprised? Probably not.

Here's another example. Men also have less oxytocin in their brains. Michael Gurian makes this observation:

Oxytocin is part of what biologists call the "tend-and-befriend" instinct, often contrasted with the "fight-or-flight" instinct.

The higher the oxytocin levels in a brain, the less aggressive the person is likely to be. Furthermore, the person with higher oxytocin levels will tend to be more immediately and directly empathic, and more likely to link bonding and empathy with verbal centers of the brain, asking, "How are you feeling?" or, "Is everything okay?"[3]

Why is your husband less likely to tune in to your emotional pain and verbalize his concern than, say, your sister, your mother, your daughter, or your best friend? His brain doesn't work the same way a female brain does; it just doesn't occur to him to connect his affection with verbal inquiry. The "mirror-neuron system" of your husband's brain, which Dr. Brizendine calls the "'I feel what you feel' emotional empathy system"—the system that helps a person get "in sync with others' emotions by reading facial expressions and interpreting tone of voice and other emotional cues"—"is larger and more active in the female brain."[4]

Men's brains also need to "rest" more than women's brains, with the result that men are more inclined to seek "mental naps."[5] Why do men gravitate toward the television screen and then launch through the channels instead of focusing on one program? Our brains get tired. At the end of the day, we often don't want plot, story, or character development; we just want escape (think buildings blowing up, cars crashing, tires squealing). All the while, *your* brain—which has 15 percent more blood flow—is still running late in the day and therefore better able to process more complex entertainment.

This is *not* to excuse a husband who escapes into Netflix or video game marathons, but it does help you see where the temptation comes from. A mature and healthy man could very well take a mental nap by going on a quiet walk with his wife in the woods at the end of the evening. It's just that the temptation is for us men to turn our minds off, or at least dial them back to a low-energy state. If you try to combat television with a high-cognitive suggestion (like, "Instead of watching television, let's go have an intense talk") you're not just fighting his motivation; you're fighting, at least in part, his *biology*.

Remember, this is true not only of your husband in particular; it's true of men in general. Be careful that you don't fault or resent your husband for being a man! Gurian notes, "As most of us have learned intuitively in our relationships with the other sex, the maleness or femaleness of the brain is not as changeable as many people might wish."[6]

If you really want to motivate your husband and communicate with him, as well as enjoy a fulfilling marriage with him and raise healthy kids with him, *stop expecting him to act or think like a woman.* He can't do that. Nor should he.

Rid yourself of every tactic and skill you use in talking to your sisters, best friends, and mother, and realize that a man's mind functions very differently. Some similarities exist, of course, so a few things will interrelate. But if you expect him to talk to you like your lifelong best friend does or your sister does or your mother does, you're being unfair. And you're going to be disappointed—and probably unhappy.

I've received a lot of positive feedback from my assertion in *Sacred Marriage* that many, if not most, problems in marriage crop up, not between two individuals, but between two genders. That's why divorce and remarriage never solve much (apart from cases of infidelity or abuse). A man still marries a woman, and until both partners accept this reality, tremendous tension will continue to exist. In fact, if a second marriage is more successful than a first marriage, it's often because one or both partners finally get it and accept that this is just the way men and women are. It's much healthier for all concerned and far more economical to learn this lesson in the first marriage.

GIVE HIM TIME

Here's another big difference in the male brain that lies at the root of many marital confrontations: neurological studies show that men may take up to seven hours longer than women to process complex emotional data.[7] Think of that: *seven hours!* Why this delay? Many physiological facts help to explain it: men have a smaller hippocampus in the limbic system (which processes emotional experiences); females have more neural pathways to and from the emotive centers of the brain; and the bundle of nerves that connects the left and right portions of the brain—allowing the processing of thoughts and talk with emotions—is about 25 percent smaller in men than in women.[8]

Consider the implications. Suppose you have an argument or disagreement just after breakfast, and you take about fifteen minutes to get a grip on why you feel so angry. Your husband may not get to that place until dinnertime. But women often find it hard to wait that long. They want to discuss their feelings right away, and they want their husband to discuss his feelings—yet all the while, his brain lags behind, stuck in the earliest stages of processing what just happened or even how he feels about it.

Let me paint a word picture. Let's say your husband invites you to an evening meeting at church. Just as you pull into your parking place, he says, "Oh yeah, I forgot. The pastor called last week and asked if you'd be willing to give a ten-minute devotional this evening right after worship. I told him I was sure you wouldn't mind."

You'd probably be furious with your husband, even if you enjoy giving devotionals. Why? You'd still want time to prepare. You'd feel your husband unfairly put you on the spot. That's *exactly* how your husband feels when you quickly click through your emotional processing and expect him to be ready for an intense problem-solving discussion just because you are. He needs time, *much* more time, to get to this point.

Here's a suggestion. If you have an emotional issue that needs to be addressed, why not give your husband a heads-up several hours before you have a chance to talk? "Honey, something's really been bugging me [or hurting me or frustrating me or worrying me]. Here it is in a nutshell. Can you think it over so we can talk about it later tonight?" By using this tactic, you'll give him plenty of time to process complex emotional data.

If you have a child who has dyslexia or has physical disabilities, your child's limitations will give you empathy instead of anger, won't they? You don't expect a child with autism to have the emotional insight of a female novelist. You don't get angry at a child in a wheelchair who can't jump over a three-foot pole. Will you look at your husband's emotional/relational challenges, within reason, as partly a consequence of neurological inability? I'm not, not, *not* excusing a husband who expresses his "brain weariness" by escaping into mindless entertainment. I'm not suggesting it's okay if he doesn't talk to you, acknowledge you, or inquire about you. These skills can be learned, and I hope this book will help you guide your husband further down the path. But healing and growth begin with *understanding legitimate challenges*.

You must deal with what is—not what you think should be or what you wish were true—with what this person is really and truly capable of being and doing.

Leslie Vernick provides a helpful corrective to women who try to sidestep this neurological reality by saying, "Well, the Bible says we shouldn't let the sun go down on our anger, so that's why we need to settle it before going to bed." Leslie responds, "The Bible never says we have to resolve all differences or problems with our spouse before going to bed. If you're still dealing with your anger, you can let that go *by yourself,* before going to bed, even if your spouse won't or isn't able to discuss the issue until later."

If a woman retorts, "But he *won't* discuss it later," Leslie works on helping wives "learn how to bring up something without attacking their husbands and while working on their own heart and approach. Most men are willing to discuss something if they're not feeling like they're being pushed into a corner or blamed for something they did wrong."

WHY DO MEN STONEWALL?

When a woman doesn't understand the way a male brain works, she risks fostering an extremely destructive male response, something researchers call *stonewalling*. Stonewalling describes how men shut down emotionally and verbally, ignoring another person and essentially withdrawing from the conversation. Understandably, few things irritate women more than being tuned out—and yet it is a stereotypically male action.

A biological reason helps to explain what's going on. Michael Gurian writes, "The male cardiovascular system remains more reactive than the female and slower to recover from stress . . . Since marital confrontation that activates vigilance takes a greater physical toll on the male, it's no surprise that men are more likely than women to attempt to avoid it."[9]

Gurian warns that most men don't immediately like to talk through distressing emotional events (frustrations at work or in relationships, disappointments in life) because talking about such issues usually brings them great cognitive discomfort. In other words, it *hurts* men to talk through hurtful experiences. Because of the way the female brain works (with the release of oxytocin), talking through emotional issues has a calming effect for most (not necessarily all) women, while the opposite is true for most men, for whom such discussions can create anxiety and distress. Since it's more difficult for males to process the data, they feel distress instead of comfort. You may feel soothed by talking through problems; for men, it can feel like torture. That's why men sometimes tune out; it's a desperate (though admittedly unhealthy) act of self-defense.

When you understand that a verbal barrage takes more out of your husband than it does out of you, and that it takes him longer to recover from such an episode, you may begin to realize that criticizing, complaining, and displaying contempt will not allow you to effectively communicate with him. Proverbs 15:1 reminds us, "A gentle answer turns away wrath."

You may well be addressing a legitimate issue, but if you address a legitimate issue in an illegitimate way, you'll turn your husband away. He'll shut you out. You'll get more frustrated because you realize he's not listening, which makes you criticize him even more and throw in even more contempt—and his stone wall rises higher and higher and higher.

How can you tell if your husband is falling into this pattern? Dr. John Gottman notes, "A stonewaller doesn't give you . . . casual feedback. He tends to look away or down without uttering a sound. He sits like an impassive stone wall. The stonewaller acts as though he couldn't care less about what you're saying, if he even hears it."[10]

In Dr. Gottman's experience, stonewalling usually happens in more mature marriages; it is much less common among newlyweds. It takes time for the negativity to build up to sufficient levels for the husband to choose to tune out his wife altogether. Gottman gives more insight into this issue:

Usually people stonewall as a protection against feeling *flooded*. Flooding means that your spouse's negativity—whether in the guise of criticism or contempt or even defensiveness—is so overwhelming, and so sudden, that it leaves you shell-shocked. You feel so defenseless against this sniper attack that you learn to do anything to avoid a replay. The more often you feel flooded by your spouse's criticism or contempt, the more hypervigilant you are for cues that your spouse is about to "blow" again. All you can think about is protecting yourself from the turbulence your spouse's onslaught causes. And the way to do that is to disengage emotionally from the relationship.[11]

The deadly trap here is that in the face of a legitimate complaint, your husband is poised to protect himself, rather than to try to understand your hurt. As long as he's in protection mode, he can't be in "How can I comfort/please/adore her" mode. You may think the greatest need is to *make sure he understands what's bugging you* when in fact the greatest need may be to *disarm his defenses so he can hear what you're saying*. Then, and only then, is it helpful for him to hear the actual offense.

Instead of reacting with fury, take a breather and ask yourself, "Why is my husband tuning me out?" The answer may have something to do with the way you're treating him. If you respond to the stonewalling with the same behavior that created it, you'll only reinforce it. Be gentle and patient, and give him time.

EMOTIONAL REST

Just as a verbal barrage can overwhelm the male brain, so too can an emotional barrage. When a woman pours her intense, deepest feelings into a man all at once, he may start to panic. She's likely been thinking about these issues for a long time, and the intensity has been building. For him, it's like going from zero to sixty in half a second, and his engine may feel like it's about to explode. And for many men, the biology of a man's brain requires occasional vacations from emotional involvement.

It is the rare man who grows in intimacy by being chased. A good, healthy marriage happens *by degrees*. So give your husband space. If he doesn't feel like talking, choose to occasionally let it go. Don't even ask him to justify it.

This is especially true after work. Most men need to decompress. Our brains have been working hard all day long (I know, your brains have too, but remember, you're thinking with a different kind of brain). We've been solving problems as we put forth our best efforts, and mentally we need some time to crash before we assert ourselves again. It's not personal; it's not a statement about you. Rather, it's a statement about our brains and their weariness.

One husband told Shaunti Feldhahn, author of *For Women Only*, "I wish I could make my wife understand that sometimes when I don't talk to her or act like a loving husband, it has nothing to do with how I feel about her. I just sometimes need to be left alone with my own thoughts."[12]

You have to wait for your husband to give more of himself to you. If you avoid panic and resist the urge to try to force him into intimacy, things will go much better for you in the long run. Let him have some times of silence. If you can just give up a little, you can gain so much more.

In fact, it's the wise wife who encourages her husband to occasionally go off on his own. My friend Dave Deur, the pastor I mentioned in an earlier chapter who asked his class members to list five ways they love to be loved, said that the third most common response (after affirmation and sex) was this: wanting the freedom to occasionally do something fun without being made to feel guilty, without a sigh of disappointment or a guilt-inducing, "So you'd really rather go scream at some football players than spend an evening with your children?"

If a guy asks for two nights out a week, I'd say he has priority issues. But a hardworking man does occasionally need some time away to do something he truly enjoys. Some men will feel guilty asking for this, but a wife can build tremendous gratitude by taking the lead. In fact, my wife did this for me recently.

Because of an approaching book deadline, several speaking trips, and a seminary class to prepare for, I canceled a planned golf outing with three friends. Lisa called me and said, "Gary, the weather is beautiful; you really need to go." I started to protest, but she said, "I don't mind making the extra trips to get the kids; you deserve an afternoon off." I went—and enjoyed the break immensely. It meant a lot to me that Lisa willingly did the afterschool pickups so I could spend a late afternoon with some close friends. In this, Lisa showed me Jesus' love.

Consider one significant episode in Jesus' interaction with his disciples. What I'm talking about is exactly how Jesus cared for these men: "Then, because so many people were coming and going that they did not even have a chance to eat, [Jesus] said to them, 'Come with me by yourselves to a quiet place and get some rest'" (Mark 6:31). Notice that when Jesus said this, there were many pressing needs still to be met and much work to be completed. People were still "coming and going." But Jesus, concerned for his disciples, told them to set aside the work and get some rest.

Lisa loves me like Jesus loved his disciples.

Author Linda Weber tells of the time she willingly sent her husband off on a trip. She initially wanted to be part of it, but she knew "he needed a little time away to enjoy reflecting on a lot of things that are important to him." She goes on to make this observation:

> Because I was happy for him to have this time away, he knew that I cared about what was important to him. In his frequent calls home, he was bubbling to share with me the fun of seeing this or doing that or just remembering good times. I loved getting excited with him, and I was glad that he wanted to share his feelings with me. It was my privilege to enter his world by being interested and showing my pleasure for him. It was good for us.[13]

That last phrase—"it was good for us"—can be difficult to understand. Keep in mind that what's good for your husband is good for the two of you. Say it out loud: *If it's good for him, it's good for us.* A healthy husband is a happier husband, a more caring husband, and a more attentive husband.

There's a positive corollary to this, of course. Few women today get the refreshment time they need. Just as your husband needs an occasional break from work and family life, *so do you.* You're more likely to get this time if you remain sensitive to your husband's need for it. I'm much more eager to go out of my way to make sure Lisa gets time for herself when she's encouraging me to take that same time. Guys may not be terribly altruistic, but we're usually sensitive to fair play.

MR. FIXIT

One of the most common frustrations in marriage is that the wife thinks her husband is nearly robotic when it comes to emotions, and the husband thinks his wife is overly emotional. This really is "a brain thing."

Every man has been told that women want us to "listen" instead of trying to solve their problems, and that's a fair request. But you need to know that holding back from problem solving is *literally* painful to a man.

The following interplay between a husband and wife is classic and informative:

> DANIELLE: "I just want Neil to listen, give me a hug, and tell me how he knows I feel. But he goes into robot mode and starts telling me what I should do."
>
> NEIL: "That's not how I see it. I already told her I feel bad about all the pressure she's under. She wants me to listen to her and be sympathetic, but then she won't listen to my suggestions . . . Seeing her cry and not being allowed to help her is torture to me."[14]

Wives, will you please consider Neil's last sentence: "Seeing her cry and not being allowed to help her is *torture* to me"? You think he's being insensitive; to him, not trying to make her feel better is what seems insensitive.

There are two emotional systems that work through our brain. Bear with the technical lingo for a moment, but basically women tend toward the MNS (the mirror-neuron system), and men toward the TPJ (the temporal-parietal junction). A woman expresses empathy by mirroring a person's distress and concern because her brain clicks toward the MNS form of emotional processing. The male brain expresses empathy by a process called "cognitive empathy," which focuses brainpower on *stopping* the problem instead of *understanding* the problem. *It's still empathy*, though it may not feel like it for you. In order to solve a problem, other areas of the brain have to be stilled, which in this case is the MNS. The TPJ system works to protect the male brain from being "infected" by other people's emotions so it can fully focus on solving the problem.[15]

Two days after writing the first draft of this chapter, my wife requested special prayers. She had a very bad reaction to a very bad antibiotic and was still suffering some side effects of neuropathy. Almost immediately after she described her numb lips and a few other effects, my first words were, "Maybe I should take you to the Mayo Clinic this summer and get everything checked out by experts."

Number one, we live in Houston. Anything you can find at the Mayo Clinic you can find here. Number two, she just wanted me to listen and to pray. And because I wrote this chapter, I *knew* that's what she wanted and what would express empathy. I had been duly warned by Dr. Brizendine and had even put some of this in writing, but my default brain response remained, "How can I fix this?"

We men can and should learn to listen first, but maybe God knew what he was doing when he wired this fixit mentality into the male brain. At the very least, you might want to give your husband the benefit of the doubt. Instead of seeing him as insensitive, consider the fact that his response is what seems most sensitive to him. He's trying to be sensitive, and it's confusing to him when you won't let him be that way. It's like having an adolescent son who is hurting, and you instinctively reach out to touch him—and he acts like your physical touch is repulsive and pushes you away. You can't imagine that he doesn't want to be hugged, and it's both hurtful and confusing to you that he doesn't. *You want to show that you care, and he won't let you!* That's how your husband feels when you resent him for wanting to get involved or offer advice.

I'm not saying you have to give in and let him fix things; I'm saying it's important to learn to understand him, talk about this dynamic, and figure out a way for the two of you to address this together. You may well know how to fix the problem even better than your husband does, and it's completely legitimate for you to just want to talk about it.

I've learned (though I'm far from perfect in living this out) that when Lisa shares a frustration, my first and only response is to be understanding and empathetic. *Several hours later*, it's all right for me to come back to her and say, "I've been praying about what you shared with me earlier. Have you thought about maybe doing this?" If there are hours between her sharing and my "solution," she typically receives it a lot better. I suggest talking over this solution with your husband. You may not want to hear his suggestions, but in stopping them, you are asking him to shut down the empathy function in his brain. That's risky. Instead you can set up a win-win by explaining, "Honey, when I share a hurt, what I really want is for you to hear me, understand me and show empathy. There's a time and a place for problem solving. When I first share the problem with you isn't that time or place. Wait at least a few hours."

WHY DO MEN MISBEHAVE?

I am *not* calling sinful misbehavior a biological necessity. The only perfect person in the history of the world lived with a male brain. The apostle Paul, who also lived with a male brain, claimed to be "faultless" in terms of human righteousness and keeping the law (Philippians 3:6). Maleness thus cannot be an excuse for sin.

But men *are* biologically less in tune with the consequences of bad behavior. The anterior cingulate cortex, which is "the 'fear-of-punishment' area" of the brain, is "smaller in men than in women." Furthermore, "testosterone decreases worries about punishment."[16] The prefrontal cortex, which Dr. Brizendine calls the "CEO" of the brain, focuses on good judgments and "works as an inhibiting system to put the brakes on impulses" and is "larger in women and matures faster in females than in males."[17]

Put all this together, and you married a person whose biological ability to process negative consequences arising from bad decisions is less than yours, whose fear of being punished is less than yours, whose processing area of the brain devoted to making good judgments is more limited than yours, and whose inhibitions are naturally less than yours.

Dr. Brizendine describes an experiment in which researchers asked mothers of one-year-old boys and girls to place an interesting but forbidden toy on a small table: "Each mother was told to signal fear and danger with only her facial expressions, indicating that her child should not touch it. Most of the girls heeded their mother's facial warning, but the boys seemed not to care, acting like they were magnetically pulled toward the forbidden object. Their young male brains may have been more driven than the girls' by the thrill and reward of grabbing the desired object, even at the risk of punishment."[18]

This neurological action can create males who can seem cuddly, affirmative, and relational and then can become astonishingly unaware and dangerously curious. One mother (named Jessica) described to Dr. Brizendine how her toddler son "picks me flowers, tells me he loves me, and showers me with kisses and hugs. But when he gets the urge to do something, the rules we've taught him vanish from his mind." Dr. Brizendine writes, "She told me that David [her son] and his friend Craig were in the bathroom washing up for dinner when she heard Craig yell, 'Stop it, David. I'm peeing.' Then she heard the distinct sound of the hair dryer. *Danger* flashed through Jessica's brain. Racing down the hall, she flung open the bathroom door just in time to get a splash of urine on her legs. David had turned the blow-dryer on his friend's stream—just to see what would happen."[19]

As a guy, I totally get this. One time, I was running on a beautiful trail that went from Virginia to Maryland along the waterfront. Passing a rock garden, I saw a sign that read, "Please don't throw rocks into the river." It never would have occurred to me to stop and throw a rock, but seeing that sign made me really want to do it. There's something about the male mind that says, *Oh yeah? What if I do?*

That male mind has helped (along with female assistance, of course) to get a rocket to the moon and solve many problems in the world, so there's a place for this cognitive curiosity. But it can be dangerous when it's not controlled. And of course, we are always accountable for refusing to control these urges. Again, I am not asking you to give your husband a pass with a "boys will be boys" mentality. You may rightly hold him accountable. What I'm asking you to understand is that what is easy for you may not be quite as easy for him.

A man can surrender to the work of the Holy Spirit, fill his mind with Scripture, and learn to walk with wisdom and discretion. But biologically, a case can be made that it actually is easier for women to "behave."

THE END GAME

If you can learn to live with and appreciate your confusing male-brain husband through his twenties, thirties, and forties, there's a surprising payoff in his late fifties and beyond: because older male brains produce less testosterone and vasopressin, the ratio of estrogen to testosterone increases, which means "hormonally the mature male brain is becoming more like the mature female brain."[20]

Your husband is gradually growing into a person who will likely be more in tune with your emotions, more capable of making sound judgments, and more relational overall. If you divorce a man in his forties, you've likely lived with him through his most difficult relational years, and you may miss his most tuned-in, empathetic years.

This isn't a promise—remember, biology isn't destiny, and though stereotypes tend to be true, they aren't absolutely true. But the potential for your husband to become a person who is more aware of facial clues and more relationally in tune with you is high.

This explains in part, but of course doesn't excuse, why older men are often able to date much younger women. It's not just the money. A younger woman may well be tired of a twenty- or thirty-something male brain with its hypercompetitive, territorial, and sexually predatory nature and find it refreshing to have an older man who is more relationally aware. God's ideal plan is that this man's new awareness should be a gift to his wife who has been with him for three or four decades. When a man leaves his wife at this stage, it's a double hit: she suffered while putting up with him in his more insensitive years, and then she misses out on what may well be his most relational years.

The younger woman's devotion may be confusing to the original wife. The ex-wife may remember what this man was and thus not understand the new wife's affection, while the new wife appreciates what he is and not understand the ex-wife's rejection. This situation is terribly sad and goes against God's creational design. What a blessing to go through the early decades together, learn to understand each other, and then appreciate those golden years when your brains have gotten used to each other and you share decades of the same memories, the same children, and the same grandchildren!

If you value relational connectedness and understand the slow evolution of the male brain, it really is true that "things are getting better all the time." A gentler, kinder, more relationally aware husband is on the way.

THE CLIMATE FOR CHANGE

As the chapter comes to an end, let me ask you to do much more than merely understand your husband's neurological differences. I want you to appreciate them and even try to learn from them. It is God's providential design that most of us will become the fullest, most mature person we can possibly become by living in an intimate partnership with someone of the opposite sex. We must learn to understand and respect each other, and not arrogantly think our brain is superior. As we age, our brains begin to resemble each other's more and more. Men gain more estrogen, and women more testosterone, and in this we become fuller and more well-rounded individuals. How astonishing it is that Jesus, while still so young (barely thirty when he started his public ministry), demonstrated the perfect balance of typical male and female strengths—courage and gentleness, forceful action and empathy, leadership and humility.

Your husband has much to learn from you and the way your brain functions, but you also have much to learn from him and the way his brain functions. Furthermore, it is God's wise plan that children be raised by two people with two different kinds of brains, thereby getting the best of both. The happiest of wives will be the one who learns to respect her husband's brain and thanks God for it, learning what she can, understanding why he does what he does and doesn't do what he doesn't do, and learning to cherish him in the midst of it.

QUESTIONS FOR DISCUSSION AND REFLECTION

1. Which one of the brain differences between genders surprised you—or enlightened you—the most? Why?
2. In what ways has *not* understanding the male mind created conflict in your marriage?

3. Are there any ways you've expected your husband to act more like a woman than a man? Do you ever resent your husband's male pattern of thinking? In what way? What are some healthier responses?

4. How can your emotionally charged discussions take into account that some men take up to seven hours longer than their wives to process complex emotional data?

5. Does your husband ever stonewall? If so, have you contributed to this response by flooding him? What advice would you give to a wife who notices a pattern of withdrawing in her husband?

6. Given that talking through difficulties tends to soothe the wife but can be neurologically painful for the husband, how can couples find a healthy balance?

7. Are there ways you may be crowding your husband emotionally? What do you need to change in this regard?

8. Do you need to demonstrate love to your husband—the kind of love Jesus showed to his disciples—by encouraging him to experience something fun or relaxing? What would most meet your husband's needs in this regard?

9. Can you think of a trait in your husband that isn't sinful but that really annoys you? What's the healthiest and most God-honoring response to such a situation?

PART 3

CONFRONTING HER MOST COMMON CONCERNS

CHAPTER 8

RAY AND JO: TAMING THE TEMPER, PART 1

Self-Respect as a First Defense against Your Husband's Anger

Do you find yourself married to an angry man?

Perhaps you saw signs of rage before you married, but in your eagerness to become a bride, you chose to look past it or excuse it as a onetime occurrence. Maybe he was really good at hiding it. Perhaps you thought you could learn to pacify him, and that marriage would make everything better. But now you're stuck in a frightening situation. You want to do the right thing for yourself and for your children, but fear, guilt, and confusion so fill you that you don't know what the right thing even *is*.

Maybe your husband's anger is more occasional. Ninety percent of the time, maybe even 99 percent of the time, he can seem like one of the nicest, most pleasant men in the world. But the remaining 5 or 10 percent? Those small windows make you shudder.

This may not be your situation, but I can assure you it's the situation of someone who attends your church, lives in your neighborhood, or works in your office. So even if this chapter doesn't describe your husband, you may want to read it anyway in your quest to become a woman God can use to reach out to others.

Remember, there's a difference between anger and intimidating violence. By "intimidating violence," I don't just mean actual physical violence. If you feel threatened, that's an unhealthy situation you need to escape, not manage. We'll talk more directly about domestic violence in the next chapter. This chapter is written for those women who want to help their husbands learn to manage and express their anger in more appropriate ways.

ESCALATING ANGER

Like so many women who have walked down the marriage aisle, Jo Franz knew her prospective bridegroom had bouts of "intensity and anger," but she reasoned that, because Ray loved God, the two of them as a couple could overcome them. Not until they became married did Jo realize just how intense Ray could be.

"His voice intensified so dramatically that it felt like he could physically hurt me, even though I didn't think he would," Jo remembers. Ray sometimes unleashed his anger over seemingly small things, like when Jo would forget to buy something at the store.

"You can't even run a house well enough so we don't run out of soap," Ray yelled at her one time.

Jo was shocked. "I had no idea he would nitpick like that or be so attacking."

In case I'm talking to an unmarried woman, let me pause to say I have never heard of a situation where marriage made a man *less* angry. You should assume you are seeing, at most, about 75 percent of your future husband's temper while dating him; it's virtually guaranteed that more temper will erupt after the wedding. If the man you are dating already seems too angry for your taste, he'll be *much* too angry after the honeymoon.

As long as a woman blames herself for causing her husband's temper, she ignores the real problem: she's the *target*, not the cause. Don't assume unwarranted blame for your husband's problem. Of course, you could be making a bad situation worse; a little later I'll talk about strategies to avoid this. But for now, you need to know that it's impossible to live with an angry man without making him angry. Make sure you catch that: *it's impossible to live with an angry man without making him angry.*

But you *can* remove yourself as the target.

"I HAVE VALUE"

Ray grew up with a very critical alcoholic father who taught him that relationships are built on extremely high expectations. Ray admits, "Sometimes I have little patience, and yes, I can be intolerant of other people's patterns, like forgetting to buy more soap."

At first, Jo responded to Ray's angry tone with defensiveness and guilt, thinking she was most likely in the wrong. But after Jo analyzed several confrontations, she eventually decided Ray wasn't always right, which led her to react with anger of her own—and that only made things worse. Ray would yell at her, and then Jo would yell back, "Don't you *dare* speak to me like that!" and the anger soon spiraled out of control.

Proverbs 15:1 is key here: "A gentle answer turns away wrath, but a harsh word stirs up anger." As I said before, you are most vulnerable to sin when you are sinned against. Your husband's inappropriate expression of anger doesn't excuse your inappropriate expression of anger. "Whoever loves a quarrel," writes Solomon, "loves sin" (Proverbs 17:19). Become spiritually grounded so that you can respond out of reverence to Christ instead of "giving more of the same." If you give more of the same, all you'll get is more of the same.

That, at least, was Jo's experience. One day, she finally said to herself, "Enough is enough. I can't live like this."

Jo took her dilemma to the Lord.

"As I prayed, I thought, *Do I deserve this?* And I realized, *No, I don't!* As a Christian, I have value to God, and my husband should value me too, but I can't force him to value me. How can I help him learn to respect me and show it to me in his communication?"

Over the next several weeks, Jo became convinced that God wanted her to learn how to communicate to Ray in such a way that he could hear her concern. As Jo reflected on her previous actions—responding to Ray's temper by letting her own temper flare—she had to admit she was making the situation worse. Then God led her to the wisdom of Ecclesiastes: "The quiet words of the wise are more to be heeded than the shouts of a ruler of fools" (9:17).

Jo sought to use "the quiet words of the wise." She explains, "What I sensed God saying to me was to use communication that was direct and nonattacking and that showed self-respect: 'This is what I need from you,' or, 'Would you please communicate in a way that isn't so frightening?'" Essentially, Jo heard God tell her to respond with a gentle and quiet spirit (see 1 Peter 3:4).

It would be an oversimplification to suggest that their disagreements changed immediately; however, over time, this quiet, gentle approach began to work. Note the spiritual foundation behind this transformation: Jo allowed God to change *her*, which resulted in her husband's spiritual growth.

Ray explains, "Before, if I was condescending to her or demeaning or critical, she would respond very quickly and angrily back: 'Don't talk to me that way! Don't use that tone of voice when you're talking to me!' Her face would get tight and tense, and I thought, *Boy, she's really hurting. I've touched a deep nerve in there somewhere,* but I didn't understand why she was making such a big deal out of it."

In the midst of subsequent blowups, Jo concentrated on being firm but gentle. "I need for you to reword that," she would say, "so I don't feel so defensive." Recognizing that Ray was raised in an alcoholic family, Jo decided she needed to tutor him on how to talk to a woman.

Ray reflects, "It's so important for the woman to share that she's been hurt, but to first take the intensity out of the response. Otherwise, we men tend to think you're overreacting. Jo put it this way: 'I care about you very much, and I need you to know that what you said was very hurtful.' She dropped the sharp, 'Don't talk to me that way!'"

According to Ray, Jo's previous method of communicating "just made me feel guilty. I already knew I had screwed up, and here she was, piling it on, making it more of an issue than it was. And when you already feel low about yourself, and then you're attacked, you're more likely to strike back and escalate the intensity."

Ray says that what made him the angriest was being misunderstood. He believes that Jo sometimes looked only at his behavior without giving him the benefit of the doubt. That perplexed and frustrated him, which escalated into anger. In fact, Ray believes he often had good intentions, but when Jo assumed the worst, he became frustrated, which in turn made him angry—and then he chose to lash out.

Looking back, Ray sees how God used this situation to challenge both him and Jo. "God may frustrate us at times, but we should give him the benefit of the doubt because we know his motivations and intentions are good."

This may seem like a small point, but I think it's a profound one: learning to love and communicate with a very imperfect man can teach valuable lessons about how to love and communicate with an absolutely perfect God. Sometimes we *do* tend to assume the worst—not just of our spouses but of God too: "He doesn't care; he doesn't see; he's playing with us." At the very least, when we know this is never true of God, perhaps it can teach us to show a little less arrogance in our assumptions and much more humility and grace in our attitude toward others.

Personally, I believe this will be one of the greatest challenges that wives married to angry men will face. It's going to be difficult for you, if you're married to such a man, not to look at every new response of his as simply "more of the same." That's why forgiveness is so crucial; we need to let go of the past so we don't keep coloring the present with it. Otherwise, the future is going to look very bleak indeed. In spite of your past hurt, can you choose to suspend your immediate judgment and try to give your husband the benefit of the doubt?

SPIRITUAL PREPARATION

There's another principle we can learn from Jo's experience: In order to confront your husband's anger, you're going to need to put your own spiritual house in order; otherwise, you'll likely lack the strength, courage, and perspective to help your husband.

Jo realizes that her marriage is about more than her and Ray; it is also very much about her and God. When you live with an angry man, you not only crave but *need* God's affirmation. Men can be very cruel with their cutting comments; if you aren't receiving affirmation and affection from your heavenly Father, you're going to feel emotionally empty and perhaps even worthless—and that will feed into your husband's response and tempt you to become even more of a doormat. Jo went to God, understood her value as his daughter, and approached Ray from a position of being spiritually loved instead of desperately empty. Had she been spiritually destitute, she probably wouldn't have had the motivation, the courage, or the will to risk confronting Ray.

So if you're living with an angry man, please accept my encouragement to spend much more time in worship, prayer, and Christian community so you can soak up the love, affirmation, and affection you need for a healthy spiritual life. From such a strong spiritual core, you can face the hurt and frustration in your marriage, as Jo did.

God is your Creator. Not only did he make you, but he can remake you, giving you all that you need for every situation you face. He is your good Shepherd. He will watch over you. He will never sleep in the face of a potential attack. He can help you escape (if need be), and he can help you heal. He is your truest friend who wants only the best for you, and even if everyone else abandons you, questions you, or refuses to believe you, God will be your certain advocate. Especially when your marriage is taxing, you need to spend extra time in prayer, worship, and Bible reading, feeding your mind, fortifying your soul, and healing your heart.

Armed with her standing before God, Jo made it clear to Ray that, while she wanted to understand his frustration, she would not put up with any more verbal abuse. Because Ray desired a better relationship with his wife, Jo's tactic worked. He started to see that letting his temper get the best of him was hurting his relationship with Jo and getting in the way of communicating his frustrations.

"I really wanted, more than anything, to be a good husband," Ray says. "I wanted to recognize Jo's needs. When she stood up to me, it told me she valued herself. So I valued her. It made me understand that Jo is a person with a lot of character; she cares about herself, which I think is what every man wants. I don't think men want a woman they can just run over. We want to value our wife's character. The way Jo stood up to me revealed a lot of character."

This goes back to the point made in chapter 1: Respect is vital in a marriage, and not just for a woman toward her husband, but also for a man toward his wife. If your husband doesn't respect you, you're going to have a very difficult time influencing him in any significant way. And if you don't respect yourself, you'll make it that much more difficult for your husband to respect you.

It took time for Jo's gentle and self-respecting approach to bear fruit, but she kept at it. "The more that I persisted in asking him to lower his intensity, the more he began, gradually, to see what he was doing."

Remember Dr. Melody Rhode's concept of functional fixedness. Men usually don't change unless their wives give them a reason to change. This requires specific, direct, gentle, and self-respecting communication.

"My husband is so grateful that I stood up to him," Jo says today. "He actually said that in one of our conversations! When he learned to lower his intensity, he started to like himself better, and he realized he was loving me better. That made him feel so much more like the man God wanted him to be that he was *thankful* I stood up to him."

Angry men sometimes tell me something they rarely tell their wives: they feel ashamed of how they've acted; they hate what they've become. In most cases, when you help your husband tame his temper, you're helping him become the kind of man he wants to be.

HELPING HIM LOVE YOU

In her role as an inspirational speaker, Jo has met many women whose husbands have cowed them into an unhealthy doormat mode. Sadly, sometimes this posture gets couched in religious language and represents a complete misreading of biblical submission. Jo observes, "Women don't tell men what they need because we've been taught that it's selfish to even think of ourselves. In fact, some of us aren't in touch with our own feelings enough to even *know* what we need. Schools don't teach females how to do this. We're supposed to be strong enough on our own, without asking a man to help us, and many families today aren't healthy enough to model it, so these women go into marriage ill equipped to relate to a man who is likewise ill equipped to love them."

This "martyr method" of marriage shortchanges both husband and wife. Your husband will prosper spiritually and personally by excelling in loving you. God designed marriage, in part, to help both husband and wife grow in character. If you do all the sacrificing, if your husband runs over you, he's not growing; he's shrinking, spiritually speaking. He's becoming lower in character. You may well become a saint after living with such a man for twenty years, but he is going to become increasingly miserable because, ultimately, any man who treats others poorly begins to despise himself. This may sound backward, but you need to love your husband by teaching him how to love you, because *it's spiritually healthy for him to grow in loving you.*

At one time, the thought of telling her husband what she needed would have sounded selfish to Jo, and she would have dismissed the thought. She has since learned that *respect matters* and that a husband won't truly love a woman for whom he has no respect. Jo realized that if she didn't respect herself, her husband would adopt that same attitude of disrespect.

Jo also came to see that a marriage that never addresses the issue of needs ultimately provides little intimacy. As I've said before, husbands can't read minds. Jo understood that if she didn't tutor Ray in how best to communicate his frustrations in a way she could hear them, their marriage would fail to fulfill either of them. Likewise, she needed him to understand that she also had certain needs; Ray could focus on changing certain things, even as he had asked Jo to change. Doing so would keep the marriage from becoming condescending and one-sided. An angry husband often acts as if only his wife needs to change. This is a false view based on a lack of respect.

SHARING NEEDS

Focusing on having our needs met can be selfish, of course, but there's a way to share needs that builds intimacy and respect. It can even become an act of humility: "I need your help. Will you help me?" Clothed in biblical humility, sharing needs can become an incredibly vulnerable and thereby courageous act that gives birth to increased intimacy. Clothed in demands, sharing needs can become a selfish accusation that builds walls: "How come you never talk to me when you get home? Why are you always ignoring me? Is that any way for a Christian man to treat his wife?"

The proper way to share needs involves having the right *motivation* and using the right *presentation.*

Motivation

Your first goal as a sister in Christ is to help your husband more fully express the image of Jesus. Of course, God calls all of us to do that; it just so happens that in this instance, such a change will make your life more pleasant. If you make gaining a more pleasant life your first aim, however, your husband will likely pick up on that and resist your selfish demand. *She's not perfect either*, he'll think, *so why doesn't she just get off my back?*

Here's the purest motivation for change: God calls us to "purify ourselves from everything that contaminates body and spirit, perfecting holiness out of reverence for God" (2 Corinthians 7:1). You call your husband to change in the context of reverence for a perfect God, not in comparison with an imperfect wife.

Get painstakingly honest with yourself in prayer before you approach your husband. Dig deep into those buried motivations. Are you praying this way because your husband makes your life miserable, or because you're concerned about how he is grieving God and destroying himself spiritually? Are you motivated out of selfish ambition, or out of selfless love? I know it is truly difficult to be altruistic in the face of understandable and legitimate hurt, but that's what prayer and the Holy Spirit's comfort, guidance, and empowerment are all about.

If selfishness motivates you, you're far more likely to give up if you don't get the immediate response you hoped for: *It's not worth the hassle*, you think. *I guess I'll just have to learn to put up with it.* But if you truly dedicate yourself to your husband's spiritual welfare, you'll stick with it and persevere.

This is not to suggest you are *responsible for* your husband's spiritual health; some men will resist the godliest advances ever proposed. Remember what we said early on. You can't guarantee success, but you can deserve it. That's all I'm talking about here.

Presentation

Ray urges wives who are married to angry men to "use a loving tone of voice and let them know you really care about them and are committed to them. If you say something the wrong way, you can kill the content. It's not what you say; it's how you say it. Tell your husband you care about his character because you see a good man in him. That tells him you're on his side. And once he knows you're on his side, you can use a word picture to show him how his angry response makes you feel."

Remember our earlier discussion about affirmation? We men feel desperate to preserve your good view of us. When you say things like, "You're a better man than that," we want to rise to the occasion. If you belittle us with words like, "You're such a despicable man I don't understand why I even married you," we won't hear anything that comes after "despicable," and in self-defense we may taste the disrespect and spit it out. I think of Ephesians 4:15 in this regard: "Speaking the truth *in love*, we will grow to become in every respect the mature body of him who is the head, that is, Christ" (emphasis added).

EXPRESSING NEEDS

Jo learned that her reluctance to speak about her own needs in a direct and straightforward manner caused confusion in her marriage. She says, "I realized that when I didn't communicate clearly, I sounded manipulative and controlling. I could be indirect—'Why don't you do such and such?'—instead of just coming out and asking, 'Please do this for me,' and explaining why it was important. The direct approach is so much better; it honors him more and it doesn't sound controlling or manipulative. It's just a simple request."

Expressing needs is certainly healthier—relationally, spiritually, and psychologically—than stewing in resentment and bitterness because the husband (out of willful lack of respect or maybe out of ignorance) doesn't seem to get it.

Ray admits that many men have this problem. He says, "I didn't understand Jo's needs until she shared them with me. I always used to say, 'What's your point?' or, 'Just give me the *Reader's Digest* version.' But Jo wanted to process everything with me, and I didn't understand that."

A case in point occurred when Jo asked Ray to go shopping. Ray became goal oriented. "I intended to go into the shirt department, find a style we liked, check the size, buy it, and leave." But Jo finally learned to express that when she suggested they go shopping, she often just wanted to spend time with him. Shopping wasn't necessarily about buying anything; it was about going out on a date.

Ray counsels women, "It would be so much more helpful if wives would just say, 'I want us to go shopping, but I want to use shopping as a way for us to spend more time together and to talk. I really don't care if we actually buy anything. We may just walk around and talk about what we're going to do with the patio or how the children are doing. So let's just relax and not rush out of the store, okay?'"

Jo admits that Ray's desire to change played a key role in their success. But she believes that a principle behind her approach remains true for many marriages: "The more we share with our husbands what we need, the more our husbands can meet those needs. Women often fail to realize that many times, our husbands don't know what we need; unless we tell them how we want them to communicate with us, they'll stick with whatever pattern they learned from their father. And if they didn't have a healthy father, watch out!"

SPIRITUAL LESSONS

In addition to changing her verbal presentation with Ray, Jo went through a threefold spiritual process to relate to Ray much differently in her heart.

First, Jo looked into Scripture to see who she was in Christ. The biblical way in which God honors women and the affirming way in which Jesus treated women contrasted starkly with the subservient description she often heard applied to women in many churches. "When I looked into Scripture and realized who I was in Christ, I started valuing that. God thinks of me as a person of value, and I needed to agree with him!" She had learned the truth highlighted earlier: *God, not your marital status, defines your life.*

Second, Jo applied this same "person of value" approach to Ray. "Not only does God value me as a woman and wife," she says, "but he values Ray as a man and as a husband. When Ray spoke to me out of anger, I didn't value him as God does. I resented him. I feared him. But I didn't value him. It wasn't until I stood up to Ray that I could begin to value him."

Again, it's good to pause here, because Jo touches on something insightful. It's far easier to *dismiss* an angry man than to *value* him. Anger attracts no one; a guy throwing a temper tantrum can look downright silly to an observer. When a woman truly values a man, she stands up to him and says, "You're better than that. Don't do this to yourself, or to us." A faithful sister in Christ challenges her husband to grow in grace, mercy, and humility.

And third, Jo realized as a co-laborer in Christ that she must hold Ray accountable for God's best in his life. It was *not* God's best for Ray to let his temper direct his relationships. "Many Christian spouses do not hold each other accountable," Jo warns. "We let things slide." A biblical marriage provides a smaller picture of the church. We should use the position and gifts God has given us "so that the body of Christ may be built up until we all reach unity in the faith and in the knowledge of the Son of God and become mature, attaining to the whole measure of the fullness of Christ" (Ephesians 4:12–13).

By holding each other accountable as brothers and sisters in Christ, we not only address issues that have the potential to wreck our families; we also help each other learn how to better relate to people in general. Genuine believers will welcome this process of sanctification.

Today, Jo raves about the changed relationship she has with Ray. "Ray has seen so much change in himself since I patiently persevered," she says. "My insistence showed him I want the best relationship with him, that I value the person he's become. He wants to continue to be that person. I know he wants to be the best husband he can be. I know he wants to love me like Christ loves the church. When I hold him accountable, I give him more of a chance to become that person."

MALE ANGER

One caution is in order as we keep addressing this issue: anger is a perfectly natural and even, at times, spiritually healthy emotion. The Bible says that even God becomes angry (Nahum 1:5–6 and many other passages). Anger in and of itself is not a sin. Responding with rage or letting anger fuel a threatening, hurtful, or abusive outburst is always a sin. You can't fault your husband (or yourself) for getting angry, but you must focus on what you or your husband do with the anger.

It also might help you to know that "a man's brain area for suppressing anger, the septum, is smaller than it is in the female brain, so expressing anger is a more common response for men than it is for women."[1] These anger circuits in the male brain are hormonally reinforced, but they will quiet somewhat as your husband ages.

At times, you must allow your husband to feel legitimately angry with you. You're not perfect, and sometimes your husband would have to be in deep denial or less than human *not* to be angry with you. If you act as though anger is always illegitimate, you'll merely confuse him, because asking him not to feel angry is like his asking you to never feel hurt. We have to manage our anger in appropriate ways, however, and for you this begins with gaining a better understanding of the dynamics of male anger.

Male anger is fueled in part by greater levels of testosterone, which makes it feel different for us than it might feel for you. That's in part why we're more likely to respond automatically by punching a wall without even thinking about how stupid that is. We "physicalize" anger and thus often need to cool down before we can process it appropriately. It will help you as a wife to learn what provokes and what soothes this response.

Anger as a feeling becomes sinful when my expression of anger scares, threatens, or hurts my wife. It is also sinful when it pressures her to give in or keeps her from expressing her own anger or feelings. It's helpful when a wife can endure a husband's anger while managing her own, as the expression of both spouses' emotions can create understanding. This is admittedly high-level relating, and it may require the help of a counselor to get a couple to this place.

When dealing with a husband's anger, it's helpful to remind ourselves of the differences between a female brain and a male brain (again, brains form along a "spectrum"; we can only address what is most typically true). Many times, women wrongly assume that talking things out always makes things better, but many men simply need time to process their anger. It's a biological fact that emotional conversation can feel very stressful for a man and actually *increase* his anger, particularly if that conversation gets pushed on him.

If you married a man whose rage seems to build the more you talk, *stop talking*! Let your husband's brain process the stress as you wait for him to come back to you. Just because conversation calms *you* down, it doesn't mean it will have the same effect on your husband. You still get to say what's in your heart, but consider offering it in bite-sized pieces. Find the most direct and succinct way to express it, and then know that he may need to go for a run, hit some golf balls at the range, fiddle around in the garage, or do some yard work while he processes his anger. His need for this activity doesn't necessarily amount to stonewalling. It may simply be his very different but legitimate way of processing anger.

Also know that in some male brains, particularly if the husband is high in testosterone, vasopressin, and cortisol, getting into an argument may activate his territorial fight reaction. This means being angry produces *pleasure*. Your husband can actually get high from an angry interlude, which can help him succeed in business or athletics but is destructive in marriage. So don't participate in it. Certainly don't reinforce it. You don't have to argue. Since testosterone is fueled by a challenge, don't glare back. Don't yell in return. Put it back on your husband to own and manage his anger by calmly saying, "Deal with your anger, and then we'll talk."

Dr. Ed Welch, who is on the faculty of the Christian Counseling & Educational Foundation, recommends some of the following "defusing" comments:

- "If it is important for us to talk about my sins, we could do that. Let me know when you are able to talk."
- "What's really wrong?"
- "What do you really want?"[2]

Dr. Welch counsels that if your husband's anger makes him incapable of having a decent conversation, wait until his anger passes and then bring these questions up when things aren't quite so tense:

- "Your anger is saying, 'I hate you.' Is that the message you want me to get? I think you are saying more than that."
- "I don't know what to do or say when you are angry. I think you care about our relationship, but it seems like you want me to get away."[3]

Far too often, women expect to argue with a man in the same way they would argue with a woman. Furthermore, they assume the way *they* handle conflict is the best way, or even the only appropriate way. In *For Women Only*, Shaunti Feldhahn asks a provocative question: "If you are in conflict with the man in your life, do you think it is legitimate to break down and cry? Most of us would probably answer yes. Let me ask another question: In that same conflict, do you think it is legitimate for your man to get really angry? Many of us have a problem with that—we think he's not controlling himself or that he's behaving improperly."[4]

The question needs to be asked: Why do women tend to respond with hurt, and men tend to respond with anger? It all has to do with the male need for respect. Feldhahn goes on to quote Dr. Emerson Eggerichs, who explains, "In a relationship conflict, crying is often a woman's response to feeling unloved, and anger is often a man's response to feeling disrespected."[5]

Feldhahn conducted her own survey, which confirmed this reality. Here's the statement:

> Even the best relationships sometimes have conflicts on day-to-day issues. In the middle of a conflict with my wife/significant other, I am more likely to be feeling:
>
> • that my wife/significant other doesn't respect me right now: 81 percent
> • that my wife/significant other doesn't love me right now: 19 percent[6]

Men get most frustrated and angriest when they feel disrespected. You can't control your husband's anger, but you can provoke it by being disrespectful. That doesn't excuse any inappropriate actions on his part, but if you truly want to be part of the solution, then try to learn how to disagree with your husband without showing a lack of respect—and that includes nonverbal routines such as folding your arms, turning away, rolling your eyes, or making mocking gestures.[7]

Also, carefully consider your words. Do they suggest inadequacy? When you continually question your husband's purchases, his ability to run the house or fix things, his choice of clothes, the way he handles the kids, and the like, you create a "frustration bomb." These things build up over time, and eventually, one more blatant act of disrespect lights the fuse that results in an increased expression of anger, perhaps stronger than you've ever seen before.

Every man is different, so study your husband to learn when you need to let go. You may not agree with how he's fixing something, or you may think it's long past the time for him to bring in an expert, but in most cases, let him make the call. Women often simply don't understand how offensive and annoying it can feel to a man to be constantly challenged and corrected, especially in a disrespectful manner.

Try to stop those little acts of disrespect—the tone that ridicules him; the teasing barbs that feel like little splashes to you and like tsunamis to him; the constant complaints to friends; the frequent questioning, "Are you *sure* you know what you're doing?" and the like. Instead, focus on the positive. Make sure he knows you believe he is adequate, competent, and capable. Talk up his strong points. Praise him in public. Show your unconditional support.

If you do all this, his anger meter may reach record lows in a surprisingly short span of time. From that platform, you can then begin to apply the principles we learned from Jo's experience.

One caveat here. In a destructive relationship, a woman has no voice or isn't allowed to express a contrary opinion. Her husband's anger thus becomes a weapon to silence and demean her. That isn't healthy and isn't something to be managed but rather challenged and confronted with professional counseling. It may even require separation. If you suspect that's what's happening in your marriage, I urge you to check out Leslie Vernick's *The Emotionally Destructive Marriage* for specific suggestions, and you'll also find help in Chip Ingram's *Overcoming Emotions That Destroy.*[8]

THE QUEEN OF THE VIRTUES

James 4:1–2 explains the genesis of every marital argument: "What causes fights and quarrels among you? Don't they come from your desires that battle within you? You desire but do not have, so you kill. You covet but you cannot get what you want, so you quarrel and fight. You do not have because you do not ask God."

According to James, we fight because we're selfish, because we're disappointed, because we're not getting our way, and because we're depending on someone other than God to meet our needs. There's one word that describes this hideous disposition: *pride*.

The ancients called humility "the queen" of the virtues because they rightly understood Scripture to teach that pride is the greatest of all sins. Humility will serve your home well, and it can also play a preeminent role in reducing angry outbursts.

Ray told me that one of the most helpful things his counselor suggested was to learn to ask for God's wisdom to compose himself so he could focus on Jo's needs, making her the center of his attention. By nature, men can be self-centered; Ray needed to learn that Jo *matters*.

This cuts to the heart of the issue, because an angry man often acts as though he is the only one who matters. An angry man tries to assert control, seizing the situation by force and trying to use his anger to intimidate or scare the other person into doing what he wants. Humility—focusing on someone other than himself—provides the best spiritual remedy for your husband.

But here's the catch for you. You must work to stay humble as you oppose pride. Maybe your side of the argument is that you don't want to put up with an angry man! Maybe what you want but aren't getting is a peaceful relationship, and so you are tempted to lash out with the same attitude of pride and expression of anger.

There's a very important spiritual principle behind this: Just because someone I'm opposing is wrong doesn't make me right. There are a hundred ways to miss a target, but only one way to hit it.[9] It's very possible that on any given day, and in the midst of any particular argument, both you and your husband are succumbing to pride, which in turn will blind you from the wisdom of God's humility. Your husband may be wrong and may be expressing himself in an improper way, but it doesn't mean you have to stoop to his level. When you respond as God would have you respond, you have succeeded and pleased God, even if your husband doesn't like it.

Pray for humility. Read books that deal directly with this topic. Pray with some friends, always keeping James 4:1–2 in mind. Pride is an ever-present foe, so make humility an ever-present friend.

THE REST OF THE STORY

Up to this point, I've purposely left out one final, but crucial, element of Jo and Ray's story. Jo's husband married her *after* doctors had diagnosed her with multiple sclerosis. A woman facing a debilitating disease that has the potential to leave her in a wheelchair faces certain temptations that other women will never know.

It would be easy for a woman in Jo's situation to feel so afraid of losing her husband—and so fearful of losing his support as she faces an uncertain future—that she would just shut up and endure the angry outbursts. After all, where would she be if her husband left her?

Jo is a woman of tremendous courage. Though her body is gradually losing some of its functions, she still knows that in Christ she is highly valued. And out of that courage, she calls her husband to value and respect her as well.

Like Jo, you are a person of *great* value to God. Paul's word of encouragement is for you: "Finally, be strong in the Lord and in his mighty power" (Ephesians 6:10).

This chapter has focused on managing a man's anger. There comes a time, however, when anger becomes more than mere anger and escalates into abuse. That topic deserves a chapter all its own, to which we will now turn.

QUESTIONS FOR DISCUSSION
AND REFLECTION

1. Did you notice any increase in the level of your husband's anger after the two of you were married? Did this surprise you? Looking back, can you see any seeds of that anger?

2. Why do women sometimes blame themselves for their husbands' anger?

3. Jo discovered that because Ray was raised in an alcoholic family, she "needed to tutor him on how to talk to a woman." Discuss effective ways you've found to teach your husband how to express his anger in appropriate ways.

4. Gary writes that "Jo went to God, understood her value as his daughter, and approached Ray from a position of being spiritually loved instead of desperately empty." Have you ever approached your husband out of need instead of out of being loved by God? Talk about the difference it makes when wives first cultivate a satisfying relationship with God before they seek to influence their husbands.

5. Gary shares that "angry men sometimes tell me something they rarely tell their wives: they feel ashamed of how they've acted . . . In most cases, when you help your husband tame his temper, you're helping him become the kind of man he wants to be." How might this insight help motivate you to finally take a stand against your husband's anger—or to persevere if your stand isn't immediately met with gratitude?

6. Have you, like Jo, ever held back from sharing your needs out of fear of seeming selfish? What do you think of Gary's contention that patiently teaching your husband to love you is providing your husband with a valuable spiritual service?

7. How might being motivated by your husband's spiritual welfare—rather than your own comfort—transform the issue of what you address with your husband and how you address it?

8. Why do you think so many women provide indirect clues or hints about their needs but rarely state them in a concrete manner? Why do you think it was so difficult for Jo to just tell Ray that going shopping wasn't merely about buying something but, even more, about being together?

CHAPTER 9

TAMING THE TEMPER, PART 2

Protecting Yourself from Your Husband's Anger

Male violence creates havoc in homes across the world. You can hardly pick up a newspaper without reading at least one account of the destructiveness of male anger and violence—in virtually all aspects of society. It may be ignored from most pulpits, but wives know from other wives, if not their own experience, just how prevalent it is. And because men tend to be stronger physically than women, male temper can become a frightening issue in many marriages. So I want to spend a bit more time on it as a general topic, beyond what we learned from Ray and Jo.

ENOUGH IS ENOUGH

There's a moment when anger becomes rage and when rage becomes physical or so demeaning that the situation calls for a more drastic response than what we discussed in the previous chapter.

In *Sacred Marriage*, I talk extensively about how God can use a difficult marriage to shape us. He uses trials to transform us, and he teaches us to respond to evil with blessing. God has used many difficult marriages to help shape people for life and ministry. Having said this, it is a misapplication of scriptural principles to believe you must stay in a situation where you are being physically abused.

God used a long-standing North American women's conference to open my eyes when I was overwhelmed by the horrific nature of things some wives are having to put up with. Between sessions, I was bombarded by heartfelt inquiries: "What does a wife do when her husband does this? Or when he does that? Or keeps doing this?" It broke my heart. I felt like I needed to take a dozen showers that weekend.

In retrospect, I believe this conference was a divine appointment. I can't get these conversations out of my mind. One wife began our conversation with, "God hates divorce, right?"

"Yes," I said, "I believe he does."

"So I've just got to accept what's happening in my marriage, right?"

When she told me what was happening, I quickly corrected her. "If the cost of saving a marriage is destroying a woman, the cost is too high," I said. "God loves people more than he loves institutions—even institutions he has created." Throughout history, God let a world be destroyed by a flood, a favored and chosen nation decimated by enemies, a one-of-a-kind temple destroyed, and church congregations disappear, though he built and called each one into being. God created the idea of a Sabbath, but when the Sabbath began being used to harm people instead of serve them, Jesus was clear: "The Sabbath was made for man, not man for the Sabbath" (Mark 2:27).

This woman's husband is a persistent porn addict (I'll address porn in a later chapter). He has neglected her sexually except to fulfill his own increasingly bent desires. He keeps dangling divorce over her head, which makes her feel like a failure as a Christian. He presented her with a list of five things he wanted to do that he observed in porn, and if she wasn't willing, he told her he was through with the marriage. She agreed to four of them, but just couldn't do the fifth. And she feels guilty.

God hates divorce, right?

This wife's situation is monstrous and vile, and it actually has little to do with sex. I've seen how porn creates angry men who use bent sexual demands as a weapon. This woman needs to be protected from such grotesque abuse, and if divorce is the only weapon to protect her, then the church should thank God that such a weapon exists.

A young wife, barely in her twenties, held a baby in a blanket and looked at me with tears. Her husband has a huge temper problem. He has forced her to get out of the car, on a highway, with her baby, *twice*. "But both times he came back for us," she said in his defense. They were now separated, and she was living with her parents. She wanted to know if she should take him back, because his psychiatrist said there wasn't anything wrong with him. Her husband doesn't think he has a problem, that, in fact, the problem is with her "lack of forgiveness."

They had been married only three years, and she had already lived through more hell than a woman should face in a lifetime (she shared more details with me than I have time to share here). My thoughts weren't at all about how to "save" the marriage, but how to ease her conscience and help her prepare for a new life—without him.

When a young man is so immature that he puts his wife and baby's lives in danger on a highway (among other things), the thought that we're worried about the "appropriateness" of divorce shows that our loyalties are skewed. As Kevin DeYoung ably puts it, "Every divorce is the result of sin, but not every divorce is sinful."[1]

Another woman told me about putting up with her husband's appalling behavior for *more than forty years*. I was invited to look at her face, see the struggle, and see the heroic perseverance, but also to be reminded that counsel has consequences. So when I talk to a young woman in her third year of marriage, and it's clear she's married to a monster, and then I see someone who wants to "save" the marriage, I want them to realize they are likely sentencing her to four decades of abuse, perhaps because of a choice she made as a teen. When these men aren't confronted and aren't repentant, *they don't change*.

Jesus said what he said about divorce to protect women, not to imprison them. Divorce was a weapon foisted on women in the first century, not one *they* could use, and it almost always left them destitute if their family of origin couldn't or wouldn't step up.

Does it honor the concept of "Christian marriage" to enforce the continuance of an abusive, destructive relationship that slowly squeezes all life and joy out of a woman's soul? Our focus must be on urging men to love their wives like Christ loves the church, not on telling women to put up with husbands who mistreat their wives like Satan mistreats us. We should *confront and stop* the work of Satan, not enable it.

I hate divorce as much as anyone. I have been married for thirty-two years and cannot fathom leaving my wife. I have prayed with couples, counseled with couples, written blog posts and articles and books, and traveled to forty-nine of the fifty states and nine different countries working to strengthen marriages in the church. By all accounts, I believe I've been an ambassador for improving and growing marriages.

Marriage isn't easy. Every marriage must overcome hurt, pain, and sin. No husband is a saint, and every husband will most assuredly need to be forgiven and will be troublesome and even hurtful at times. I'm not talking about the everyday struggles of living with a common sinner. Few things inspire me as much as tales of a grace-based love that draws a recalcitrant spouse back to God.

Please understand what I'm trying to say: I love marriage—even the struggles of marriage—but I hate when God's daughters are abused—physically or otherwise. And I will never defend a marriage over a woman's emotional, spiritual, and physical health.

Some evil men are using their wives' sense of guilt and the

church's teaching about the sanctity of marriage as weapons to keep harming them. I can't help feeling that if more women started saying "This is over," and were backed by a church that enabled them to escape instead of allowing the abuse to continue, other men in the church who are tempted toward the same behavior might finally wake up and change their ways.

Christians are more likely to have one-income families, making some Christian wives feel even more vulnerable. We must clean up our own house. We have to say, "Enough is enough." We must put the fear of God in the hearts of these terrible husbands, because they surely don't fear their wives, and their lack of respect is leading to ongoing deplorable behavior.

We are called to love marriage, but when marriage enables evil, we shouldn't value it over a woman's welfare. As a pastor, I hold to a strict view of Scripture, particularly with regard to divorce and remarriage. I've seen God completely turn men around. But there are times we must realize that a woman is going to be destroyed unless she (at the very least) separates from her husband. And, sadly, there may be times when it ultimately leads to a divorce. In these instances, women from abusive marriages need encouragement and consolation, not rebuke and guilt.

If you're wondering whether the treatment in your marriage rises to the level of abuse, I recommend the ministries of Leslie Vernick (www.leslievernick.com) and Megan Cox (herself an abuse survivor; www.giveherwings.com).

PRACTICALLY CONFRONTING ABUSE

Some women spiritualize domestic violence. They assume it's their duty to bear up under the assault and certainly not to report it to anyone, lest their husbands get in trouble.

You are not being unfaithful to your husband when you seek help. It is not gossip (regardless of what your husband or others might say) to share your hurt or concern with a person capable of helping you, especially when you share it in a redemptive way (that is, to genuinely seek help or to work toward a healthy marriage). Ridiculing your husband in front of a bunch of friends just to vent or elicit laughter is gossip; going privately to a counselor or trusted friend who can provide godly feedback and help is called *fellowship*.

You are, in fact, acting in love by helping your husband confront a behavior that offends God and could prove fatal. Paul writes, "Have nothing to do with the fruitless deeds of darkness, but rather expose them" (Ephesians 5:11).

Biblical submission *never* means you must serve as someone's punching bag. We are called to submit to one another "out of reverence for Christ" (Ephesians 5:21), which qualifies our response. If my wife asks me to do something or participate in something that offends Christ, I am not compelled to join her. On the contrary, I have a duty to God to resist her. The same is true for you as a wife.

While separation is usually necessary to end domestic violence that has become physical, please seek advice from trained professionals first. Sometimes when a woman separates from an abusive man, she puts herself in even more danger of abuse. You need to work with an experienced person to help you choose the wisest and safest course of action. That's why couples' counseling is often an unwise choice in the face of abuse. First seek counseling on your own with a counselor who has experience helping wives evaluate and confront their situation. Many who have been through this have told me that couples' counseling made things worse.

You need protection and wisdom, and your husband needs accountability. Once his problem no longer remains a secret between the two of you, he will be less likely to escalate the harm. He knows he's finally "on record" and could be in big trouble if he continues acting out. If you try to solve this "just between the two of you," you put yourself at increased risk. Your husband may become afraid of being found out and do something desperate to silence you.

So please, please, please—get help! And if you feel threatened, call the police.

While some women spiritualize domestic violence, others live in denial, dismissing it as a joke that got out of hand. Ximena Arriaga, an associate professor of psychological sciences who studies relationship commitment and domestic violence, gives this explanation:

> We hear people say my partner was joking when he hit, kicked or burned me. They also may excuse degrading comments as simple jokes. When a partner is violent, the victim must wonder, "Why is this person who is supposed to love me also hurting me?" One way to make sense of this puzzle is to view the violence as benign. If the person can explain it as something else—something less negative, such as joking, and attribute it to their partner's sense of humor—then they can deny that they are abused and don't have to put up with the possible shame that goes with staying in a violent relationship.[2]

It pains a woman so much to know that her husband is hurting her that she might try to pass it off as "rough humor" or "an accident." An "occasional joke" is easier to face than the fact that you married a wife abuser. But physical harm is never funny. There is no humor in hurt.

If you're in this situation, don't be ashamed. You are not alone. Though domestic violence is less prevalent in marriages than it is in cohabiting relationships, it still happens far too often, which is why churches can do great good by posting in their women's restrooms notices of helpful programs. When you courageously step forward and talk to a pastor or counselor, you could become the lead person in helping your church confront an issue that is all too often kept in the shadows. If no one talks to the pastor, they may not realize there's a problem and never address it from the pulpit.

Don't let the fear of your financial needs and parental responsibilities get in the way of confronting this problem, because it devastates your children to remain in a violent home. Allowing yourself to be abused "for their sake" is a contradiction in terms. My friend Megan Cox, who is a pastoral counselor, shared a helpful spiritual insight with me: "Standing up to and sometimes leaving an abusive husband will help to keep your children from having a skewed view or understanding of our Father God, Abba Father, because you will show them that your husband's abusive behavior does not represent real fatherhood. The children will find solace in God, as their Father, without confusing their earthly father's behavior with God the Father's heart."

Other couples have worked through this. Ignoring it or putting it off will only make things worse. The habit will become more ingrained, and you and your husband may reach a point where the marriage cannot be salvaged.

Many groups and organizations can help you face the immediate financial implications. If you can't find adequate help through your church, consider calling the National Domestic Violence Hotline at 1-800-799-7233 (or visit www.ncadv.org for information on the National Coalition Against Domestic Violence).

Reporting your husband may, indeed, make him very angry. If as a result of this confrontation he chooses to repent and seek to grow, in the end he'll thank you. After he confronts his behavior and begins to make changes, he'll find it far more fulfilling to love, nurture, encourage, and support a woman than to abuse one. If he doesn't repent, you certainly do face some dark days ahead, but in the end, it will be better than remaining in a home where you fear for your life. Furthermore, you'll teach your children that their father's behavior simply isn't acceptable. Your daughters will learn to refuse to put up with that kind of behavior, and your courageous action can help stop a generational pattern of destruction.

FROM STRENGTH TO STRENGTH

I appeal to women in healthy marriages to become advocates for their sisters in unhealthy marriages. Because some abusers are clever and manipulative, many wives aren't taken seriously when they try to address this. And frankly, many men don't understand how terrifying it is to live with someone who could physically hurt you, so they don't take these allegations seriously enough. That's why an abused woman may throw out a "half clue," perhaps a semi-joke about her own marriage to other women in a desperate cry for someone to take her seriously. She may be afraid to openly admit what's going on and is hoping to prompt someone who will draw her out.

Please be that friend. Help her walk out of this valley of violence. Be the good Samaritan who takes the time to stop and care for a wounded stranger. If you're reading this book in a group, please stop right now and ask if anyone needs to share their story, perhaps even to find out if they are being abused (caution: depending on the group dynamics, it may be wise to do this one-on-one).

When a respected woman in a healthy marriage helps shed light on an unhealthy situation, it's far more likely to be taken seriously than when an abused woman in an unhealthy marriage brings charges and her abusive husband tells everyone she's just crazy. Being made to feel crazy for admitting the truth is one of the cruelest weapons that abusers level at women and it's frighteningly common.

If you're in a difficult marriage and are fearing a tough road ahead, let me encourage you. I've been part of a marathon training group for many years. I've seen women who had never run five miles slowly work their bodies into shape so that five or six months down the road they complete a marathon. I'm not talking about women in excellent physical shape either. You'd look at some of them and think, "The last thing they'll ever do is run twenty-six miles in a day." But through months of small decisions and patient preparation, they do it.

If you live with an angry man, this is your spiritual marathon. You're going to be challenged in ways that may terrify you. You may feel terrified, but think with me about a future in which you are supported instead of threatened, in which you feel adored instead of attacked and appreciated instead of insulted. Isn't it worth the risk, for you and your children, to work toward such a marriage?

Furthermore, God can use this situation to help you become much stronger. Sadly, it's often only when we feel like we're in over our heads that we fully throw ourselves on God's mercy and learn to walk with his empowerment and grace. Let faith and spiritual resolve win out over any understandable (and legitimate) fear. Remember, courage is not the absence of fear; it is expressed as you put your faith in God and move forward, even when you are terrified and convinced that everything will go wrong.

Your situation may resemble Jo's—anger, but no violence. You need the courage to accept God's view of yourself as a valuable person and then the wisdom to teach your husband how to respond to you appropriately. If your situation is beginning to become violent, you need to act now, find some help, and be part of creating a crisis that can lead to change.

Above all, remember that while you might feel frightened, uncertain, guilty, or confused, you are *never* alone. Your God is with you, and his people will surround you. Spend some time asking God to bring helpers into your life before you act; this may be the wisest step you can take. And then move forward from there. If you keep stepping out in faith, you'll discover just how strong you can become in Christ—and that's a valuable life lesson. If you persevere, you won't even recognize yourself several years down the road. I've witnessed timid, fearful, victimized personalities vanish in favor of strong, wise, bold, and courageous women of faith.

As the apostle Paul wrote, "To this end I strenuously contend with all the energy Christ so powerfully works in me" (Colossians 1:29). This is your refuge and your hope.

QUESTIONS FOR DISCUSSION
AND REFLECTION

1. How can the church do a better job of helping women who are in abusive relationships?
2. Discuss why it's not in a child's best interest to be in a home where domestic violence takes place.
3. Ask if any women need help understanding whether they're in an abusive relationship.

CHAPTER 10

RICH AND PAT:
THE MAGIC QUESTION

Helping Your Husband Become More Involved at Home

Although Rich and Pat have three children together, they led mostly separate lives for some time. According to Pat, "We did little together except argue about the kids."

Rich concurs. "Home life was pretty combative," he says.

Pat once complainingly described Rich as an overinvolved worker during the week and an avid hunter and fisherman on the weekends. Any other free time he had he spent watching TV or using the computer, making him a relatively uninvolved husband and father. When Pat brought up Rich's frequent absences on weekends, Rich would say, "Don't worry, honey. Hunting season is almost over." But Pat soon learned that fishing season was just around the corner.

From Rich's perspective, life seemed much easier *outside* the home—a view shared by many men. "I probably was overinvolved in work, and when I wasn't working, I wanted to hunt and fish. Outside of home, there were all sorts of things to succeed at: birds to shoot or issues to solve at work. There's great satisfaction in getting my limit of trout or ducks and resolving issues at work. Also, these were *solvable* problems that I could tackle with a certain degree of success; the problems at home didn't seem all that solvable."

We men tend to avoid battles we know we can't win or that make us feel incompetent. I've met professional athletes who freely admit that the reason they avoid golf is that they want only to play something in which they can excel. The thinking is, *If there's no chance of winning, there's no chance of me even competing.* Unfortunately, this means that when we start to feel like we're in over our heads in our family life, home may become the last place we want to be—*if we can't succeed, we don't even want to try.* Sadly, we may end up slowly increasing our hours at work and extending our involvement in recreational hobbies, perhaps not even realizing we are virtually hiding from our families.

Pat realized what she was up against when she asked her husband to take care of their infant son, Ben, one evening a week so she could get some work done or have some relaxation time without being interrupted. Rich declined, telling her, "I'm not really that interested in babies." By Rich's reckoning, since he worked all day, the evenings belonged to him, and he shouldn't have to bother with child-rearing. By the same token, since he worked all week, the weekends were his to relax and recharge. What's more, since he worked all year, vacations allowed him to pursue hunting and fishing or camping. In Rich's view, watching the kids and taking care of the house were solely Pat's responsibility.

Meanwhile, Pat saw her job as twenty-four hours a day, seven days a week, with no vacations and little or no help.

Pat blames herself for letting this go on for so long. "I didn't have negotiating skills or boundaries," she says as she reflects on her marriage. "I kept thinking that if I worked harder, it would get better somehow—but it didn't, and then I'd explode, and that just made things worse. I didn't know how to confront people in a good way or look for alternatives. For example, I could have hired a babysitter to take the kids to the park while I stayed home. And I should have set better limits on my children, like setting a timer and having a one-hour flat-on-bunk time every day or having a list of chores to get done and then going to the park. Fortunately, I did start seeing my hours as flexible and Rich's as inflexible. I decided to start having some fun during the day so I'd feel more rested when Rich came home."

Shortly after their oldest child turned fifteen, "things began to fall apart," she said. "Our house was characterized by arguing, yelling, and busyness. Our children fell into the classic pattern of rebellious child, overpleasing child, and withdrawn child. Rich was usually gone and didn't really want to be home—and I had given him every reason not to! I greeted him with a list when he came home, was in a chronically bad mood, and was usually either depressed or angry."

Pat tried to talk to Rich about becoming interested in family activities (besides hunting and fishing), but Rich responded, "Look, I work hard, I don't drink, I don't gamble, and I don't chase other women. All in all, I'd say I'm a pretty good husband."

"He did provide well for us," Pat admits. "In his eyes, that made him a good husband and father. He also went to lots of the kids' games. He just couldn't see that he was cold and distant and was avoiding problems."

CARVING OUT A NEW PATH

Eventually, Pat realized that even after years of confrontation and arguing, Rich remained overinvolved at work and relatively absent at home. Now in her early forties, Pat didn't want to spend the rest of her life with a man who always had his mind somewhere else.

"To be honest," Pat admits, "I wanted a divorce, but I knew the only biblical grounds was if he committed adultery or left me. So I prayed he would die or find someone else."

Instead, *Pat* found someone else—the Lord, whom she credits with saving her life. "Without God, I would have ended up in jail or the insane asylum," she said. Pat assumed she had always been a Christian because she went to church, but a frustrating experience with her pastor had led her to visit Bethel Church in Richland, Washington, where she encountered a rich, deep, and authentic faith.

At her old church, Christianity seemed more of a cultural thing. Most of the congregation considered those who actually read the Bible as either strange or religious zealots. People just didn't use phrases like "God spoke to me" or "the Bible says." Pat started listening to Christian radio, reading the Bible, applying her new pastor's teaching, reading popular Christian books, and growing spiritually by the hour.

When she started reading about biblical submission of wives to husbands, Pat initially felt wary. "That was a radical, new thought for me," Pat says. "I wasn't raised that way, and I was more into the women's liberation philosophy of equality. Furthermore, I felt pretty nervous about submitting to someone who wasn't reading his Bible. Doing so will either break you or develop your faith in the love and power of God."

Pat's church also introduced her to basic Christian virtues, such as being thankful in all circumstances and pursuing love, joy, peace, patience, goodness, and kindness. "I thought I deserved to be cranky; anyone who had to put up with what I had to deal with would do likewise. It was hard to admit that, regardless of circumstances, people can choose their response."

THE MAGIC QUESTION

Pat began this journey of reorienting her marriage by asking Rich what she now calls the "magic question." Doing so went against every fiber of her being. It was actually the opposite of what she thought would best serve her marriage, but she decided to give it a try anyway.

"Rich, what things would you like me to do that I'm not doing?" Rich's answer caught Pat completely off guard.

"Somehow I expected him to tell me he would like the house to be cleaner—I could have dealt with that. But he asked me to start preparing meals that the kids would like. I was in shock. I was raised with the notion that there is only one thing worse than a murderer, and that is a picky eater. 'You've got two options: take it or leave it!'"

When the kids didn't enjoy what Pat made, she insisted they eat it anyway, regularly creating friction and confrontation around the dinner table. Rich just wanted peace. When Rich was a boy, if any of the kids in his family said, "I don't like this," they never saw it again. If Pat ever were to give that response in her family, she would have been served the same meal, in double portions, for breakfast the next morning!

"I was appalled that Rich let the kids eat dessert if they didn't like the main course. But over time, he helped me see there is wisdom in the fact that people do feel loved when you give them the things they want; and he's come around to my view too—that healthy eating and polite table manners also matter."

Previously, Pat made the kids' lunches, and that was that. Now, at Rich's request, she became more aware of what they liked and didn't like and started customizing their sack lunches. "Before, I simply ignored what the kids liked. My attitude was, 'I made it; you eat it.'" One of Pat's daughters liked her sandwiches cut in a fancy way; the other kids didn't care about such niceties. For the first time, Pat began to regularly accommodate this daughter's preference, and years later, she was glad she had. On a high school retreat, someone asked this daughter to name something that someone had done to make an impact on her life, and she said, "My mom cut my sandwiches like I liked them. It made me feel special and loved."

"At the time, I thought it was crazy," Pat remembers, "but listening to Rich helped me demonstrate love to my daughter in a way she could receive it. Also, I remembered as a child that I wanted my sandwiches cut a certain way. It seemed a small thing to ask because it requires no money and almost no time. But my mom refused. I felt stupid and insignificant. Unless I had submitted to my husband, I would have done what my mom had done. I never would have learned to balance practicality with graciousness."

Pat's question can transform a marriage. Perhaps you're reading this book because you want to see something change in your husband. It's always a good exercise in humility, however, to occasionally put the spotlight on yourself. Do you have the spiritual fortitude to put aside your own frustration and disappointment long enough to ask your husband, "What would you like me to do that I'm not doing?"

I know—if you're as disappointed as Pat was, asking a question like that seems counterintuitive. But you're about to hear of some rather impressive results.

Notice, Pat didn't ask this of a perfect husband; she asked it of one with whom she felt very angry, one who seemed to be ignoring her and the kids. *But she also believed that if change was going to transform her home, it would have to begin with her.*

Let me challenge you to take some time in the next few days to offer a simple, yet potentially marriage-changing question, "What would you like me to do that I'm not doing?"

"THE LAST THING I WANTED HIM TO ASK"

After getting used to meal changes and seeing some good results, Pat decided to repeat the question. Once again, Rich's answer astounded her. "I don't care if the house is clean." he said. "I just want you to be in a good mood when I walk in the door."

"That was the last thing I wanted him to ask of me," Pat admits.

"I could see how it was theoretically possible, because if all I had to do all day long was to be in a good mood when he walked through the door, I figured I should be able to do that. But complaining, criticizing, and arguing were old, faithful friends. Be in a good mood? That was not me!"

Rich also asked Pat to focus on having more fun with the kids instead of correcting them all the time. Pat's constant admonitions kept pouring tension into the home, and Rich craved peace.

Beyond these things, Rich was reluctant to talk about what Pat could do for him, so she thought up a few things on her own. Instead of complaining about Rich's fishing trips, Pat started going with him. And not just the fishing trips—she'd accompany him to the sporting goods store and even to Rod and Gun Club meetings (where, according to Pat, "they eat venison, moose, or bear, and some speaker shares slides of his latest hunt").

"This was real hard for me because I felt that fishing and hunting was something my husband should give up," Pat acknowledges. "At first, it sort of felt like wanting an alcoholic to give up going to bars and then going out drinking with him; to me, it felt the same anyway. This was a real idol in his life, and I didn't want to support it. I still think hunting and fishing have a bigger place in his life than they should have, but I finally had to admit that there *is* a difference between fishing and drinking. It wasn't sinful for me to go fishing with my husband. I had to learn to let God be God and let *him* work on things with Rich."

After adopting this very difficult transformation, Pat laughs about how she now drives past places and thinks, *That would be a great place to fish*. "I actually *enjoy* some fishing," she says in a surprised tone of voice. "We went to Sun Valley for our twenty-fifth wedding anniversary and had a great time fly-fishing."

For both of them, it's been a long transformation by degrees. "Basically, when I asked Rich what he wanted of me—regarding us—what he wanted sounded really difficult. He just wanted me to be in a good mood, to be more fun, and not to complain about things that don't get fixed." Some of those things, Pat now fixes herself. And as for her mood—well, Rich will tell you she's a lot more pleasant to live with.

OVERWHELMING BENEFITS

Much to Pat's surprise, when she started focusing on helping Rich instead of fighting and resenting him, he became more involved at home. "Home became a lot more pleasant place to be, so I'm sure that had something to do with it."

Pat heard two guys on the radio joking about a 1950s home economics textbook that encouraged women to serve their husbands, but their comedic exchange affected Pat in a different way. "Most men, if they're honest, really would like that in their wives," she says. And she's trying to provide some of that loving service for Rich.

Pat decided to focus on helping Rich. She cleared her calendar to cut out a lot of her outside activities, so that, as she says, "instead of trying to find fulfillment in other things, I could focus my energies on my home and my family." It's a bit ironic that in her efforts to get her husband to be more involved at home, Pat began by making sure *she* was more involved at home—not just present, but emotionally, spiritually, and relationally engaged.

Pat doesn't sugarcoat the difficulty of any of this. "It's impossibly hard to put so much energy into a home and marriage when you don't enjoy your home or family. At first, you feel like you're dying. We all crave recognition, power, and honor. Sacrificing and serving seem to move us away from those desires."

But Pat fought off the resentment. She explains, "I felt that, in one sense, what I was doing was contrary to everything I am. I felt like I was dying, but the paradox is that I am more me now than I ever was. I am kinder, gentler, and more submissive, but I am also more strong-willed and opinionated than I ever was. I used to think those were contradictions, but now I see how they work together. Although at the time, I thought I was giving things up, I can see now I was gaining. I wouldn't go back to the way I was for anything. I have more joy, forgiveness, and grace, and more friends as well—*a lot* more friends! My family has changed dramatically, and for the first time, I get along with my siblings, Mom and Dad, and my in-laws."

Pat added, "The way I moved my husband was by changing myself. I honestly believe that when you do what your partner wants you to do, you heal yourself in the process. God gives you your spouse as the person who can fix those things in you that you really don't want to fix."

Rich agrees. "Pat softened a lot," he said, "and that made a big difference to me. It's a lot easier to feel empathy for someone who is soft than for someone who is coming on hard."

"You can't do this without faith in the Lord," Pat adds. "And though, like me, you'll probably feel like you're dying, all I can say is that it's *so* worth it. By submitting to my husband and doing what he asked me to do—even though there was so much I wanted *him* to do differently—I became the person I wanted to be: a more loving wife, a better friend, a better mother. And then I found that those things bring me a lot of joy. The benefits to myself have been overwhelming. Even if my husband acted like the biggest jerk from now until the day he dies, submitting to him has brought an incredible change in me, and I wouldn't go back to the way I was for anything."

THE BIG ADVENTURE

To wives whose husbands play darts on the weekend, constantly haunt the golf course, or accompany their buddies to the local bar, Pat advises, "Consider how you might be driving your husband out of the house and over to the basement workshop, the golf course, or the computer."

Think very honestly about this past week. Put yourself in your husband's shoes. What did it feel like to be greeted by you? What kind of mood do you set in the home? Are you pleasant? Confrontational? Apathetic? *Would you like to be welcomed home in the way you welcome home your husband?*

Maybe you get home from work after your husband does. You can ask yourself some other questions. Do you regularly complain about your day instead of listening to him about his? Do you pour out your resentment that other women have it easier than you do? Do you make him feel as though he doesn't measure up? Are you preoccupied with unanswered email? What are you doing to make your husband your "buddy"? Are you a pleasure to be around?

Pat says that since she's experienced these changes, "Rich now *wants* to come home. He *wants* to be with me; he wants to support me if I'm going through a bad time. When he does go away on trips, he's careful to organize them in such a way that he can see the family as much as possible before and after."

Pat adds, "If you want a big adventure, submit to your husband. That will be the greatest adventure of your life. It will be more exciting than rocketing to the moon. It will open up a whole different way of looking at things—a way you perhaps can't envision right now. Few topics are more controversial than that of submitting to your husband, but it's absolute truth—and it has worked so well in my own life."

RICH'S PERSPECTIVE

Rich points to three factors that influenced his evolution from absentee father and husband to a man eager to come home at night:

- Pat's renewed commitment
- Pat's expression of her own hurt
- Rich's renewed faith

"To me, the big change occurred when I felt that Pat was really *committed* to the marriage," says Rich. "I had begun to wonder just how committed she was. There were times she said she didn't love me—that she even hated me—and suggested I might want to leave, which I did not want to do. But I think what became important was when she realized we have a commitment. Marriage isn't just about *feelings* of love; there are times when only a commitment carries you through. When marriage is based on a Christian faith, it's much more solid. You can depend on it. That, to me, was the foundation that was most important—after we both realized we were committed to this marriage, I wanted to change, and I always had hope after that point."

Rich brings up a good point. Why would a husband change for a wife who shows no commitment to him, who might, in fact, even leave him or encourage him to leave? From a guy's perspective, that's like filling up the gas tank just before you sell your car. If your husband has no confidence that the marriage will continue, why go through the hassle of character transformation?* Most men need to know their wives will be there before they feel motivated to make a change. Once again, however, bear in mind that this principle needs to be adjusted for destructive marriages. A woman cannot commit to coming home or having a husband return home until she sees a consistent change over a period of time.

Second, Rich was genuinely surprised when Pat finally got through to him about how badly he was hurting her. Rich obviously enjoys being around his wife, and he really didn't want to lose her. "Pat is an extraordinary woman," he says. "She once asked me why I wouldn't leave, and I said, 'Because I like you.' There's just something about her that's different that I really like. This may not be true of every marriage, but I personally couldn't ever see myself

---

* I believe husbands should be motivated "out of reverence for God" (2 Corinthians 7:1), not out of their wives' reactions. I'm describing here what *usually* happens, not what *should* happen.

being married to or dating another woman. I had no interest in other women."

When a man feels this deeply about a woman and then sees how his actions cause her deep pain, he's going to feel motivated to change. Before then—as much as this may frustrate Pat—Rich says he really didn't understand just how much pain he was causing.

The third major stage of Rich's evolution came about when he saw Pat's renewed faith. Her renewed relationship with God became contagious. Like Pat, Rich exchanged a cultural Christianity for a real faith. If you ask him why he's more involved at home now, Rich says, "There's no treasure in the other activities, no inheritance; it all gets burned away! I still put in a good day at work, and I still love to hunt and fish, but I realize that, from the standpoint of eternity, they'll all pass away."

How interesting! The man who once threw himself into work and outdoor sports because of their solvable nature and tangible rewards now recognizes that their rewards pale in comparison to God's promised rewards in eternity.

In my view, that's why Pat's mission worked. Instead of trying to change Rich for her own sake, she drew closer to the Lord, captivated Rich with her own example, and in a godly way encouraged Rich to reevaluate his priorities according to God's standards. Rich needed another measuring stick. Marriage, faith, and family life take more effort than work and fishing—but they offer much greater rewards: "Everyone who competes in the games goes into strict training. They do it to get a crown that will not last, but we do it to get a crown that will last forever" (1 Corinthians 9:25).

Rich has some simple counsel for wives married to overinvolved husbands: "First, they really need to let their husbands know how it feels to be left alone. Second, I would tell them that their man needs to get into an accountability group. Doing so helped me to see other role models at church. Our small group evolved into an accountability group, and those guys started challenging me about how much time I spent with my wife compared to time spent at work or hunting. Plus, it was very helpful to see what other successful couples were doing."

Rich and Pat's story emphasizes the importance of a healthy Christian community. It'll go much easier for you if other men can challenge your husband. Some men resent it when they think their wives want them to change for the wives' sake; it's a different matter entirely when some committed friends say, "Hey, buddy, you need to do this because *God* calls you to do this."

Rich also urges wives to follow Pat's example of entering into their husbands' world. Pat says to wives, "Find a way to be his buddy and do the things he wants to do," and Rich affirms this wholeheartedly. "It really helped find common ground on things we like to do," he said. "I really appreciated it when Pat made the effort to start fly-fishing with me. After she did that, I thought I had an obligation to spend time shopping with her and doing the things she likes to do."

I believe marriage involves a commitment to "fall forward," as I say in *Sacred Marriage*. Just as I started following figure skating (something I have zero natural interest in) when figure skating became important to my daughter; and just as I'll occasionally watch HGTV (Home and Garden Television) with my wife, even though finding the "right" shade of white paint ranks one millionth on the list of things that interest me—so you might think about doing something or becoming informed about a topic simply because your husband enjoys it. Doing so creates momentum for your husband to also fall toward you.

Rich freely confesses that conversation doesn't rank high on his list of favorite things. "The hardest thing for me is just sitting down and talking," he says. "Oh, that's hard!" But he's at least willing now to give it a try.

Rich emphatically says, "Wives need to understand the commitment part. Marriage is love *and* commitment; a husband won't stay or even want to stay in a marriage if the wife isn't committed."

Commitment is about more than simply staying put; it also requires moving toward someone. If you want your husband to move toward you, ask yourself how you are moving toward your husband. This goes far beyond staying legally married to include the spiritual commitment of continuing to love, pursue, and serve.

Your first movement toward your husband should be, as it was for Pat, a movement toward God. Paul praised the Macedonians for this: "They gave themselves first of all to the Lord, and then by the will of God also to us" (2 Corinthians 8:5). When you give yourself first to God, you open yourself up to his correction, affirmation, and redemption.

How might God be using the situations in your life to help you reevaluate yourself, your priorities, and your actions? For Pat, the answer came loud and clear that she needed to learn the meaning of biblical submission. I doubt she could have given herself to Rich if she hadn't first given herself—including her emotional desires, relational frustration, and personal despair—to God.

And then follow this up with the second question: "What would you like me to do for you that I'm not doing?" If you heed your husband's words instead of taking offense, you can slowly transform your home into a more pleasant place for him to be and therefore make him *want* to come home.

QUESTIONS FOR DISCUSSION AND REFLECTION

1. Gary notes that men tend to avoid battles they can't win or that make them feel incompetent. How can wives support their husbands so they'll feel just as competent at home as they do at work?

2. Pat confesses that when Rich came home, "I greeted him with a list, was in a chronically bad mood, and was usually either

depressed or angry." Identify and talk about some realistic expectations for wives so that they can do a better job of getting their husbands to become more involved at home.

3. Discuss the magic question: "What things would you like me to do that I'm not doing?" Are you comfortable asking this of your husband? Why or why not?

4. Pat entered Rich's world of fishing, even though she initially had no natural interest in it. What are some of your husband's favorite hobbies or activities, and how can you build intimacy by joining in with him?

5. Pat says, "God gives you your spouse as the person who can fix those things in you that you really don't want to fix." This may be a hard lesson to accept, but what are one or two things God is using your husband to fix in your own life?

6. How can small groups in particular, or churches in general, help challenge underinvolved husbands?

CHAPTER 11

PURE PASSION

Cementing Your Husband's Affections and
Protecting His Spiritual Integrity

Wives, there's something you need to know about your husbands that many women don't know. Your husbands aren't likely to tell you about it, because they fear it might sound self-serving or maybe terrify you. So let me be your husband's advocate and tell you something you need to know if you want to truly understand your husband: *sexual struggles are different for men than they are for women.*

They just are.

Wives, if you want a connected marriage, an intimate marriage, a marriage based on understanding, a marriage in which your husband is grateful to you for knowing him and getting him, you have to avoid comparing your sexual struggles and temptations to his.

They're not the same. They will never be the same.

They're just not.

Dr. Louann Brizendine's research has found that "men have two and a half times the brain space devoted to sexual drive in their hypothalamus. Sexual thoughts flicker in the background of a man's visual cortex all day and night, making him always at the ready for seizing sexual opportunity."[1]

Yes, women struggle with porn, as men do. Women have affairs, as men do. Women struggle with same-sex sexuality, as men do. But the underlying causes are usually very different. For example, it is rare that a happily married woman will have an affair, while many men who say they are very happy in their marriage end up in an affair. Why do you think this is?

The ongoing levels of interest in sex between a male brain and female brain are widely different. Dr. Brizendine explains, "Women are surprised that the penis can operate on autopilot and even more surprised that men don't always know when they're getting an erection. The autopilot penis is part of a man's daily reality for most of his life, though it happens less as he gets older."[2]

Stereotypes can be hurtful and unhelpful if your husband isn't typical, but for the vast majority of wives reading this, sexual integrity is a more intense struggle for your husband than it is for you. I have worked with many men in many different decades of life, and many are somewhat terrified of their sexual desire. They want to live lives of integrity but for them it's a constant battle that few men can forget about.

Famed illustrator Robert McGinnis (who is now ninety-one) confesses, "All men are . . . hooked and helpless in the face of female beauty."[3] You may hate that quote, thinking I'm giving guys a pass with a "boys will be boys" mentality. I'm going to try my best not to do that, but even so, this may well be your least favorite chapter of this book. I was tempted to just get rid of it, but that would be doing you and your marriage a disservice. You deserve to know the truth if you want to know your husband.

Speaking as a man in his fifties, I do think the battle changes somewhat as we get older, but it doesn't end. All men are exposed to material that seeks to pull us away from our wives, and I'm no exception. And please understand, I'm not excusing sexual sin.

A wife should not just accept ongoing, unrepentant sexual sin. Any form of sexual sin will destroy marital intimacy, assault integrity, diminish worship, handicap ministry, detract from our parenting, and sap our spiritual energy and desire. Every form of sexual sin should be confronted, and if the man doesn't repent, the church needs to support the wife, not imprison her with an unrepentant and increasingly bent husband. She should never be asked or guilted into just putting up with shameful treatment to keep the peace.

This is about pleading with women married to struggling sinners, helping them understand that they're not doing their husbands justice if they think, "Because sexual temptation is, for me, a two on a scale of one to ten, then it shouldn't be higher than a three or a four for my husband."

That's not a fair comparison. That would be like a weight-lifting husband saying to his wife, "Because I can bench press three hundred pounds, you ought to be able to do two hundred fifty pounds."

I am *not* making excuses for your husband by saying his sex drive is likely different from yours. I'm simply saying I want to help you understand him, to realize that it is different for him, to pray for him, to be watchful for him in a caring, cherishing way rather than showing him a judgmental, condemning attitude.

FIRE ANT THERAPY

While I love many things about Texas, what I like least—it's fair to say I even hate—are fire ants. They're not native to Texas, so when I want to kill them all, I'm merely cooperating with God's creative intentions. Fire ants are tiny, but their bites are brutal. It takes a couple hours to feel them, but then the burn and the itch are with you for *days*.

Some of these insects invaded our house recently and assaulted my wife. She was bitten all over her body, in a dozen different places. She was miserable. I felt sorry for her, but not sorry enough.

It wasn't until one of them got me a few days later, on one of my hands, that I was reminded of the intensity of their devilish assault.

When I faced my own struggle (just one bite kept me from sleeping one night) and then multiplied it by ten, I realized just how awful the struggle must have been for Lisa, and how I should have had one hundred times the empathy and compassion I demonstrated. I had one bite; she had a dozen. I knew what a little sting was like, but she had to live with multiple stings. That made me more sensitive, not less.

Can you have that attitude with your husband? You know what sexual temptation and bent desires are like. Multiply that struggle by a dozen, and you'll begin to understand what it's like for your husband.

Most of us Christian men want to love our wives with purity and walk with God with integrity. We want to let the light and life of Jesus Christ change, not just our actions, but our very desires. But all this takes time. Sanctification is a process. You don't help us by ignoring sin or accommodating sin, but you also don't help by shaming us or by acting as if your relative lack of struggle is proof that we shouldn't struggle as well.

Of course, whenever a writer makes generalizations, there will be exceptions. There are an increasing number of marriages where the wife's libido seems higher than her husband's, but in many cases this is because the husband has sinful sexual activity happening on the side.

Which means, wives, if you happen to be married to a man who takes his sexual integrity seriously, who fights to save all his sexual interest and desire for you, who makes himself accountable to rein in his untoward desires, and who is committed to being faithful, please don't take him for granted.

A good friend of mine is one of the godliest men I know. He loves the Lord and his family with an intense, infectious passion.

Yet he opened up to me recently in an offhand comment that he is terrified about sexual temptation. He and his wife canceled a free monthlong Netflix subscription after just two days because, he told me, "I don't trust myself." He's not weak. He's strong in the Lord, but he still feels very vulnerable.

In this chapter, I'll discuss how you can use the sexual relationship within marriage to cement your husband's affections and help protect his spiritual integrity, which I believe is vital for a healthy marriage. But I also want it to be a chapter that opens up new doors of sexual enjoyment for you. I'm not one to excuse sexual selfishness in men, nor do I believe it's healthy for a marriage to be bent toward "feeding the husband's beast." The best marriages focus on mutual enjoyment and caring for each other's needs even above our own. I will always hold men to that standard and goal.

If your husband lives with the thought that sex is mainly for him and if your marriage is bent in this direction, all it will do is create and grow a self-absorbed husband. Your husband needs to learn to serve and to give in this area as much as in any other. For him to be whole in Christ, he will have to die to certain desires and not be driven by internal demands. This is where it can be very difficult to be a wife. Your first concern for your husband should be his growth and wellness in Christ, not the fulfillment of your husband's every sexual desire. You can't change your husband and you shouldn't take responsibility for his poor choices, but you can at least pray toward the goal and encourage him toward the goal of a healthy, mutually satisfying sexual relationship within marriage. The best defense really is a good offense.

We also need to discuss the increasing threat of porn and why it can be devastating to your marriage. This has become such an important discussion that it will require an additional chapter of its own to fully understand how destructive it has become and to offer practical help for confronting it.

THRESHOLD TO INTIMACY

The good news is that the majority of married Christians feel "satisfied" or "very satisfied" with their sexual relationship. According to a survey published in *Today's Christian Woman*, 63 percent of respondents fit those two categories; only 17 percent felt "dissatisfied" and 5 percent "very dissatisfied."[4]

These aren't bad numbers, especially when we consider that we ought to expect many of the stated causes of dissatisfaction in the course of a normal married life: busy schedules, children in the home, occasional sexual dysfunction, or a current illness.

This is doubly good news in that a satisfying sexual intimacy is a key component in your husband's emotional availability. Dr. Melody Rhode has seen more than her share of couples in her two decades of family counseling, and from her perspective, "most women want more emotional involvement from their husbands, but most husbands can't connect with their wives emotionally if their sexual needs aren't being met. So if women want a deeper emotional connection, they *must* provide the sexual one."

I fully realize this sounds like it puts the burden on you. Part of this is just realism—if your marriage is at a standstill, somebody has to make the first move. If you know your husband isn't going to and you want a different kind of marriage, your only option is to take that first step and see what happens or learn to be content with the status quo. No, it's not fair. Yes, it must hurt—a lot. But not moving—whether out of fear, spite, or frustration—will simply cement you where you already are. If you don't want to stay where you are, I don't see any other alternative.

Of course, for many women, participating in a fulfilling sexual relationship is a joy, not a burden. There will always be times when the weariness of raising a family can dampen anyone's enthusiasm for particular sexual episodes, but most women value the intimate connection formed through years of generous physical affection.

It may surprise you, however, to learn how closely connected your husband's emotional availability is to expressions of physical intimacy.

We've already talked about oxytocin, the "relational bonding" chemical more predominant in women than in men. While women normally have oxytocin levels up to ten times higher than those of men (in extreme cases), a man's oxytocin levels match those of his wife in one particular instance—following a sexual encounter. Neurologically, reports Michael Gurian, "one of the primary reasons that men want sex more than women (on average) is because it feels so good to them to have the high oxytocin—it feels great to feel so bonded with someone . . . In male biochemistry sex is the quickest way for a man to bond with a woman."[5]

Another wonderful aspect of oxytocin in your husband's brain is that its release makes him find you more attractive and other women less attractive. This means that a vigorous and active sexual relationship literally trains your husband's brain to see you as the most beautiful woman in the world. It's God's wonderful design to cement a man's affection for his wife on a regular basis.

After the honeymoon and the first year or two of marriage, it is so easy for couples to begin to coast in this area. Sometimes they coast because a baby comes along and they're both too tired to think about another physical activity. On occasion, couples may coast because one or both partners simply lose the desire they had at the beginning. Yet sexual coasting, no matter what the reason, endangers the relationship. Studies reveal that coasting physically usually leads to drifting apart relationally.

I stress this because if your husband feels frustrated in this regard, if he feels his sexual relationship with you has waned to such a degree that his sexual advances will likely receive a "you've got to be kidding" response, then he'll have a difficult time maintaining the emotional bond so crucial to a fulfilling marriage.

To illustrate how this works, let's turn the tables. Say a man gave his wife the silent treatment for a week and then expected her to have sex with him. We would naturally assume that such a man knows little about either women or relationships, that in fact his request is cruel, selfish, and absurd. But when a woman consistently turns down a man's physical advances and then expects her husband to open up to her emotionally and engage in long conversations, essentially the same dynamic is taking place: "We haven't had sex for a week, and you want to *talk*? Why would I *want* to talk to you?"

Sex may *feel* like a physical need to your husband, but it's inherently emotional and even spiritual. Michael Gurian believes that, neurologically speaking, a man's "self-worth is linked, to a great extent, to how often and how well he engages in the sex act."[6]

One husband told Shaunti Feldhahn, "When [my wife] says no, I feel that I am *rejected*. 'No' is *not* no to sex—as she might feel. It is no to me as I am."[7] The wife thinks she is rejecting an activity, but her husband feels she is rejecting *him*. This not only cuts off the opportunity for the oxytocin chemicals to create a refreshingly new bonding experience, but it will tempt him to shut down emotionally. Another man told Feldhahn, "[My wife] doesn't understand how even her occasional dismissals make me feel less desirable. I can't resist her. I wish that I, too, were irresistible. She says I am. But her ability to say no so easily makes it hard to believe."[8]

I know you probably don't feel as though you are rejecting your husband when you say no to sex or when you seldom initiate physical intimacy—but the lack of initiation carries a tremendous emotional impact, whether you intend it to or not. Feldhahn makes a good point:

> I believe that most of us aren't manipulatively withholding something we know is critical to our husband's sense of well-being. Much more likely is that after a long day at the office or with the kids, we just don't feel an overwhelming desire to rip off our husband's clothes and go at it. I suspect we simply don't realize the emotional consequences of our response

(or lack of one) and view his desire for sex more as a physical desire or even an insensitive demand. Once we truly comprehend the truth behind our husband's advances, we're more likely to *want* to respond.[9]

A man who feels sexually fulfilled is much more motivated to become emotionally and spiritually intimate with his wife, as well as to want to please her. He is far more likely to be more heavily invested in the home if his wife pursues him sexually. By being considerate, thoughtful, creative, generous, and energetic in this area, you can create a more stable foundation on which to make over your marriage and open the door to the emotional intimacy you rightly desire.

THE ONE TIME MALE PRIDE WORKS IN YOUR FAVOR

Learning to enjoy each other sexually is one of the great gifts of marriage. There is nothing like a married couple enjoying a special morning of intimacy, seeing each other later in the day, and smiling at the memory shared only by them. It's a beautiful, intimacy-building thing.

Which means one of the best gifts you can give your husband is to learn to be enthralled by the sexual experience. This is the one time in marriage when your husband's pride may work in your favor. If you're exhausted, panting, and smiling after a sexual encounter, your husband gets a certain satisfaction, thinking, *I did that to her, thank you very much.*

The challenge is that sex is like any physical activity in that it takes time to master. And every woman's body and mind are vastly different. There's no way your husband can possibly know how to please you, because you are truly unique. One husband found that making his wife wait, with extended foreplay, made it more difficult for her to reach orgasm. "She likes to go from zero to sixty in less than five minutes, to be honest," he said. "And once she's revved up, it's cruel to make her wait." That goes against conventional wisdom, to be sure, but there's no right or wrong when it comes to his wife's body. He needs to learn what fulfills her and then work from that vantage point.

Find a way to help your husband please you. Show him. Tease him. Ask him. Affirm him when it works. This isn't selfish. You're giving him one of the best gifts any man could ever have—a sexually satisfied wife.

Sheila Wray Gregoire, a popular blogger (tolovehonorandvacuum.com) and author of several books, including *The Good Girl's Guide to Great Sex*, told me, "The message that women often hear is, 'We have to have sex, or he'll be tempted, or he'll stray, or he'll be a bear.' These threats aren't exactly aphrodisiacs. Obligation sex isn't sexy. But what if we're missing the bigger picture? So often sex is framed as something that men need and women have to provide. What we women often miss, though, is that we need sex too. We may not feel the physical pull in the way that many men do. But God created sex to be the pinnacle of intimacy—a deep 'knowing,' as it says in the Hebrew, where we long to be totally and utterly connected to another person. He created us so that sex wasn't just sex; it was also making love. Oxytocin, which is released during sex, bonds us, increases affection, and makes us feel safe.

"Plus, sex can also feel wonderful! It helps us relieve stress. It wards off many illnesses, including mental illness and some cancers. And my personal favorite—it helps us sleep better! For exhausted women being pulled in all directions, making love is often the best cure. Yes, our husbands desperately want sex, but we need it too. And God created us to be just as physically responsive as men are. The question, then, shouldn't really be, 'Do I owe him sex?' The question we really need to ask is, 'If God created something this great, why would I want to miss out on it?'"

THE SPIRITUAL GOOD
OF A PHYSICAL ACT

For your sake, your children's sake, and your husband's sake, the best way to influence your husband is to encourage his growing *intimacy with God*. A man who is deeply in love with God, who regularly listens to God's voice, and who seeks God's kingdom above all else will feel more motivated to love you, keep his focus at home, and purify himself out of reverence for Christ. Probably 90 percent of the changes I've made in my marriage have come out of prayer and Bible study, not out of conversations with my wife. This isn't to diminish the importance of conversations between husband and wife; it's to elevate the importance of prayer in your husband's life. God can be your truest advocate in marriage, pleading your case and convicting your husband in ways you never could—if, that is, he's praying and is connected to God in a listening way.

An experience of compromised sexual purity is one of the great threats to your husband's spiritual intimacy with God and therefore to the welfare of your marriage.

Let me be clear: there is no excuse and no reason for a man to use pornography. I don't care if his wife refuses to have sex for six months in a row. I'm not blaming any woman for a man's failure in this regard. Wives shouldn't have sex primarily out of fear that if they don't, their husbands won't be faithful; that's coercion, not intimacy. The goal should always be a *mutually satisfying* sexual relationship. But having said this, it is also true that a wife's seeming indifference to her husband's sexual needs does make a man's struggle more intense and less easy to bear. Where some wives see sexual relations as a burden or a chore, I as a pastor see God's sons wanting to be faithful, trying to be pure, working harder than anyone can imagine to keep lust at bay.

I realize many of you are married to men who prefer porn over reality—this isn't the kind of man I'm talking about here. We'll get into that in the next chapter. I'm talking about men pursuing a real relationship with their wives and wanting to honor God in their choices while also feeling besieged by temptation. These men often don't tell their wives how difficult the sexual struggle can be. It's embarrassing, and when they fall by viewing porn, it feels shameful. Many of them truly hate straying. And if they don't understand grace (and get some help to stop the sin), it can wreak havoc on their relationship with God. Satan will try to use your husband's sexual temptations to drive a wedge between your husband and you *and* between your husband and God. Illicit sexual activity, once chosen, tends to escalate in all the wrong directions. The husband soon finds himself spending far less time thinking about pleasing his wife and far more time trying to figure out how to hide and how to indulge in his fantasy life. Furthermore, a man whose mind brims over with inappropriate sexual fantasies will have a difficult time praying, studying the Bible, and meditating on God's truth. Temptation will bombard him every time he closes his eyes or tries to quiet his mind. Thus his sexual sin will bleed out into other areas of his marriage. When he stops spending intimate time with God, he will probably become, in general, more impatient and more critical, as well as more selfish and a lot angrier.

And it will devastate your marriage. One of the many reasons porn is so destructive to a marriage is that it makes a husband resent his wife's proximity, because when she's around, he can't indulge. Instead of desiring you, he'll resent your presence that keeps him from his desire. This is nuclear-warfare-like in terms of marital harmony and peace.

I know you don't want that for your husband! God doesn't want it either. He broods over your husband's welfare with a passionate concern. He has called your husband to a holy lifestyle, and he zealously desires the growth of your husband's integrity. That's why he has anticipated your husband's sexual drive. He created marriage, after all, and while marriage is about much more than a holy sexual outlet, such an expression is part of it—and even provides one reason for considering marriage, as the apostle Paul observes: "But if they cannot control themselves, they should marry, for it is better to marry than to burn with passion" (1 Corinthians 7:9).

God knows exactly what it's like for your husband, because every day he sees every thought, every temptation. In the midst of your many responsibilities, you can easily forget about your husband's struggles. But God sees every one.

Knowing what it's like for a man, God created marriage as a holy and healthy outlet for a man's sexual desires. In the ideal world, a man would marry a woman who understands her husband's situation, who cares about his spiritual integrity, and who lavishes her affection on him (while the husband remains thoughtful, unselfish, caring, and romantically inclined). She realizes that her husband will, at times, feel in desperate straits spiritually as he tries to remain faithful to his God, his family, his marriage, and his own integrity. She also will realize that she, by God's design, is the only appropriate outlet for her husband's desires. Anything she denies her husband becomes, by definition, an *absolute* denial, because he has no other place to which he can go to find satisfaction in a healthy or holy manner.

This believing woman may, at times, resent the fact that God gave her husband such frequent desire. At various stages in her life, she may even resent the fact that only she can meet that desire. At times, she may even contemplate the benefits of the Old Testament concept of a concubine! But if she's a mature Christian, she'll understand that God called her into marriage to help her husband—and in this area, he may need special help. She might wish this weren't so, but she reminds herself that God's design, God's will, and God's explicit instructions from the Bible are foundational here.

Lest I lose you here, let me state that I know some of you may have an entirely opposite situation. Maybe you've made yourself more than available, even regularly initiating sexual relations, but your husband's lack of awareness of and sensitivity to your needs keeps your sex life from becoming even remotely close to satisfying.

The situation in your marriage may not be a wife's lack of interest but a husband's laziness or selfishness regarding how to please a woman. Some women have made themselves more than available to their husband sexually, only to have their hearts broken when they discover his lack of interest for them hasn't dampened his interest in pornography. In many cases, this abuse of pornography is a lifelong habit, indulged in long before the man even met his wife. Any man who tries to blame his wife for his sin is in serious denial.

Regardless of the situation in your marriage—whether it means there's a need for you to become more generous with your affection or to woo your disinterested husband into more significant intimacy—let me stress the spiritual health benefits of your working to maintain this threshold to marital intimacy, as well as the gift you present to your husband when you work with him to see this area of the marriage excel.

May I ask you to consider a bold question? *How well does God think you're helping his son walk in sexual holiness?* The sexual life you foster, create, and maintain in your marriage isn't merely about you and your husband; it's about your husband's relationship with God, as well as about his ability to provide a godly example for your children.

More important than how your husband feels about your sexual relationship and about how you feel about your sexual relationship is how God feels about you and your husband's sexual relationship.

If you'll persistently pursue this side of your marriage, you'll reap tangible, practical, and long-lasting rewards. Your husband will feel emotionally closer to you than at any other time, while finding spiritual reinforcement to go out into a world of constant sexual temptation and be an overcomer.

THE LIMITS OF DESIRE

Sheila Wray Gregoire believes one of the main challenges women encounter in embracing an active sex life is that the media today tells us that women's sex drives work a certain way—and they don't. "Whether you're watching a TV show or a movie," says Gregoire, "the plot when it comes to sex always goes something like this: the couple's together, and they start to pant. Then they kiss. Then the clothes come off, and they end up in bed.

"They pant, they kiss, they take off their clothes, and they end up in bed.

"Pant. Kiss. Clothes. Bed.

"That's what we're taught desire looks like. Many of us women, then, are at home with our husbands, *waiting to pant*. And when we don't, we figure we're just not in the mood. But what if the media is wrong? What if women's sex drives work very differently? God created us, in general, so that women don't feel aroused until we start making love. While men tend to be aroused before sex, women need to start touching and kissing first. But it's even more complicated than that. We need to *decide* to be aroused. For women especially, our sex drives are primarily in our heads. If our heads aren't engaged, our bodies won't follow.

"That can be ever so frustrating when husbands seem to want sex all the time, and women don't always feel the same physical need for it. But God made us so that in order to truly enjoy sex, we women had to decide we were going to. We don't only physically 'let him in'; we have to mentally and emotionally decide to as well. Sex isn't supposed to be only physical; it's also emotionally and spiritually intimate, and women's libidos actually promote the other aspects of intimacy too. The good news is that when our brains are engaged, sex can be amazing. And if God made sex to be that great for women too, then why would we want to miss out on it?"

There's plenty more of this kind of great teaching in Sheila's fine book, *The Good Girl's Guide to Great Sex*.[10]

Clearly, desire matters, but from Sheila's perspective, desire has to be desired! It doesn't just happen. When you understand that sex can also be a *ministry* that feeds the marriage, with the added benefit of providing stability for your children and pleasure for you, hopefully you'll realize that desiring desire is something to be desired!

Let me end this chapter with one more plea on your husband's (and your) behalf: If God came to me with a proposition—"Gary, I have a chore for you that will take just two hours a week. It'll secure your wife's affections, thereby providing great security for your children. It will make your wife feel loved and will be a crucial part of building a stable home"—I can't imagine turning him down. I really wouldn't care *what* the chore was; if it meant shoveling manure, I'd say, "Where's the shovel?" I'd do it gladly, knowing that my wife, children, and I would receive tremendous benefits.

Women who ignore this aspect of marriage because they're too busy with their children have it backward. They risk exposing their children to the devastating wound of divorce, a spiritually sick father, or a spiritually compromised father by not tending to the stability of their marriage. A wise woman understands her husband's desires and uses them to strengthen the relationship. She anticipates his needs and gives him something to look forward to when he comes home, reinforcing his need for her, his desire for her, and his focus on her.

Sexual desire can knit a man to a woman, or Satan can use it to build an ever-growing reliance on things outside the home. Satan has one goal in sexual temptation: to take that man's heart away from his wife and his family and to get him to desire something, or someone, else. The Devil doesn't care what or who it is, as long as this desire weakens the Christian family's foundation.

God calls you to entice your husband and make his desires, thoughts, and fantasies center on you. Then his physical longings will build up the family (and your children's well-being) rather than putting it at risk.

Yet some wives read something like this and say, "You know, he's right. I need to do better." And for a couple weeks, they'll try. But then they'll forget or get frustrated with their husband's lackluster response, and things will return to the subpar level at which they used to be.

As a husband, if I knew that a vicious enemy lurked outside the door, waiting until I fell asleep to strike his blow against my family, I'd stay awake all night. I'd do everything I could to keep that threat away—particularly if I knew this enemy had one aim, namely, to tear my family apart. I'd keep focused. I'd build up the defenses. I'd keep watch.

Wives, such an enemy really *does* lie in wait at your family's door. It's called "sexual temptation."

The Proverbs 31 woman "watches over the affairs of her household" (31:27). She is diligent and alert. You may grow weary of meeting your husband's needs, but know this: neither natural temptation nor the spiritual tempter of our souls ever sleeps. In fact, the apostle Peter describes Satan as a "roaring lion looking for someone to devour" (1 Peter 5:8). Today, Satan even has the internet on his side. And the challenge of pornography has never been greater. It's time to give this topic a chapter of its own.

QUESTIONS FOR DISCUSSION AND REFLECTION

1. Do you believe that husbands experience sex more personally than do wives? How might this affect the relational dynamics in the bedroom?

2. Does Michael Gurian's assertion that a man's "self-worth is linked, to a great extent, to how often and how well he engages in the sex act" surprise you? How does it affect the way you might look at your husband's advances in the future?

3. Gary suggests that a husband "is far more likely to be more heavily invested in the home if his wife pursues him sexually,"

and that by making an effort at physical intimacy, wives "open the door to the emotional intimacy you rightly desire." Do you think this is a manipulative use of sex, or a God-ordained function of sex?

4. Discuss how sexual promiscuity is affecting the spiritual integrity of men. Then suggest ways that wives can help their husbands avoid this trap.

5. Were you surprised by Gary's suggestion that many wives simply don't understand how much effort it takes for some men to remain sexually faithful to one wife? Do you think this is true of *your* husband? Have you ever thought about how you can make it easier for him? Or thanked him for remaining faithful?

6. How can wives say no to improper sexual demands while still being generous with regard to pure expressions of physical intimacy?

CHAPTER 12

THE PROBLEM OF PORN

Helping Your Husband Overcome
a Most Destructive Habit

Pornography has crept into many homes, crippling countless marriages. Here's why you should care: high-speed-internet pornography can literally rewire a man's brain, making it difficult, if not impossible, for him to be completely sexually satisfied (or sometimes even aroused) by his wife. Pornography works on the neurological trigger of offering something different, something new. If a man sees a familiar video or picture, he'll usually click right over it. It's "used up." It's the "something new" that titillates him.

You can quickly see how this is the antithesis of marriage, where a person finds full satisfaction in their spouse over the course of a lifetime. The same God-ordained sexual desire that can knit a man's soul to his wife can get diverted to create a lust for women in general rather than for his wife in particular.

A man who is sexually faithful to his wife is training his mind, whenever they are sexually intimate, to find his wife more attractive than all other women. We cultivate sexual appetite every bit as much as we cultivate a taste for certain foods.

In this chapter, we'll look at how several couples confronted the increasingly common problem of porn and also consult a few experts to provide wives the best advice for what to do if it has entered your marriage.

Let's be clear at the outset: *your husband's porn addiction is not about you*, though it may feel that way. It was never about you. Most men who struggle with porn become users long before they meet their wives. Your husband's continued use of porn after marriage is not your fault. It is not a reflection on your beauty or body. It is not about whether you have gained weight or about how well you perform in the bedroom. It is not about your desirability. It is, first and foremost, about your husband's addiction or bad habits. You cannot and should not own this, and it is not on you to deliver your husband from it.

In fact, if your husband is not motivated by God and self, there is nothing you can do to deliver him. I'll offer plenty of advice for wives married to men who are motivated to change, but if your husband is not motivated to change, you may need to respond as if he is having an affair, not just an addiction. When porn use replaces sexual intimacy with a wife, it *is* an affair.

SANDY'S STORY

Robert started looking at porn when as a young teen he discovered magazines at his uncle's house. That led to high-speed-internet porn and a lifelong struggle.

When Sandy found out her husband had gone back to porn, she was firm and told him, "It's me or the porn. You can't have both."

Sandy may not have realized it at the time, but she initiated a textbook-perfect conversation with her husband.

Sandy had made it clear to Robert before they got married that porn use wouldn't be tolerated. Robert said he wanted to give it up, but after the wedding, Sandy had her suspicions. When Robert left his computer signed on to his Amazon account, she checked his past history and saw the videos.

"I told you I wouldn't tolerate this," she said, "and I'm not going to."

After dealing with the relational issue, Sandy stressed the spiritual angle. This wasn't just about their marriage; it was about Robert's relationship with God. She showed empathy and understanding about his past and the unfortunate way he was introduced to porn, but she made it clear again, in case there was any doubt, "You will lose me if you continue doing this."

My good friend Dr. Steve Wilke (this book is dedicated to Steve and his wife, Rebekah) told me that one of the most important things a wife can do in situations like Sandy's is to be strong and ensure "healthy boundaries following clinical recommendations while being open and accountable for qualified counsel."

Steve says, "She needs to be like Deborah, Rahab, or Ruth—the kind of woman who will look at her man and say, 'No mas!' Too often, spouses don't appreciate the severity of the situation they find themselves in, and they end up perpetuating the problem instead of resolving it." He adds, "These circumstances are serious and should be treated as you would any serious illness, with the same time and energy put into finding the best clinical care possible. If you want your marriage to survive, you have to commit to actively engaging in a treatment plan."

Steve's son, Dr. Ryan Wilke, a physician certified by the American Board of Psychiatry and Neurology, explains the current understanding of the biological and psychological components of addiction, including pornography. "Addiction is more than just bad behavior and poor judgment. The brain registers all pleasurable experiences in the same way—whether it's from enjoyable music, a walk with your spouse, or behavior necessary for survival, like eating and sexual activity (which can be healthy or pathological), as well as from intoxicating chemicals. The result of repeated exposure to intoxicating substances or behaviors is a conditioned response driven by the memories in your brain from repeated exposure.

Eventually, this newly acquired brain pathway overrides our logical and rational mind. In essence, through habituation, addicts become slaves to a master they themselves created. This is a major reason addicts seemingly can't just stop their behavior."

Both of the Wilkes believe this is best represented in Romans 1. They explain, "When choices are made that are contrary to God's original plan for our lives, as biological science demonstrates, what was a choice is now less so. God is a gentleman, and he allows us free will to make our own choices. But if we persist in making poor ones, eventually he steps back and makes way for the consequences of our free will. At that point, we're no longer entirely free; we've become slaves."

The reality of ignoring God's consistent warnings is that our rebellious choices eventually shape our minds into rebellious brains. This is why a wife can't afford to be weak or passive in the face of such a challenge. Dr. Steve Wilke explains, "She's going to have to balance her fear of what has taken place in her life with her need to be strong in her marriage and for her children."

The reason you want to get control of this addiction as soon as possible is that the longer it goes on, the more it will change your husband's brain. The good news is that following abstinence, the brain appears to begin to heal—but neuroscientists don't yet know how much it heals. It may never go back to the pre-addiction phase. But it certainly can get better.

Recovery specialists are fond of saying that "recovery involves relapse." Dr. Steve Wilke agrees but adds, "Guys with stronger wives tend to have more positive outcomes." In other words, if a man thinks you'll go easy on him, he may try to find out how much you're willing to tolerate to manipulate you. Dr. Wilke says, "When a wife says to her husband, 'If you touch anybody or look at that stuff again, then I'm gone—and I'm going to tell everybody who asks me exactly why I left you,' well, guys who get that speech have a better chance at a positive outcome."

It's important to distinguish between urges, habits, and addictions. These are three different things. When the word *addiction* is used too loosely, it can make men feel they have a pass, as if they are not able to control themselves. They may have strong urges or a bad habit, but you can learn to fight both of those. When we slip into the addiction language as if the man has no power over his behavior, he may be more likely to just accept it.

This requires professional care and diagnosis. Since porn often starts in pre- or early adolescence, it's likely your husband will need to seek professional, board-certified help at the highest level. You don't have time to give amateurs a try. Our church has a board-certified counselor I refer guys to who suffer from a long-standing addiction. Most of us pastors aren't trained to understand the brain science behind breaking what has become a physiological addiction.

In Sandy's case, Robert knew he would lose her and also knew she was watching. For instance, Sandy knows how she can use Google to look at where anyone in her family goes on the internet. So when Robert clicked on a picture of a swimsuit model, Sandy knew it— and she immediately asked Robert about it. She says, "He realized I can see everything he's doing, and that has certainly helped."

Here are some things that have helped Sandy and Robert:

- They won't watch movies or television shows containing nudity, and whatever they watch, they watch together. Sandy realizes her husband's brain needs to heal. It's not about legalism; it's about wisdom.
- Robert has focused on growing in God. Porn addiction is a spiritual issue as much as it is a neurological issue. The best defense is a good offense. They suggest getting into a good church, joining a solid Bible study, reading solid Christian books. "Make your spiritual intimacy soar," they say.
- Sandy offered a clear ultimatum: "You can't have me and porn." She took the choice away from Robert. "If you want me, you can't do that," she said.

- Sandy uses Google to keep Robert accountable. It puts her mind at ease, and it helps reinforce Robert's conviction.
- Sandy made it clear to Robert that if he was willing to do the work, she was willing to walk through this with him. She'd give up watching the movies she didn't want him to watch. She'd give up playing the risqué video games she likes. She would choose not to shame him. In essence, she fought the addiction with increased marital intimacy, telling him, "I'm on your side. I'm with you, and we'll do this together." That attitude means so much to a man.
- Sandy and Robert also worked their way through a video series that teaches about building sexual purity.*

AN ANCIENT BATTLE

Dr. Wyatt Fisher is a Christian psychologist who has worked with many couples struggling with the husband's use of porn. Dr. Fisher points out that while lust is an ancient problem and is nothing new, "easy access to sexually explicit content through the internet *is* new," and "the combination of a lustful heart plus easy access has created an explosion of pornography addiction over the past few years that's destroyed marriages, devastated families, wrecked employment, and in some cases even caused imprisonment. As most addiction specialists know, the three A's to addiction are accessibility, affordability, and anonymity and porn provides all three. It's accessible because it's everywhere on the internet; it's affordable because the majority of it is free; and it's anonymous because you can view it without no one ever knowing."[1]

Because men can be exposed to this threat as boys, they may not have realized how devastating it can be to their sexual health before

---

* One such program that helps couples understand what is at stake was created by Dr. Wyatt Fisher and is available at www.christiancrush.com/p/pornography-addiction-help.html (accessed May 30, 2017).

they become addicted. According to Dr. Fisher, "Porn has been shown to be as addictive as heroin or crack cocaine because it lights up the same reward center in the brain. Combating porn is not as simple as just deciding to stop. It's a neurological addiction akin to alcohol or drug addiction, making it very complicated."

Dr. Fisher urges wives to balance their reaction when they find out their husband has been looking at porn. "Wives need to try to balance their reaction by not overreacting but also not underreacting. A wife who overreacts threatens divorce and has no empathy for her husband's porn addiction. This type of reaction often encourages the husband to dive deeper into secrecy to ensure his wife never finds out again. At the same time, a wife who underreacts is also detrimental. She responds by being a bit disappointed but knows it's a 'guy thing' and not that big a deal. This type of reaction often doesn't create enough motivation for the man to stop looking at porn because it doesn't seem to really bother his wife."

He also urges couples to adopt a unified front on battling porn. "Similar to discovering that your husband is an alcoholic," Fisher says, "wives must spend time understanding why pornography as a neurological addiction is so powerful for their husbands, what the triggers are, and what there is about their marriage that may influence it. For example, husbands who feel sexually satisfied in their marriage often have a decreased risk of pornography. However, it's never the wife's fault that her husband looks at porn because it's ultimately his choice to cross the line. But, chronic sexual dissatisfaction within marriage can certainly increase a man's temptation to turn to porn for fulfillment."

Dr. Fisher is a strong proponent of internet filters, such as Covenant Eyes, on all devices. "For men who struggle with porn, if they have access to it somewhere, it's usually just a matter of time before they view it. Similarly, an alcoholic trying to recover would never leave a bottle of Jack Daniels in the closet. In addition, it's important to have the man's wife set up the password for their account so they're never tempted to login and disable the filter. Also, it's ideal to set up their wives as accountability partners who will receive a weekly report with all of their online activity. Knowing that their buddies who also struggle with porn will receive their accountability report may increase motivation somewhat, but knowing that their wives will receive a report of all their online activity will send their motivation through the roof."

Bear in mind, though, that not every wife can handle this information. If you prefer not to know what your husband has looked at, you shouldn't feel guilty. Dr. Melody Rhode has a different perspective than Dr. Fisher's. She thinks most wives should just step away from their husband's addiction and let him fight it on his own rather than try to be his mother. Experts can and do disagree on this issue. Certainly, if the thought of being your husband's accountability partner is ruining your mental health, you shouldn't feel obligated to sacrifice yourself. There are other ways for your husband to hold himself accountable.

Another approach Dr. Fisher takes—one I particularly support—is urging men to prioritize time with God daily. The best defense is a good offense. Wives, whatever you can do to help your husband reconnect with God, study God's Word, engage in worship, and spend time with other believers is a huge part of recovery. And I believe it's entirely legitimate for a wife to require that her husband pursue such activities as part of the agreed-on recovery plan.

Dr. Fisher is a firm believer in couples having "a sex fast with no masturbation each time he falls into pornography for a period of time. Doing so can serve as a natural consequence and provide an opportunity to regain mastery over his sexual behavior because it has just mastered him. It also can provide time for his wife to heal from the breach of trust. In addition, men must learn how to have intimacy-oriented sex rather than body-oriented sex. Porn viewing makes men overly focused on body parts, and sexual encounters become more about them getting their high than becoming one with their wives. Instead, men need to learn how to connect with their wives emotionally through sex. One excellent way to facilitate this is for men to share some of their loving feelings toward their wives before sex, focus on their pleasure during sex, and look into their eyes occasionally during the encounter and especially during orgasm. Eye contact will help men connect to their wives' souls rather than just to their bodies."

Dr. Fisher cautions wives, "Remember, overcoming porn addiction is often a journey and not a destination. There are going to be setbacks, so expect them."

Dr. Fisher speaks not only as a psychologist who helps men overcome pornography addiction, but also as a someone who once fell into this sin himself. His wife, Alia, shares a bit about how they overcame it as a couple. Be prepared! Alia warns that the majority of wives who have stumbled onto their husband's porn addiction met the criteria for posttraumatic stress disorder.

"The way you respond to your husband when he tells you about this or when you find out is really, really important," says Alia. "I don't want you to misunderstand what I am saying at all, so please try to hear me out. All your feelings—the hurt and the devastation—are valid. We want our husbands to understand how much this really hurts us. We don't want them to breeze over it and not get it. But the way you respond when he tells you is key to him moving forward with this. He wants to feel safe with you knowing. He needs to be able to know that he can come to you, so if you respond overly strong and in a way that will make him fearful of telling you again, he's probably going to want to go back to secrecy. So it's this very fine line that you have to walk in the middle of the hurt and in the middle of wanting to be a team with him."

Alia points to a team approach, but let me stress that these strategies assume the husband is *repentant and willing to change*. You can't be soft with a husband who thinks it's no big deal and who wants you to just accept his addiction. Alia's words are for those wives married to men who genuinely want to change.

"Remember that we live in a sex-saturated culture," Alia says. Everywhere your husband goes, these images come up—whether in a grocery store line, at a magazine stand, or on the internet browser on his phone. So he can't fully escape all the sexual stimulation coming at him. This problem is a bit harder to break than, say, alcohol addiction, where you would keep all the alcohol bottles out of the house. This one seeps in by means of many more places. The problem with the internet is that he can get the same high as heroin with just one little click of the mouse. So it's easier to access than a drug fix, and that makes the battle much harder.

"Women's bodies are man's greatest desire. Men look at a woman and are turned on within ten seconds. It just takes a little bit of stimuli to get a man ready to go. And God made men to have this visual orientation, which women don't typically have. It's not necessarily a bad thing in and of itself, but it goes up against a man's nature—and so the struggle is partially biological. We wives have to remember that visualization of women's bodies isn't the problem or a sin per se; we just want it to be directed at us, not outward at other women. But it's okay that he has that bent.

"You have to strive together toward a daily check-in on this battle with him. Check in with him every day. I guarantee you it's on his mind, so you need to ask him, 'Are you struggling today? Is there anything going on with you today that's going to make you susceptible to wanting to look?' [Let me add here that I'm not sure I would recommend this if your husband hasn't already fallen or if this isn't a daily battle for him. If it isn't a constant struggle for your husband, discussing it on a daily basis, as opposed to every couple weeks or so, may not be a wise thing to do, as it will only bring it to the forefront of his mind.]

"Receive a weekly accountability report. If you're going to battle this, you need to get a filter put on every single device your husband has access to—whether it's at home, his phone, or your phone. This will help you build trust so that you can see that your husband is being clean while he is at work and being clean when this trust issue right now is between you and him.

"Recovery is a journey. It is not exactly a straight-shot destination at this point. There are all kinds of tendrils that we've talked about. You've got to give him some ability to have some setbacks, but you're going to keep on moving forward together as a team."

Let me jump back in here with a comment that Alia's husband desired to change and was willing to change. Some of you may be married to husbands who are more frustrated with your frustration than they desire to change. Of such husbands, Leslie Vernick counsels, "You can't build trust with someone who you have to put a control on their device. The husband is not a child. He is an adult, and unless *he* decides to put a filter on his device, he will get around any device a wife puts on home devices. An addict has to take responsibility for his treatment—including implementing important accountability measures to make it less likely that he will fall. If a wife feels like it's her responsibility, it will be an unrealistic call or burden to put on her. She can take responsibility to help him, but not to monitor or control him."

As with all marital advice, the challenge is to discern your husband's heart and proceed accordingly.

In her seminar, Alia seeks to help wives build compassion for truly struggling husbands. "There is no justifying his behavior," she says. "However, you have to understand the roots of the problem to be able to heal and to become a team."

Here's what Alia suggests you do to build greater understanding (note that these are Alia's words that she has graciously allowed me to quote verbatim):

- Think of all the things in his background that predisposed him to porn. For instance, did he have exposure to explicit sexual content as a child? Did his parents have porn in the house? Did he see it modeled by his father? Any type of exposure like that can make it a lot harder for him in this battle. This is partially why he may be in the battle. Is there any sexual abuse in his background? Sexual abuse can sometimes lead men into sexually deviant interests and behaviors. Does he have a promiscuous background? Did he have a lot of experiences with women before you got married? Did he lack nurture from his mother? Is he seeking to satisfy some hole in his heart through viewing porn?

- Think of things in his life right now that may be encouraging him to use porn. Is he alone a lot? Is he in his basement or in a hotel room with nobody to hold him accountable for what he is doing? This is why the filter is so important, because it lets him know he is accountable, even when he is alone. Has he been under increased stress or pressure? A lot of times we want a release—some sort of relief from all this pressure—and so those can be things that contribute to his use of porn right now.

- Think of anything you may have done to contribute to his temptation with porn. There is no justifying his behavior; however, we do have to look at all components, and I have to ask how thriving your sex life with your husband is. Husbands value a high-thriving sex life, and if they're not feeling like they're getting it at home, they are much more susceptible to going elsewhere to find it. I [Alia] know firsthand because when we got married, I had a lot of negative sexual baggage from my past. I believed that sex was dirty. *Men are pigs. Sex is shameful. There is no love in sex.* If you have any of those thoughts and don't like sex or don't want to have sex or don't have much sex with your husband, I encourage you to get healing for it. It's very important because we have to work with our husbands—not just let him do his thing, but taking ownership of the parts where we are broken or where we cannot do what we know our husband needs. So please try to get help from a counselor and deal with your own wounds from the past.

Healthy couples have sex one to three times a week on average, and of course it will sometimes be less and sometimes more often. But if you are far from that, then it may be a sign that your husband needs you to try to work on this area for him.

- Think of anything in your upbringing that may be influencing your reaction to his porn use. If you've been betrayed or have trust issues because of your experience, it may significantly impact how you're responding. And it may be important to look at those areas, so your husband feels safe coming to you, knowing your reactions won't be as severe and strong. It's really important for you to discern how much of your reaction is about your husband's behavior and how much is from your own wounds from your past. Don't forget your own weaknesses. Romans 3:23 reads, "All have sinned and fall short of the glory of God." You may not struggle with porn as your husband does, but we all have our weaknesses and sin areas. It is important to remember that God views them all the same and that God loves us all the same. We need to remember our own brokenness so we can have empathy for our husband's weakness in the struggle.

Let's look now at how this teaching plays out in the stories of two other couples.*

JODY AND MARK

Mark's involvement with pornography began in his uncle's garage when he was a young boy. When that exposure was followed up by two experiences of sexual abuse, Mark entered, as he puts it, "a healthy marriage with a virgin bride," and he says he "felt completely unworthy." Because of his sordid past, he didn't think he

---

* I realize this is a long chapter, but if your marriage is struggling in this area, you need extra attention. If this isn't an issue in your marriage, feel free to skip to the next chapter.

deserved Jody. That sense of shame only served to fuel his growing addiction. When sexual shame drives a man into the darkness, it leads him to all the wrong places.

Throughout the next decade, Mark struggled with magazines, store-bought adult videos, and movies, but before the advent of the internet, he could contain it to a rare occurrence—like when he was traveling. All that changed with the advent of high-speed internet connections and smartphones. Porn soon became an ever-present battle.

In Mark's case, sadly, it was even worse than porn. After a while, as the consistent compromise with porn slowly eroded his defenses, Mark ended up in a full-blown physical affair. This was all done in the shadows. His wife, Jody, "had a check in my spirit that something wasn't right, but I didn't ever really pursue it." When a doctor checking her out for a different medical issue offhandedly mentioned that she had a sexually transmitted disease, Jody thought he must be joking. She was a virgin on her wedding day, and Mark had told her he was a virgin too. She confronted Mark, who sidestepped the real issue by confessing to a sexual relationship prior to marriage without mentioning the affair during their marriage.

We don't have time or space to get into the life events that led Mark to face up to his addiction and destructive behavior, but it all came out in an intensive, all-day counseling session designed to save imperiled marriages.

When Jody found out about the affair and the use of porn, she insists, "Divorce never crossed my mind." She was, however, hurt and angry that Mark couldn't see what he was doing to her.

Why didn't Jody even consider divorce? "I had seen the repercussions of my mom's divorce, and she had made it clear that divorce is not a good thing," she says. "It's not the easy way out. And frankly, I knew my husband's heart; I had watched him make other mistakes and try to overcome them by beating himself up and by working very hard. I knew that, other than this, he was a good man with a good heart who always tries to look out for other people. When the counselors helped me understand some of his history and vulnerability, I was able to put my anger aside long enough to commit to saving the marriage."

A painful side effect, however, was that Jody found herself feeling extremely inadequate. "When I began thinking about the two women I had never known about—I never thought Mark could compare me to anyone—and then the actresses in the porn movies, I couldn't get away from the fear of how could I ever measure up to that?" Jody admits that this remains a struggle for her on occasion, even today. Sadly, a husband's history with porn doesn't just go away when it's revealed; it's often a burden the wife carries for the rest of her life.

Mark was touched by Jody's grace. "I knew Jody had a biblical reason to divorce me," he says, "but she hung in there. And I will spend the rest of my life trying to earn her trust, including telling her how beautiful she is. She's not always ready to receive it. It's like there's a wound there, and I take it as a challenge that it's a lifetime of earning that trust back."

Jody's grace hasn't come without consequences. There has been increased accountability. Mark uses the app from xxxchurch.com and lists both Jody and his son as accountability partners. He also meets regularly with another man who knows how to ask specific, direct questions that won't allow Mark to be evasive, including asking Mark to hand over his cell phone. "If the browser history has been emptied," says his friend, "it means a guy is trying to cover something up. Don't fall for that. An empty browser is almost always an admission of guilt."

Mark believes the biggest deterrent for continued porn use has been that he now, as he puts it, "lives in the light. Now that I'm caught, that's my biggest help. If I see something, I have to tell Jody." He urges men who struggle in this area, "Make it so you will get asked and get caught, and it'll help keep you from doing it."

As most counselors recommend, Mark and Jody entered a season of sexual abstinence as Mark sought to regain control. This was healing for both Mark and Jody. They both needed a break to set things right and to heal.

Mark credits Jody's turning to God, her commitment to the marriage, and her insistence that "this is going to stop" with helping him stop looking at porn. In the early days, if he relapsed, he immediately went to Jody and told her. It took their marriage a couple steps back, but the relapses became less and less frequent and less and less serious.

In her own healing process, Jody got plenty angry with God. "I was like a child beating on her daddy's chest. I read psalms to him, shaking my finger at him and being mad. I'd say to him, 'I've spent my life loving you, and you allow *this* to happen?'"

This is all to show that the hurt was deep and lasted for a long time, and the effects still bring some pain to Jody's soul even today. But she is glad she pursued reconciliation rather than divorce. And years later, their sexual relationship is actually better than ever.

Jody eventually realized that, early on in their marriage, sex wasn't given the priority it deserved. "My extreme lack of knowledge about sex prior to marriage led to minimal intimacy, which was not fulfilling to Mark. Though this doesn't excuse the choices he made, he had very little help at home to fight it. He was sort of on his own."

Once Mark was in recovery, Jody started asking him, "What would be exciting for you?" She found that Mark revels in the anticipation—that if Jody has given sexual intimacy some prior thought, like choosing to wear a certain kind of underwear, Mark gets lost thinking about his wife, anticipating being with her, and has no room for other fantasies. So now, when Jody leans over at a public place and whispers to Mark, "Think red," he knows *exactly* what it means. Other times, he comes home from work and finds

Jody wearing a robe—with nothing on underneath. The fact that Jody thought of this and initiated it has been very helpful to Mark, leading to a positive and healthy anticipation.

Here's what Jody would tell those women who find out their husbands are viewing porn: "If you really love your man and your God, staying in the marriage can be the right thing to do—and it was so worth it in my case. It was not and will not be easy. There were tears. There were so many emotions involved in the journey but, again, it has been worth it. I am daily amazed at this point at the man of God that Mark has matured into. His guilt and shame over pornography and all the other things used by Satan kept him trapped, but he is no longer trapped. He is free to be who God created him to be. Is he perfect? Of course not—none of us are—but he is very, very good. Even amazing in many ways. We say that we would not want to go through it again, but we would not want to go back to the old us either. So I want to tell you that this is an opportunity to live out the faith you say you have in God. It's a chance to watch God work, but it's also a chance, not just for your husband to work on himself, but for you to work on yourself. I challenged God to show up, and he did. Not as fast, not as neat and clean as I would have liked, but he did show up and did work, heal, and provide for us."

Some of you may not be ready to hear this. Your hurt may run so deep that you don't even want to contemplate a future together. But I include Jody and Mark's story to show how some couples have gotten through this together and have found healing and redemption. Yes, it requires a repentant man. But keep in mind, Mark was purposely evasive early on. Even so, with grace and strength, professional counseling, accountability, a renewed passion for God, and a recommitment to their sexual relationship (after a season of abstinence), Mark and Jody have discovered a better life and a better marriage than they ever had before.

MARCUS AND TARA

Like so many others we've talked about, Marcus's first exposure to pornography came when he was a young boy. Sexually explicit magazines flooded his house, and his dad subscribed to an explicit cable channel.

I hope you can understand, wives, when I say that it's not a fair fight for a young boy to be exposed to pornographic material—though this is never an excuse. Natural curiosity ("What does a naked woman look like?" "How does sex happen?") can lead to a fairly innocent "click," and without the spiritual or intellectual sophistication to fight what happens next, a young boy can be sucked into a world he may never feel fully free of. I grieve for the battles younger men have to fight—especially those who are growing up in the era of high-speed internet.

Marcus and his wife, Tara, had talked about his struggles with porn before they got married, but when high-speed internet and smartphones became standard, temptation increased—and Marcus fell. Tara found out when they started to get an increasing number of unsolicited, sexually explicit emails and pop-up ads—a telltale sign that someone using that computer has been visiting sites with suggestive material.

Marcus's description of how Tara responded was nearly textbook perfect. "Tara has been incredible through it all," he said. "She has been both intolerant and supportive at the same time."

By supportive, Marcus means she has known this was a problem and was willing to listen to what triggers the temptation. At the same time, she's made it clear she will not have it. "She would rather have me come to her when I'm tempted so we can talk about it," Marcus said, "and she's created an environment where it's safe to do that."

Tara has learned about Marcus's triggers. For him, it's stress. The use of porn releases tension—a very common cause and effect of porn use. The last several years have been an uncertain time of employment, so Tara knows Marcus is vulnerable.

I was struck with Tara's commitment, compassion, and grace in the face of a struggle that so many women understandably resent. She says, "My dad had the same magazines and same cable channels in our home, so I grew up knowing about that stuff."

She dealt with her husband's fall as women often do. "I was a little hurt, a little mad," she says. "Having him fall again certainly re-creates that bit of mistrust. And, of course, especially early on, self-esteem issues came into play. *Am I not enough for him? Am I doing something wrong in the bedroom?*"

What helps Tara, in my opinion, is that she understands this is a common temptation, and it's rooted in addiction. Such awareness has given her a little space to not just be firm but also understanding. And it puts her on the lookout. If Marcus suggests they watch an explicit movie, Tara is firm. "I tell him we're not going to open that door; we're not going to invite that temptation into our house." And that's a good reminder to Marcus that, while she is understanding, she isn't going to accept continued, unrepentant involvement in porn.

Tara told me she would counsel other wives whose husbands struggle with this to love him, pray for him, and listen to him. I asked her, "How can you be so gracious? I've seen so many women get angry, and I understand their anger." Tara responded, "Because I love him. Everything in me loves him, ever since we met, so I'll fight for him."

This doesn't mean—please hear this!—that you don't love your husband if you find it difficult to show understanding at the outset. It's your love for your husband that may make you so angry. But Tara allowed her love to overcome all other emotions.

"I try to be firm and forgiving," she says, "and then help him find a healthier way to deal with his stress. He'll play a video game, or our family will go for a walk." Marcus says that just getting outdoors with the family can do wonders to make the temptation go away.

There were times in Marcus's recovery where they needed to take a sex break—but no longer than a month. "We both needed the break to reset expectations," says Tara. "After that break, it becomes a period of rediscovery with each other instead of taking each other for granted."

Tara would never *choose* to have to face this throughout her marriage, but she says that doing so has made them closer and also encouraged her to make their own sexual relationship more of a priority—not just by being available, but also by being creative and initiating.

Marcus would tell other wives that what helped him most was Tara's willingness to have the painful conversation, as well as his confidence that she wouldn't push him away when she found out. Rather, she was on his side and was committed to helping him. Marcus would also urge women to understand what Tara does. "This is a legitimate addiction," Marcus says. "Too many people in the church don't see it that way, but porn use is as controlling as alcohol, drugs, or gambling." He still calls it "a daily fight."

For maintenance, if they happen to be watching a movie where a surprising scene comes on, Tara goes on hyperalert. She says, "I immediately think, *Where will this take him?* and try to get his attention." One of the ways she does that (which Marcus appreciates) is to snuggle up to him and either give him a little kiss or whisper something. It's a touching way of Tara reminding her husband, *I'm here. Focus on me. This—what you and I have—is real. Don't let your thoughts go somewhere else.*

THE WAY FORWARD

I have to be honest. If your husband is dealing with this addiction, the way forward is longer and more painful than most would like to admit. Dr. Patrick Carnes's seminal books on pornography addiction suggest that most recovery programs involve a *five-year* cycle (with the second six months being the most likely time for a relapse).

Some wives expect their husbands to drop a lifelong habit without any relapses, and in most instances, this may well be unrealistic.

There's a major difference, of course, between a repentant, struggling husband and one who is in denial. If your husband refuses to enter an accountability group or to take steps to address his behavior, then I think you have every right to set clear boundaries, including exposure to appropriate professional counselors or clergy and perhaps even separation. It is that serious. If a man has an unrepentant and persistent use of pornography that eclipses sexual intimacy with his wife, that seems to me like the very definition of an affair. You deserve, as a wife, to be adored, cherished, desired, and pleased sexually.

It's not enough for a man to merely avoid sinning against you; a good husband should be focused on *serving* you sexually. You're not selfish for wanting that. It's a clear call for both a wife and a husband, and if the husband's choices make him incapable or unwilling to serve you in this way, he has broken his marriage vows—even if only mentally. There may come a time when you need to say, "Look, for our marriage to continue, this behavior must stop, and that stopping point is *now*. If you refuse to address it, I have no choice but to take it before our church and begin to seek their counsel as to my next step." Ephesians 5:11 tells us, "Have nothing to do with the fruitless deeds of darkness, but rather expose them."

And let me add that "fruitless deeds of darkness" can include sexual activities featured in porn that hold no interest for you. Acts depicted there are never obligations for a wife to agree to. The reality is that if a man wants to be healthy sexually, there will be things he desires that must be denied. Your denial serves him in God's eyes (even if it frustrates him), as it's never appropriate to accommodate sin. Acting on harmful, bent desires usually just increases them or fosters even worse desires.*

---

* Please do not contact me via email to discuss these issues. I am not a trained therapist. Email counseling is as ineffective as it is unwise. Approach someone who can sit down with you face-to-face and spend the necessary time with you—perhaps over the course of several months.

A BLESSING OR A BURDEN

In some ways, sex seems like a very heavy burden. At other times, it may seem like one of the top two or three blessings. And if so, why then does it cause so much hurt, pain, and confusion?

It is not for us to question our Creator's design. If he has called you into marriage, he has called you into regular sexual relations with your husband. Biblical marriage isn't a cafeteria in which we can pick and choose the dishes we enjoy. It's more like a soup—a lot of ingredients mixed together—and we must take the dish as a whole. God's design calls you and your husband to sexual fidelity and loyalty, as well as to sexual generosity and service, regardless of whether either of you feels like it. Anything less betrays marriage as God laid it out for us. To withhold one element of marriage is to rebel against God himself.

Be careful then. Your first argument may be not with your husband but with the God who created marriage! He knew, going in, that men and women are built differently. He knew, going in, that our levels of desire will often conflict. Yet he still created marriage. He designed the sexual relationship. He created you, and he created your spouse. And he blessed your union.

A mutually satisfying sex life does wonderful things for a marriage. It knits a man's heart to his wife. It helps protect his sexual integrity and keeps him from sinning against his God. It motivates him to please his wife, and it cements his loyalty to his home. And as an added benefit, it helps a wife learn how to love in a godly and selfless way.

QUESTIONS FOR DISCUSSION AND REFLECTION

1. Gary describes what porn does to a man's brain. Were you aware of porn's harmful effects? How will this information motivate you to be more vigilant in your own marriage?

2. Discuss how wives can walk the middle line that counselors talk about—being firm about seeing porn addiction overcome while still demonstrating commitment to the relationship and encouraging their husbands to keep talking with them—understanding through it all that this addiction can and often does involve occasional relapses. In other words, how can you avoid being either too soft or too firm?

3. Talk about the best way a wife can go about raising the issue of accountability software for her husband. What are potential pushbacks from husbands, and how can they be countered?

4. How can understanding porn as an addiction affect the way a wife addresses this temptation/failing with her husband?

5. Alia Fisher talks about the importance of maintaining a flourishing sexual intimacy within marriage, suggesting that most healthy couples experience sex one to three times a week. What can a wife do if she realizes this is a weakness in her marriage?

6. Discuss warning signs that a husband may be using porn, and how to best respond.

7. What should a wife do when her husband is asking her to try sexual acts that feel distasteful or demeaning? Where is the line to be found between joyful exploration and seeing to it that "the marriage bed [is] kept pure" (Hebrews 13:4)?

8. Gary ends this chapter by saying that a mutually satisfying sex life knits a man's heart to his wife, helps protect his spiritual integrity, and helps a wife learn how to live in a godly and selfless way. How has God used the sexual relationship in your marriage to teach you how to love?

CHAPTER 13

KEN AND DIANA: AFFAIR ON THE INTERNET

Winning Back the Husband Who Strays

The crisis in Diana's house finally erupted when Ken told Diana that he cared about her but didn't love her.

Three months earlier, Ken and Diana had discovered that their daughter, Hillary, was cutting herself. Doctors later diagnosed her as clinically depressed. In the wake of Ken's shocking declaration, Diana decided to keep first things first. "It doesn't matter what you feel about me," she told Ken. "If you leave now, Hillary might not make it. *You will not leave this house*, for Hillary's sake, if nothing else."

Ken agreed, but the couple's long ordeal had just begun. They shared the same house and even the same bed, but emotionally, they lived miles apart.

Early on, Diana sought solace in her faith. She read Psalm 55, about how a companion, a close friend "with whom I once enjoyed sweet fellowship" (verse 14), betrayed the writer, and her copious tears permanently stained her Bible. "The next seventeen days were horrible," Diana admits, "but God was so faithful."

As Diana looks back, she can predict the drift, including the part she played in Ken's dwindling affections. Earlier in the year, Diana's company suffered a major computer meltdown. It took a full month for Diana to get things back up and running. She regularly stayed late at the office and brought work home.

The first night after Diana finally solved the work crisis, Hillary overdosed on prescription drugs. A boy Hillary really liked had said some cruel things to her. Heartbroken, Hillary turned to drugs to tune out the pain. To make matters worse, shortly after the overdose, another young man eagerly pursued Hillary, and in the wake of her hurt and recent abandonment, Hillary started sleeping with him.

Diana was devastated when she discovered all that had happened. Every maternal nerve fired Diana's indignation, and she all but swore off sex in her marriage. Every time Ken proposed physical intimacy, Diana thought about Hillary losing her virginity, and she just couldn't respond.

It doesn't take a PhD to predict this one—overwork, serious problems with a child, no sex at home, and little communication. *Of course* one partner began to feel he was no longer in love. "If you don't water your plants," Diana admits, "eventually they're going to die. You *have* to nourish your relationship."

"DO YOU REALIZE WHAT YOUR HUSBAND IS DOING WITH MY DAUGHTER?"

For years, Diana and Ken had separate interests they rarely shared. Diana loves going to the movies; Ken tolerates them. Ken enthusiastically follows NASCAR; Diana has never quite understood the fascination of watching cars drive in circles for hours on end.

Diana sensed that Ken was pulling away, but a friend assured her that it was probably just pressure at work and that she shouldn't get paranoid.

But Diana *knew* something was wrong. When she pressed Ken for details, he finally came clean and told her he cared about her but didn't love her.

"Is there anyone else?" Diana asked.

"No," Ken said, much to Diana's relief.

Unfortunately, Ken was lying.

On June 11, just a few weeks after Ken had declared his lack of feelings, Diana found herself praying that God would use whomever and whatever to save her marriage. She never expected it to come from "the other woman's" mother.

That very day, a woman phoned Diana and asked her, "Is your husband Ken Franklin, who works at Grizzly Industries?"

"Yes."

"Do you realize what your husband is doing with my daughter?"

Diana felt her heart beat its way out of her chest. "What are you talking about?"

"Your husband and my daughter met in a NASCAR chat room. They started out sending emails to each other, and now they've exchanged pictures. They're even planning to meet on the Fourth of July weekend."

Diana couldn't believe what she heard, but sadly, it all added up. Ken had already arranged for Diana to spend time at her parents' house while he went on a "business trip" over the holiday.

And then came the kicker: "And my daughter is married and has two kids!"

Diana could hardly believe that her husband had planned an affair with a married woman. Would Ken really rip apart two families, just when Hillary needed him the most?

That's when Diana took the action that both she and Ken believe saved their marriage.

A FRIEND IN NEED

As Diana drove to a friend's house, her mind was racing with questions and prayers about the future. "What will happen to me?"

"Oh God, what will happen to Hillary? Will she make it all right?"

"Okay, God, technically this is adultery. I can leave this marriage, right?"

And yet Diana had a strong sense that divorce played no part in God's plans.

Diana's mind launched into such a whirlwind of speculation that when she got to her friend's house, she blurted out the entire story on the front porch, venting her rage, yelling at Ken, asking how much more she was supposed to take, and calling Ken some nasty names she hopes he never hears about.

Diana's friend had survived a similar situation. Her husband had an emotional affair several years before, so she could understand Diana's feelings of betrayal.

Today, Diana believes that "venting my anger, disgust, and disappointment on Darla instead of on Ken saved my marriage." Darla patiently listened as Diana worked through her emotions. Once Diana gained control of herself, she risked returning home to her husband.

She arrived at about ten o'clock. Ken's car was in the driveway. Diana immediately went up to him and said, "We need to talk."

"Why?"

"Cheryl's mother called."

Ken's face went white.

Diana and Ken went out onto the porch—and here the story becomes remarkable. With incredible detachment, devoid of accusation and fiery emotions, Diana talked through everything with Ken. Because she already had vented her emotions with Darla, she could be objective and dispassionate in this conversation that possessed the potential to either save or wreck her marriage.

"Okay, tell me about Cheryl," she began.

Ken slowly described how he had met Cheryl on the internet. The two shared a love of NASCAR. They had never met, but Ken admitted they planned to do so. They had even talked about a possible future together.

"You mean to tell me you've actually contemplated a life with this woman?" Diana asked.

"Haven't you ever wondered what it would be like to be with someone else?" Ken said.

"Let me get this straight. You're prepared to tell Hillary you won't be her daddy every day, but you'll be Daddy to these two other kids whom you've never met?"

Finally, Ken began to see how ridiculous and foolish he sounded. Diana's eyebrows lifted, almost comically. "You can't be serious about ending nineteen years of marriage for someone you met on the *internet*," she said with a laugh, and Ken laughed with her. The entire evening went like that. Diana spoke forcefully but maintained a light enough air to raise her eyebrows and elicit some comic relief at just the right moments.

Not once did Diana swear or call Ken any of the names she had uttered on Darla's porch—even though Ken expected exactly that. Later, Ken told Diana that if she *had* reacted to him in the way she had talked to Darla, he would have bolted. Instead, he saw a picture of God's grace and mercy through Diana—and it made all the difference.

Diana recalls, "When I first walked out onto the porch with Ken, the disappointment and sadness were still there, but the anger was gone, replaced by God's peace and the confidence that if Ken chose to stay in our marriage, it would eventually be better than it was before. It was so totally God, because I did not expect to act that way. I was very hurt and disillusioned."

The evening concluded with Diana saying to Ken, "My challenge to you is to be obedient to God's Word and contact Cheryl and say it's over—and then go to work on our marriage. If you do that, I believe God can give you astounding feelings for me again."

The next day, Ken told Diana he was through with Cheryl. He closed the email account he had used with Cheryl and gave Diana the password to the new account so she could keep tabs on what happened from then on.

Despite Ken's attempt to put the situation behind him, Cheryl continued to pursue him. Diana even received a couple of calls from Cheryl. But in the end, Ken ended the relationship, and Diana's words proved true. Ken's feelings for her came back.

WHAT WENT WRONG?

In the aftermath, Diana spent a good bit of time trying to dissect what had gone wrong. She asked Ken, "When things got tense, why weren't you talking to *me* instead of to a stranger on the internet?"

Ken doesn't have an answer, but Diana does. She believes Satan saw a foothold and used it. Because of Diana's work schedule and their problems with Hillary, Satan took advantage of these challenges in their relationship and tried to force a permanent break.

Diana wisely understood that Ken's breakup with Cheryl was just the first step. She needed to follow through and do her part to patch up an obviously shaky relationship. I asked her how she would counsel wives in similar situations. When you sense that your marriage is drifting apart because of events you can't control (a work crisis, a child-rearing crisis, or both), how can you keep the intimacy going?

"First," said Diana, "you have to keep working on your marriage, because ultimately everything else is going to be irrelevant if your marriage falls apart. I don't mean to diminish the importance of child-rearing, but if you put the children first to the neglect of your marriage, what will happen to them if the marriage falls apart? It was for Hillary's sake that I realized I needed to take better care of my marriage. An intact marriage provides better support and resources with which to face everything else.

"Second, I'd say don't forget the small things that keep a

relationship going. Keep your finger on the pulse of your marriage. If you haven't gone for a walk in a couple of days, do it! Just be up-front about it and say, 'Honey, we need to get connected again. Let's go have a cup of coffee.' Make sure you really are communicating. It sounds like such a cliché to say that communication is important, but it is! Regularly ask each other, 'Are we okay?' Do a periodic checkpoint. Use a scale of 1 to 10, or empty to full—whatever works. But don't forget to watch out for relational drift."

While Diana admits she really couldn't have put her job crisis on the shelf, in hindsight she does believe that she probably didn't need to bring home as much work as she did. "I thought I was the only person who could fix what needed fixing. It was egocentric, and it almost cost me my marriage."

Hillary presented a tougher challenge. With a child's life in peril, it's hard to keep tabs on the pulse on your marriage. "I just wasn't asking how Ken was because I was singularly focused on how Hillary was," Diana admits. It had been almost a year since the two of them had gotten away. Then add to that Diana's and Ken's wildly different reactions to Hillary's problems, which only seemed to push them further apart. Ken simply couldn't understand the emotion that would lead Hillary to hurt herself "over a boy."

Even so, Diana stresses that you cannot let your children's main base of support—their parents' marriage—crumble just when they need it most. It may sound crazy to think about breaking away for a walk or a cup of coffee—or even a weekend away—when your child is in crisis, but to keep the family going, that may be exactly what you have to do.

The book of Proverbs talks about setting priorities: "Put your outdoor work in order and get your fields ready; after that, build your house" (24:27). First, you take care of the life-sustaining needs (like food), and then you worry about things like comfort (shel-ter, for example). Relationally, you must maintain the life-giving relationship of the home—the marriage—out of which you can provide emotional and spiritual sustenance for the children. If you starve the marriage, you risk creating a spiritual hunger that ends up injuring everyone else in your home.

Almost inevitably you will endure stresses at work, concern for the health of your parents, and anxiety over the choices your children make. Virtually everyone faces these kinds of issues at one time or another. But in no case should they distract us from the duty that is of prime importance—*feeding our marriages.*

The third part of Diana's recipe for keeping intimacy going involved making a greater effort to enter Ken's world—a theme that keeps surfacing in my many talks with couples who have renewed their marriages.

When we allow common interests to fade, over time we slowly drift apart. Diana went to her movies and Ken watched NASCAR, and both of them were fine with that for a while. But when Ken met another woman who was enthusiastic about NASCAR, he realized that shared intimacy is far more fulfilling than solitary fun. That's why Diana now counsels other wives, "Find a way to be interested in the things your husband is interested in, because it shows him you care about things he cares about."

Will doing so be easy? Hardly. Diana admits that when she went to her first race, she was bored silly. She says, "I was asking myself, *Why am I here?* And then I remembered, *I'm doing this to please Ken.* And it got better."

During that fateful conversation on the porch, Diana had asked Ken, "So what would you do if you left?"

"I'd go to more NASCAR races," Ken answered.

Keeping the conversation light, Diana half laughed, half inquired, "So you'd leave me to go do NASCAR?"

"It's not just going to NASCAR," Ken said. "It's about being interested in the standings, the driver, who won the last pole, who's in line to win the championship."

So Diana has chosen a favorite driver, and on most weeks, she can tell you who leads the points race. She even enjoys the races—just as Pat learned to enjoy fly-fishing and Catherine (you'll meet her in the final chapter) learned to enjoy biking.

I can readily imagine many readers thinking, *That's all well and good, but when is he going to start doing the things I like to do?*

Give it time. Diana freely admits, "In the beginning, some of my needs were in the backseat, and I asked God to love me so I could focus entirely on loving Ken." Remember that Rich (from chapter 10) said he felt more inclined to engage in Pat's favorite activities once Pat started going fishing with him. Sometimes the person who is more invested in the relationship must accommodate the other. The apostle Paul wrote, "We who are strong ought to bear with the failings of the weak and not to please ourselves. Each of us should please our neighbors for their good, to build them up" (Romans 15:1–2). By pleasing your husband, you're winning the intimacy that you can use to influence him in a positive way, including his building an interest in *your* life.

PROBLEMATIC PRIORITIES

There's another underlying issue we need to address. What if a husband is so consumed by recreation that he loses his heart for eternal priorities? I can imagine some wives asking me, "We're called to seek first the kingdom of God—and I have to go to a *NASCAR race*?" Or, "I'm praying for the salvation of my city—but I'm supposed to put that on the sideline because my husband is obsessed with *whether the Red Sox can beat the Yankees*?"

God tends to be far more patient than we are. He waited centuries for just the right time to send his Son to earth. And then Jesus spent thirty years doing menial tasks before he launched his public ministry. By engaging in common interests with your husband, you're winning his heart so that you can influence his soul.

I have found that authentic spiritual passion is contagious. A close friend of mine serves as a missionary to Japan, and his worldwide concern for the lost inspires me. We'll go golfing together, and in our prayer before our lunch afterward, I hear him pour out his heart to God for the person we played with that day, even though we'll likely never see that man again. Being around him reminds me of God's passionate concern for unbelievers.

The same principle can work for you and your husband. The best way for you to stimulate his spiritual concern is by living out your own. Paul used this model in his own ministry. He told the Corinthians, "Therefore I urge you to imitate me" (1 Corinthians 4:16). In case they didn't get it, he repeated himself seven chapters later: "Follow my example, as I follow the example of Christ" (11:1). To the Galatians, Paul gives essentially the same advice: "I plead with you, brothers and sisters, become like me" (Galatians 4:12).

But before Paul could *say* this, he had to *live* this.

Take a deep breath, enter your husband's world, and trust God to use your example in a way that will challenge your husband's heart. The apostle Peter urges, "Wives, in the same way submit yourselves to your own husbands so that, if any of them do not believe the word, they may be won over without words by the behavior of their wives, when they see the purity and reverence of your lives" (1 Peter 3:1–2).

Besides, where better to meet the people who most need God's love than by occasionally going to a NASCAR race or a professional baseball game? Also remember that you're going to compromise your message of reconciliation if your own marriage blows up. By staying fully engaged in your marriage, you're creating a solid base for spreading God's kingdom—even though doing so may require some activities that seem frivolous to you.

LESSONS LEARNED

Most affairs or divorces don't occur as the result of one big decision; far more often, they take place after a series of mini-separations that lead to the final, permanent destruction of the relationship.

Diana unwittingly began separating from Ken when she put work ahead of her husband. She then made another choice toward emotional distance when she allowed the hurt she felt over her daughter to entirely extinguish her marriage's sexual intimacy.

Ken made numerous mini-decisions himself. He chose to enter a chat room. He chose to keep writing to the same woman. He chose to exchange a photograph. And then he chose to make plans to get together.

Diana and Ken teach us that we endanger our marriage when we put it on the shelf—even if only for a season—and then expect our spouse to put up with our temporary separation. Few people in our culture willingly endure loneliness for long stretches of time, and we no longer live in small villages. With the internet, cell phones, and air travel, the world is literally at our fingertips. Whatever causes us to ignore our spouses—work, a sick mother or father, a troubled child, a busy church, a growing ministry—makes little difference to the neglected spouse. If they feel ignored, they become achingly vulnerable. One internet chat, one long lunch at work, one phone call from an old high school girlfriend, one chance meeting at a sporting event or a business convention, and suddenly they see an instant cure for their loneliness—a cure that has the potential to destroy a marriage.

We grow together by degrees, and we grow apart by degrees.

Diana realized that if NASCAR was so important to her husband, it must become more important to her. And Ken must realize that as Diana attends some of his races, so he needs to take her to the movies now and then. Of course, our primary interests and efforts should center on the kingdom of God, but we're talking about recreational times. When a marriage loses its shared interests, it becomes utilitarian, and many people will not stay in a marriage that has lost its emotional core.

Finally, we need to understand that marriage provides the foundation for our relational lives. Work is important. Parenting is crucial. Hobbies are healthy. But when work or hobbies or even parenting causes us to neglect our marriage, the whole house may fall down—and often work, parenting, and everything else will come down with it.

Here's a helpful "Ken and Diana" exercise. Look at the little decisions you've made over the past six months. Are you consciously growing toward your husband or away from him? Are the two of you building areas of shared interest, or are you slowly and unintentionally cultivating separate lives?

We have to be realistic—I know my wife is *never* going to run a marathon with me—but we also must be intentional. The two of us take walks together all the time and bike rides some of the time. You may not be able to share every interest with your husband, but you must cultivate several others.

A NEW START

Two months after the lid got blown off his internet affair, Ken finally could tell Diana he loved her. They took a twentieth-anniversary trip to Vancouver and Victoria, British Columbia, to see the sights—and the whales. They toured the Butchart Gardens, had high tea with "the *best* strawberry preserves," drove up the coast and saw the tide pools, and overall had a "wonderful, really good time."

Throughout the trip, Diana marveled that she still had an intact marriage. Twelve months before, the thought of her and Ken celebrating two decades of matrimony seemed far from a done deal.

"In fact, it was kind of weird," she admits. "We were having such a good time that our problems felt like they had taken place ages ago; but then at other times, I'd be reminded that everything happened months, not years, ago. But mostly, I kept saying, 'Wow,' because God really *has* made us even stronger than we were before."

God also has begun using their healing to reach out to others. "We've been able to share our testimony, and that's been a really neat thing," says Diana. "It really is a remarkable story when you think about it. If I had to produce the recipe for our healing, I'd say it all came down to God's grace and our obedience."

Hillary has never found out about "the incident." She recently took a college course in psychology and made Diana smile when she talked about how unusual it was that her two parents "never had the types of problems you usually see in middle age."

"Listen, the last thing Hillary needs right now is something else to feel insecure about," Diana explains. "I'm relieved she hasn't had to carry this burden."

But Ken and Diana have shared their story discreetly, in ways that have helped other couples face similar crises. One young couple recently disclosed their struggle with internet pornography. Since Ken's struggle included the internet, he could confess some of his own temptations and the things that God had shown him.

As Ken reached out to this hurting, repentant man, he could offer more than sympathy or prayer; he provided practical help that was gained from experience. He talked about how he keeps the words of 1 Corinthians 10:13 taped to his computer and about how he's reorganized his office so that visitors can readily view the computer screen the moment they walk into his office.

Diana ministered to the man's wife. Because this young wife had heard Diana's story, she knew that Diana could understand her pain and help her confront the question most wives in such a situation fear the most: *How do you ever trust again?*

Though Ken seemed to put the affair out of his mind quite readily, Diana has struggled to do so. "It's hard. Even though this incident happened three years ago, sometimes the old suspicions still creep up, and I find I have to put my trust in God anew. Maybe I won't ever completely trust Ken again, but I trust God, including firmly believing that if Ken makes some bad choices, God will take care of me. Even Ken recognizes that it may never be the same."

Diana is thankful that Ken patiently accepts her need to

occasionally talk about the situation. "He understands that he made a huge mistake," she says, "and that we will deal with it at some level for the rest of our lives."

But Romans 8:28–29—"We know that in all things God works for the good of those who love him, who have been called according to his purpose. For those God foreknew he also predestined to be conformed to the image of his Son"—has proven true in their lives. Diana and Ken are stronger and wiser today and more like Christ. Their family remains together, and they provide hope and healing for other couples who, in the midst of their process of reconciliation, wonder how they will ever make it.

"It was *so* totally God," Diana says today. "I was very hurt and disillusioned, but we're still together, stronger than ever. God is soooo good."

QUESTIONS FOR DISCUSSION AND REFLECTION

1. To what extent are you and your husband cultivating shared interests? What are some practical ways couples can grow in this area?
2. How can wives help husbands take an interest in *their* hobbies?
3. How did Diana's solid faith help her maintain the right attitude while confronting Ken?
4. How can couples guard against Satan taking advantage of a natural lull in a relationship and trying to turn it into a permanent break?
5. Discuss practical ways in which you can engage in "winning [your husband's] heart so that you can influence his soul."
6. Are you and your husband currently growing together, or are you slowly growing apart? How can you reinforce the former, or if you are growing apart, how can you reverse this?

CHAPTER 14

JOHN AND CATHERINE: FINDING FAITH

Influencing a Nonbelieving or Spiritually Immature Husband

About four hundred years ago, when Elizabeth married John, she unleashed a love story for the ages. John's full name was John Bunyan. He eventually wrote *The Pilgrim's Progress*, one of the most influential books ever published on the topic of the Christian life. John (a widower) already had four children; Elizabeth became pregnant with their first child just months after exchanging vows.

John passionately preached the gospel during a time when the state church regulated the faith with a heavy hand. Since the church didn't license John, it was technically illegal for him to preach, but rather than accept such a prohibition, John freely and publicly proclaimed God's truth—and promptly went to jail.

He and Elizabeth had been married for less than six months.[1]

In the seventeenth century, if your husband got sent to jail, you didn't have the luxury of simply visiting him once a week and forgetting about him. Family members had the sole responsibility to supply prisoners with food, clothing, laundry services, and everything else. So get this: married less than six months, the *pregnant* Elizabeth had to care for four children from John's previous marriage, as well as regularly travel to the jail to keep her new husband alive.

Some ungodly husbands refuse to work or can't seem to stay sober. Some can't stay away from a casino or quit playing video games or get off a golf course. But John Bunyan—man of God—proved unable to stay out of jail. As soon as he got out, he started illegally preaching again, only to receive another visit from the church authorities and another no-expenses-paid trip right back to prison.

In fact, John's zeal for preaching meant that during the first twenty years of his marriage to Elizabeth, the couple lived together for less than three years. During those seventeen years of John's incarceration, Elizabeth had to raise the children on her own, earn the family's income, and supply her husband with the necessities of life.

George and Karen Grant describe Elizabeth this way: "Tempered by suffering and privation, bolstered by persecution and stigmatization, and motivated by faith and devotion, she was a voice of encouragement, comfort, and inspiration to her husband. Their marriage was marked by the strong bonds of covenantal friendship as well as the emotional bonds of love."[2]

LOVE HURTS

I chose to begin this chapter about loving a spiritually immature man with the love story of Elizabeth and John Bunyan to give you some perspective. If you're unable to share your spiritual journey with your lukewarm or nonbelieving husband, I'm sure you feel deeply hurt. Of course, you experience a sense of loss when you lack the intimacy inherent in pursuing God as part of a couple. But don't overestimate how easy two mature Christians might have it! Faith can be a risky business, with its own set of sacrifices.

Whether your husband is spiritually mature, immature, or in between, your heavenly Father likely will call you to love him and to sacrifice on his behalf. Whether you feel frustrated by his apathy or burdened by his zeal, in the end it all comes down to the same thing: every marriage requires great sacrifice.

We sometimes forget how radical Jesus' words are, but consider this passage in the context of marriage:

> If you love those who love you, what credit is that to you? Even sinners love those who love them. And if you do good to those who are good to you, what credit is that to you? Even sinners do that. And if you lend to those from whom you expect repayment, what credit is that to you? Even sinners lend to sinners, expecting to be repaid in full. But love your enemies, do good to them, and lend to them without expecting to get anything back. Then your reward will be great, and you will be children of the Most High, because he is kind to the ungrateful and wicked. Be merciful, just as your Father is merciful.
>
> *Luke 6:32–36*

Jesus couldn't have said it any clearer. If you manage to love only an easy-to-love husband, why do you need God? Even a non-Christian woman can love a thoughtful, caring, unselfish, and mature man. What credit is that to you? If you serve your husband, expecting to be served in return, what spiritual rewards can you hope to gain? In that case, you're merely trading personal favors. But when you give and don't receive; when you love those who don't know how to love or who refuse to love; when, indeed, you can love even the wicked and the ungrateful—well, at that moment you exhibit the same love that God showed to us when he loved us in our sin and rebellion. And Jesus promises that he will richly reward you.

If your husband is spiritually weaker than you are, your job is to bear with his failings in such a way that you build him up, not tear him down. Instead of assuming the worst, call him to his best. Some women, rather than building up their spiritually weaker husbands, expend their verbal energy discouraging their husbands and tearing them down, berating them for their perceived lack of spiritual leadership.

This exactly reverses the counsel of the apostle Paul in Romans 15:1–2: "We who are strong ought to bear with the failings of the weak and not to please ourselves. Each of us should please our neighbors for their good, to build them up."

The time to obsess over your husband's character is *before* you get married, not after. Once you exchange vows, you should focus only on your obligation to love.

To love well, you have to be honest and ask some tough questions: "How do I love an emotionally distant man?" "How do I love a guy who never seems to pray?" "How do I love a man who doesn't even know how to spell 'spiritual leader,' much less be one?" "How do I love a man who loves his congregation more than he loves me?" But ask such questions in a spirit of humble and prayerful inquiry, not resentful complaint.

If you find yourself in a spiritually imbalanced marriage, expect pride to become your greatest temptation. You may forget that God is working on both of you, and that in the light of God's perfect holiness, the difference in righteousness between you and your husband wouldn't buy a cup of coffee. Philippians 2:3 tells us, "In humility value others above yourselves."

Later in the same chapter, Paul urges believers to "continue to work out your salvation with fear and trembling, for it is God who works in you to will and to act in order to fulfill his good purpose" (2:12–13). Just as God may use you to move your husband toward rebirth and salvation, so he may use *even your unsaved spouse* to move you toward greater holiness. A big part of that holiness includes developing a Christlike attitude. Christ always maintained a tender heart toward the weak and immature (though to the proud and deceitful he was strong and truthful).

Please don't get me wrong. I don't want to minimize the real loneliness and legitimate heartache of living with a person who doesn't share your faith. But I do want to open your eyes to the incredible opportunity for growth that such a marriage offers. I know of no better way to do that than to tell the story of a remarkable woman who spent more than two decades praying for her nonbelieving husband. The story is true, and all the quotes factual, but the names have been changed to protect the children.

JOHN AND CATHERINE

John and Catherine were both twenty-one when they entered what many might have considered a surprise marriage in 1968. Catherine had seriously considered becoming a nun and had even spent seven months in the novitiate, but in the end, she dropped out of the novitiate and married John, whom she had dated in high school.

John never shared Catherine's religious inclinations. Though early on, John attended church services on special days, shortly after they married, John made his intentions as clear as possible. "Going to church doesn't mean anything to me," he told Catherine, "and I'm not going to go anymore."

For the next couple of years, Catherine didn't go much either; but that changed when she had a baby at the age of twenty-three. Two years later, Catherine underwent what she calls a born-again experience. She told John that she had received Jesus Christ as her Lord and Savior and that life would be much different from now on.

"We'll see how long this lasts," John replied. "You do a lot of impetuous things, so we'll just see."

John flew for the United States Navy, so for twenty of the next twenty-four months, he lived away from home. During that time, Catherine expressed her newfound faith by going to church "continuously." When John returned home, Catherine recalls, "God began to train me to become a Christian wife." For the previous two years, Catherine had focused on being a Christian mother; now she had to add "wife" to her résumé.

Catherine admits she made many mistakes early on. "I marvel at the grace and mercy of God," she says. "Without him, I think I would have destroyed our marriage single-handedly. I did lots of things wrong."

For starters, she went to church too often, leaving her husband to fend for himself. "I was at church every Sunday morning and Sunday evening, Tuesday morning, Wednesday evening, and Thursday morning. I was neglecting my husband, which was wrong, especially since he had just returned from deployment."

John's salvation became a focal point of Catherine's prayers. Early on, God gave Catherine assurance through the book of Acts that, just like Cornelius, she "and all [her] household" would be saved (Acts 11:14).

Catherine occasionally asked John to come to church, and though John always responded graciously (he never ridiculed her faith or told her not to go), he made it clear that when it came to "religion," he wanted to be left alone. "Don't let it cloud our relationship," he said.

One time, John agreed to come to a children's program in which his kids had a part, but in addition to the program, he heard a lot of singing and praying and a short but pointed evangelistic message. John felt as though he had been tricked into coming. "Don't you ever, *ever* do that to me again," he told Catherine.

During the long season of John's eventual march to faith, Catherine had to learn a number of personal lessons. Chief among them, she said, came from Jesus' words about how the kernel of wheat must fall to the ground and die (see John 12:24). "The main premise for me in applying that verse to my life was that my needs were not the most important needs," she said. "His had to come before my own. If I were willing to put my emotional needs aside and trust God to meet those, there would be a harvest."

Catherine freely admits that her "emotional neediness" ("I was very needy; *nobody* could meet those needs") caused tension in their marriage. Catherine came from an emotionally expressive home, and while John's home also enjoyed deep affection, feelings seldom got expressed in the same way.

John cites Catherine's patience as a primary reason that he finally became willing to reconsider the faith. "Catherine's patience was the key, especially the way she trusted in God and his timing. She did her best to live her life as God wanted her to and to quietly demonstrate those values," he said.

It's not as though Catherine was perfect. "She had periods of impatience when I wouldn't listen," John admits. "But she never tried to push it on me when I told her I just wasn't interested."

RELEASING JOHN

A turning point came after Catherine gave birth to her third child. She and John had moved back to Denver, and Catherine was lonely. John was gone most of the time, trying to find a new job. Catherine faced the hormonal readjustment that follows every birth; and she had just landed in a new community. "I told the Lord how I was feeling. I knew I was building up resentment and that my marriage was kind of on shaky ground."

God spoke very clearly to Catherine, telling her that as long as she expected John to do things for her that he couldn't do, she was setting him up for failure and herself up for resentment. God challenged her with the words, *If you will release him through forgiveness, then you will open up the door for me to work in his life.*

For the next several years (no short journey!), whenever Catherine's feelings got hurt, she said out loud, "Lord, I forgive him, and I release him to you and ask you to work in his life."

One day, Catherine got tired of praying this prayer. "That's great for John," she confessed to God, "but who will meet *my* needs? What about me, God?"

She heard God reply, "Catherine, I will *always* meet your needs."

Catherine explains that surrendering to God's care and provision was "like a miracle." Each time she spoke forgiveness into John's life, she could walk back into a room without playing mind games or punishing John for any perceived slights.

John understood how much his lack of faith hurt Catherine. One time, he dropped her off for church, and Catherine walked into a service that had been prepared by husbands to honor their wives. As Catherine saw husbands giving roses to their spouses, she just lost it. She wasn't prepared for the emphasis on couples worshiping together, and she grieved over not having her husband by her side. She felt so distraught that she skipped Sunday school and cried during most of the worship service.

When John picked up Catherine and the kids, he could tell she was sad, and he said, "I'm sorry I can't do this for you." Though Catherine still was hurting, it meant a lot that John somehow was able to plug into the pain she was feeling over his absence.

Catherine occasionally shared the gospel message with her husband, but sparingly—maybe ten times in twenty-three years, "when something would come up." For instance, when Continental Airlines went through difficult times, John, who was one of their pilots, lost his job for three years. John and Catherine finally exhausted all their savings.

"John, this is a perfect opportunity to trust God," Catherine said. "I know God is faithful, and he *will* meet our needs. Will you watch with me and see what he will do? Will you acknowledge it when he answers our prayers?"

Over the next three days, three families independently gave John and Catherine more than a thousand dollars total.

Still, John didn't give in. "I can't believe like you do," he told Catherine. "I just can't."

Then God unleashed the plan that would ultimately bring John to faith.

A FAMILY CRISIS

John and Catherine's two girls sailed through youth group without a problem, but their son, Brian, had a difficult time connecting with the new youth pastor. To make matters worse, Brian got beat up at a church camp. And what's more, he began identifying with his same-gender parent who had absolutely no interest in faith.

As Catherine watched her son make some dangerous choices, she grew angry at her husband. She told John, "To see our children serving God is the most important thing in the world to me. Our son looks up to you. You're a hero to him, and the two of you have a very good relationship. If anything happens to his Christian faith, I'm holding you personally responsible, and I will never forgive you"— this was the first and only time Catherine ever threatened John.

"Are you saying this will affect our relationship?" he asked.

"Yes," Catherine answered.

The conversation took place as John and Catherine were on a bike ride, and as John surged ahead, Catherine thought, *That was too harsh.* She started to peddle harder to try to catch up and apologize, but Catherine believes God quieted her down and told her not to say anything more. *Maybe I shouldn't have said it, but I may well have made things worse by talking about it more,* she speculated.

As Brian began to experience disciplinary and drug problems, Catherine sensed the Lord saying something to her in prayer that at first made no sense: "You're no longer to be the spiritual head of the home."

"Well, if not me, then who will it be?"

"I'm going to lay the mantle of spiritual headship on John, and I want you to tell him that."

"How can that be? He isn't even born again!"

But Catherine eventually gave in and told John what she perceived that God had told her in prayer. John was just as shocked as Catherine had been. "I can't do that, Catherine! How can I do that?"

"I don't know, but that's what God said, so that's all I can tell you."

Later, the Lord directed Catherine to pray for John every day, specifically that he would learn to walk in spiritual headship as God himself came alongside to teach him. None of it seemed to make any sense, but Catherine chose to follow along.

Today, she's very glad she did.

After Brian got caught smoking marijuana, John and Catherine went to see a counselor. While praying about this visit, Catherine once again sensed that God was speaking to her: "You are no longer to discipline Brian; John is to do so. I want you to pray every day for John's disciplining process."

John had *no* problem with this! In fact, he was glad to hear it, fearing that Catherine would be too soft. *For once*, he thought, *God had a great idea.*

As Catherine looks back, she realizes, as she puts it, that "this was one of the most important pieces for God to set in place; what John did not know was that he was assuming spiritual headship."

A very difficult year and a half went by. Brian continued to abuse drugs, and he got suspended from school in his senior year of high school. John and Catherine pursued more serious counseling, but Catherine had become busier than ever after having just started nursing school. About this time, Catherine sensed God directing her to pray earnestly for John's salvation. Catherine had prayed for John for most of their marriage, but it often went in spurts. For a time, she would contend strongly for her husband but then get discouraged and pull back; after a time of healing, she would begin another period of fervent prayer. Catherine remembers telling a friend, "I'm entering a new season of praying for John to become a Christian."

"WHO IS IN BED WITH ME?"

Back at home, Brian's troubles became topic number one.

"Catherine, what are we going to do?" John asked one night.

"Honey," Catherine answered, "you have to figure that out. I'm struggling to keep my head above water with my studies at school, but I know God will help you."

John checked out two videos on drug abuse from Brian's school and watched them. He came to bed late that night and started talking about them. "This police officer talked about how we're losing kids because we are made of spirit, mind, and body. While we're touching our kids intellectually, we're not touching them spiritually. What do you think of that?"

Catherine felt as amazed as she did pleased. She admits thinking, *Who is in bed with me?*

John went on. "Do you think we could talk to Brian about this? About how he's vulnerable to drugs because we're not appealing to teens as whole persons, about how his spiritual side is being ignored?"

Catherine got very direct. "John," she said, "why would Brian listen to you when you've ignored that part of your own life?"

"Yes, that *does* worry me," John confessed.

"I'd be worried about that too. Do you want to pray together about it?"

There was a slight pause. "Yeah," John said.

Catherine's heart started beating so hard and so fast that she was half afraid the fire department would somehow take notice and pay an emergency visit. For the first time, she was going to be praying with her husband of more than twenty years!

Thankfully, God kept her calm. "I don't think John sensed that my excitement was for him as much as it was for Brian," she says. "I think he felt the responsibility that dated back six years when I said I would hold him responsible if Brian rejected God."

The very next day, John had a long talk with Brian about the importance of spirituality, even though—as he admitted to Brian—it hadn't been important to him in his own life.

BORN AGAIN

In retrospect, Catherine considers it a blessing that her studies kept her so busy, or she might have gotten more involved and possibly frustrated God's plans. God seemed stern in his warnings to Catherine: "You are not to put your hand to this; this is *my* sovereign hand at work!"

Catherine did suggest a book that, based on her husband's political interest, she thought John might like—Chuck Colson's *Born Again*.[3]

John looked at it and said, "I think I'd like to read that."

Catherine went—in her words—"nuts." "I was *so* excited," she says. "We had been married for over twenty years, and I had never seen him show interest like this."

Catherine called her pastor and asked him to pray; then she kept her mouth shut. "I *did* sneak a peek now and then to see if the bookmark was moving," she confesses, "and though it moved slowly, it *did* move."

John started reading the book in October. In December of that same year, when Catherine noticed that Christmas was going to fall on Sunday, she asked John, "Would you like to come with us to Christmas services this year? If it's not the time, I understand."

John's answer shocked her. "I'm so sorry you had to ask me," he said, "because I've been meaning to tell you I want to come."

The ever-emotional Catherine broke down on the spot and cried. "Thank you," she said. "This means so much to me."

For the first time ever, all five members of Catherine's family went to church together on a Sunday. Catherine felt a bit like a spectacle. She had helped to pioneer this church, so she knew everybody was watching them, as well as sharing in her excitement and joy. For Catherine, it seemed almost surreal. She says, "I felt like it was somebody else's life that I was watching in a movie. I had waited so long; I just couldn't believe it was happening."

Catherine was absolutely amazed at how God had orchestrated everything: God's call for her to pull back and stop being the spiritual head of the house; God's directives to let John handle the discipline; Catherine's renewed season of prayer; John's viewing of the videos; the way John related to Chuck Colson. Even if Catherine had *tried* to orchestrate each element, there was no way she could have.

"It was an amazing thing to watch," Catherine confesses. "I still marvel at God's faithfulness."

John returned to church the following Sunday and then every Sunday after that. Catherine gave him a book containing a portion of Scripture from the New Testament and a devotional, which John read almost every day. He asked Catherine lots and lots of questions. Together, they attended a new believers class, and it thrilled Catherine that John seemed to hit it off with, and eventually become friends with, the teacher.

Finally, during a church service in March, the pastor asked at the end of a sermon if anyone wanted to make a profession of faith in Christ. Catherine saw John's hand go up. When the pastor prayed with John, John explained that he wanted a specific date for his conversion, though John believes he may have come to faith earlier, as he read about Chuck Colson's salvation experience.

LESSONS TO BE LEARNED

I spoke with John and Catherine about some of the lessons they learned along the way—in particular, about how other "unequally yoked" wives might gently move their husbands toward faith.

Building Bridges

Catherine often wondered how two people who shared so little in common could ever make it. Sometimes she even asked John,

"Are we going to make it? We have so little in common. My faith is so important to me, but you don't even share it!"

John would say, "Catherine, where our relationship is good, it's very good. Let's concentrate on that." John wanted Catherine to concentrate on the good places in her marriage rather than become consumed by her disappointments.

Catherine honestly admits she endured a trying and difficult season that went on for decades. "Being unequally yoked is extremely lonely," she says. "You're guiding your children by yourself. You try to stave off resentment and build a good marriage—it's just very, very difficult."

Most women in such a situation will, like Catherine, find themselves tempted by self-pity. Philippians 2:14 gives some help here: "Do everything without grumbling or arguing." The word *everything* includes marriage, even marriage to a nonbeliever. Resentment and bitterness will only keep us from being spiritually productive in that relationship.

Catherine realized that since she and her husband didn't share a faith in Christ, she would have to work extra hard to find other things to share. Unfortunately, John was most excited about things in which Catherine had little or no interest—like riding bikes, for example.

"I had to make the decision," she says. "Would I start riding bikes with him, or would I sit home by myself and let the gap between us widen?"

Catherine's initial attempts didn't encourage her. She says, "It was ridiculous. I was so out of shape. But you know what, a year and a half later, I loved it more than he did! We did 'Ride the Rockies' together—that was four hundred miles through the Rocky Mountains, a seven-day bike ride with two thousand other people. It was a blast, and we spent hundreds of hours together training for the ride."

Catherine just kept focusing on the positive. "We didn't have a family together at church," she admits, "but we did have a family together on bicycles."

Some wives might be tempted to punish their non-Christian husband by becoming even less accommodating, thinking, *If you won't share my faith, I won't share any of your interests.* But such pettiness, while understandable, does nothing except widen the gap. Catherine adamantly counsels other women married to nonbelievers, "You must find out what he loves doing and learn to do it with him."

That's not a bad lesson for wives in general.

John also loved fishing, another activity that held no magic for Catherine. Early on, when the kids were little, Catherine stayed by the campsite with the kids while John went fishing. As the kids got older, they started going fishing with John. One year, Catherine realized that she could either stay at the campsite by herself or join her family for an activity that didn't hold much interest for her.

She grabbed a pole and joined them.

Now, years later, she loves going fly-fishing with John; in fact, it's become one of her favorite things. "It's funny," she says. "What was once something I did only out of obligation is now one of the greatest delights of my life."

It took years for Catherine to learn this valuable lesson. "I'm as selfish and reticent as anybody," she confesses, "but I know that the Holy Spirit was leading me. Once in a while, I still say, 'Are we going to be okay?' We'll *never* be two people who like to do the same things. We have some areas of mutual likes, but there are many strong differences. Marriage is about choosing to allow the strong points of your marriage to be the dominant points, the areas you *choose* to focus on. Where you absolutely can't meet, you find a way to detour."

In other words, Catherine learned contentment. "Instead of spending my whole life complaining about what I wanted," she says, "I started enjoying what I already had."

You can begin this process today. If you find yourself mentally rehashing your spouse's weaknesses, counter this tendency by meditating on what you like about him. Instead of obsessing over your differences, think about the one or two things you truly enjoy doing together.

Being Realistic

Catherine warns, "Wives can be so dominated by thoughts of 'This won't work; we're too different. We have different ideologies, different passions, even different ways of looking at things.' Ultimately, we have to learn that we'll never have some of the things we've yearned for, but God will give us ways to develop strengths already there—strengths we may not be recognizing. Along the way, we slowly mature and figure out that Jesus is the one we delight in. My greatest pleasure is my relationship with God."

Catherine had to realize that God never intended John to meet all of her needs. Even if John had been a Christian for their entire marriage, some needs would still go unmet. No husband, Christian or not, is God.

How will you face disappointment with your husband? Will you allow a toxic mixture of bitterness, resentment, and anger to slowly poison your home, or will you learn to delight in what you already have? Consider this. As a Christian married to a non-Christian, you are much better off than being a non-Christian married to a Christian. You have your faith, the Holy Spirit, the hope of salvation, God's grace, your ability to worship, and a love of Scripture to fill your soul and season your mind. Realizing how rich you are spiritually can help ease the frustration you're enduring relationally.

Changing with John

Catherine eventually realized that, as she puts it, "this waiting period for John to become a Christian was about me too." She wasn't waiting just for John. She adds, "The whole process was as integral to *my* growth in Jesus as it was for him. God made it very clear that I was not to consider myself a spectator or a martyr or someone who was just waiting. God had lessons for me to learn too."

Even if you're further along than your husband, spiritually speaking, you still haven't fully arrived. None of us have. Your own character and maturity must continue to grow. Paul told Timothy, "Be diligent in these matters; give yourself wholly to them, *so that everyone may see your progress*" (1 Timothy 4:15, emphasis added). Perfection lies beyond us in this world, but every maturing believer should be showing some positive spiritual movement.

God used Catherine's marriage to teach her how to better handle fear—in her case, the fear of a failed marriage—and how to be less controlling. As Catherine grew in these areas, God did something wonderful not only in her life but in her family as well, testifying to the truth of 1 Timothy 4:16: "Watch your life and doctrine closely. Persevere in them, because if you do, you will save both yourself and your hearers."

When your husband isn't a believer, one of the biggest spiritual traps you will face is being more concerned about his conversion than your maturity. Why is that a trap? Because your increasing spiritual maturity can help foster his conversion (1 Peter 3:1)! Whenever you find yourself obsessing over your husband's spiritual state, say a prayer for him *but then pivot into this*: "And Lord, please show me where I need to grow to be the kind of person who makes faith attractive to her husband."

Being Honest

Catherine found it extremely difficult to learn how to, in her words, "live two lives": "You have two things that are passionately important to you—your relationship with God and your deep desire that your marriage be viable and strong. It's very difficult when you can't merge the two. You feel divided."

Financial giving to the church presented a particularly thorny issue. Catherine wanted to give money to her church, but she didn't work outside the home, and initially she feared what John might say. So she began saving the change from the grocery money and giving that as a contribution—something she now regrets.

"Finally, I just had to tell John how important giving was for me," she says. "I'd tell young wives to be honest about the things that are important to you instead of hiding them." Once Catherine explained why she wanted to give and how much it meant to her to be able to do so, he agreed that she could donate a hundred dollars a month. Catherine wishes she had been more up-front all along. As the book of Proverbs observes, "An honest answer is like a kiss on the lips" (24:26).

Being Patient

Some foolish women greatly wounded Catherine when they told her, "Your husband should have been saved long ago. What are you doing wrong?"

Yet when you talk to John, he keeps coming back to how much he appreciates Catherine's patient spirit. If she had tried too hard, if she had kept pushing, she most likely would have moved John further away from the faith rather than closer to it.

Keep in mind that a cosmic spiritual battle rages inside your husband. Eternity is at stake. In the light of eternity, one or two decades aren't all that long (even though twenty years can seem like forever). John remembers times when he saw Catherine and the kids getting ready for church and then pulling out of the driveway, and something inside of him would be saying, *Go after them*—but he didn't know how. It took time. If Catherine had tried to force the issue, she would have made things worse, not better. Jesus tells us in Luke 8:15 that "by *persevering* [we] produce a crop" (emphasis added).

THE ULTIMATE SURRENDER

Few things present more difficulty for a bride of Christ than being the wife of a man who is outside the faith. Catherine admits to feeling pulled hard in two directions. She loved her husband and wanted her marriage to work, but she also loved God and wanted to put him first. It hurt deeply when she couldn't immediately bring the two together.

The reality is, no easy answers exist. I can't give you an ironclad recipe that will guarantee your husband's conversion—and anybody who tells you differently, frankly, is lying. But a gentle and quiet heart—mixed with a patient spirit and a growing, flourishing soul fixed on worship and emboldened by the Holy Spirit, resulting in a woman who keeps praying and who finds ways to connect with her husband—greatly increases the possibility that she will one day pray to the God of her dreams *with* the man of her dreams.

I can tell you this: The Bible makes it abundantly clear that God does not desire anyone to perish (2 Peter 3:9), and 1 Timothy 2:4 declares that our Savior "wants all people to be saved and to come to a knowledge of the truth." When you combine the favor of God, the guidance and conviction of the Holy Spirit, and the persevering love of a believing wife, I *like* that man's chances.

God bless you in this glorious task! The most important place you can ever move your husband toward is *God*. When you consider the eternal benefits and your husband's spiritual health, nothing else comes close. It's not an easy battle, nor is there a guaranteed victory—but in the end, it's a fight worth fighting.

QUESTIONS FOR DISCUSSION AND REFLECTION

1. Discuss the impact of Jesus' words in Luke 6:32–36 about loving those who aren't always easy to love, specifically as they relate to a woman married to a nonbeliever or a nominal Christian.

2. How can Christian wives who are married to nonbelieving or spiritually immature husbands follow Paul's directive in Philippians 2:3 to "in humility value others above yourselves"?

3. How might God use an unsaved spouse to help a Christian wife grow in godliness?

4. Do you agree with Catherine that it's possible for a Christian wife married to a nonbeliever to err by going to church functions too often? What might be some other common errors of Christian wives in such marriages?

5. How might Christian wives be setting up their nonbelieving or spiritually immature husbands for failure, expecting them to do things they just can't do?

6. Catherine urges wives, "You must find out what he loves doing and learn to do it with him." How can wives move past the frustration of having different faith expressions while still being open to sharing other activities?

7. What are some of the practical issues—such as money management or time at church—that could be problematic in an unequally yoked marriage? How can a believing wife act and speak in such a way to promote redemption instead of contention?

8. How can wives balance patient perseverance—waiting for the right time—with direct sharing of the gospel?

EVERLASTING BEAUTY

As a new country began to take shape, a new child began to form in Abigail Adams's womb. The year was 1776. The colonies had declared their independence from England, and their breakaway leaders were working hard to create a new nation.

It's a wonder that Abigail and her husband, John, ever had time to conceive a child, given that John had to be away from home so frequently. But they did, although shortly after the conception took place in the early weeks of 1777, John had to leave once again, to attend yet another session of the new Congress.

The pregnant Abigail knew she could have persuaded John to remain home. She said as much in a letter to a friend: "I had it in my heart to dissuade him from going and I know I could have prevailed, but our public affairs at the time wore so gloomy an aspect that I thought if ever his assistance was wanted, it must be at such a time. I therefore resigned myself to suffer some anxiety and many melancholy hours for this year to come."[1]

Though Abigail knew she needed her husband nearby, she also believed their new country needed him even more. She willingly inconvenienced herself for the sake of her land.

John appreciated his wife's sacrifice. He recognized her unselfishness, and he respected it. Abigail had a legitimate claim, and no caring husband could deny the hardship of a pregnant wife left alone during the winter. A famous pamphlet had called the revolutionary period a time "that tried men's souls," to which John responded that they were "times that tried women's souls as well as men's."[2]

And it's not as though this inconvenience remained limited to a single season. In another letter, Abigail confides, "'Tis almost fourteen years since we were united, but not more than half that time we had the happiness of living together. The unfeeling world may consider it in what light they please, I consider it a sacrifice to my country and one of my greatest misfortunes."[3]

Abigail paid a heavy price for her love and devotion. Not only did she have to share her husband with his country, but she also had to endure many vicious attacks leveled against government officials, telling one friend, "When [my husband] is wounded, I bleed."[4]

The couple also suffered their share of marital disagreements. John could be obstinate. Though he sought his wife's counsel, he didn't always follow it. In fact, early in their marriage, the couple had an opportunity to prosper financially. Unlike today, succeeding in government back then held no guarantee of financial security. John Adams believed that land would make the best investment for their savings. When the opportunity arose for the couple to invest in newly available government securities, Abigail urged her husband to take advantage of them. But John remained suspicious of investing in "coin and commerce." He understood land, the value of agriculture, and the importance of food, but he didn't trust banks. As it turned out, "Had the Adamses invested in government securities as Abigail wished, they would, almost certainly, have wound up quite wealthy."[5]

Yet there appeared to be no lasting bitterness over this lost opportunity. Abigail was a realist, as well as a passionate partner in her husband's pursuits. She recognized that, though her husband excelled at diplomacy, his investment acumen fell far short of genius.

Like all men, he had his limits. Abigail had made her choice, and she continued to support John in his strengths while remaining magnanimous about his weaknesses.

Abigail's unswerving devotion cemented her husband's heart to hers. When John became the second president of the United States, he wrote a long letter, begging Abigail to join him without delay:

> I must go to you or you must come to me. I cannot live without you . . . I must entreat you to lose not a moment's time in preparing to come on, that you may take off from me every care of life but that of my public duty, assist me with your councils, and console me with your conversation.
>
> The times are critical and dangerous, and I must have you here to assist me . . . I must now repeat this with zeal and earnestness. I can do nothing without you.[6]

John Adams was desperate for his wife's presence. He needed her conversation and her counsel so much so that he asserted, "I can do nothing without you."

I've spent a couple of hundred pages talking about how a woman can influence a man, but Abigail Adams obviously cornered this market more than two centuries ago.

When Abigail lay mortally ill in October 1818, her husband remained constantly by her side. In her last few days, she awoke from a delirious haze, saw John next to her, and gently confessed that she knew she was dying and that if it were God's will for it to be so, she was ready. She desired to keep living, she said, only for John's sake. When John heard that even death's door hadn't dampened her devotion, he became an emotional wreck, stumbling out of the room in a stupor. Downstairs, he told a friend, "I wish I could lie down beside her and die too."[7]

Two days later, Abigail did die; but John's respect, loyalty, and remembrance lived on. Years later, when people complimented

John about his son's rise to the presidency and the pride he must feel about the role he had played as a father, Adams emphatically responded, "My son had a mother!"[8]

THE ROMANCE BEHIND THE LABOR

By now, some of you may be thinking, *This entire approach Gary has been talking about seems like so much work! Where's the romance? Where's the fun?* I've told the story of John and Abigail Adams because I believe their marriage had the best of romance encased within the reality of sacrifice and personal struggle.

I believe in marriage—with all of its work, obligations, and sacrifice, along with all of its joy, pleasures, laughter, and romance— because it's what God calls most of us to do. If you're reading this book, I suspect you're not called to celibacy. God designed you to live—physically, emotionally, and spiritually—in a lifelong, committed relationship with one radically imperfect man. Can you trust God enough to believe that surrendering to this life—both the good and the seemingly negative or difficult—will, in the end, produce the most satisfying life possible: a love based in faith and built on a lifetime of memories, esteem from your children for holding your home together, and rewards from your heavenly Father for creating a family that testifies to his redemptive and reconciling love?

A lifetime of romance lies hidden in the work of marriage. In your own relationship, you may occasionally feel tempted to get lost in romantic comedies instead of studying how to love a real man. It may seem easier to withdraw from love, to get lazy in your affections, to coast in your marriage—but such an indulgent, soft way of life will ultimately steal your sense of well-being and even your happiness. You'll lose any romantic feelings you once had for your husband, and you'll eventually despise the person you've become.

God built us in such a way that, early on in a relationship, romance is unearned and often unappreciated. Intimacy is immediate and electric. In a mature marriage, romance is maintained only through hard work, deliberate choices, and concrete actions. You can't force feelings, but you can choose to act so that feelings usually follow. If we act like we're in love, we'll keep falling in love. It's a process of growth—toward God, toward each other, and toward personal holiness.

I look at it this way: Everything that God asks of me is what I ultimately want to become—a loyal, loving spouse; a sacrificing, affectionate, and involved parent; an enthusiastic worker for the gospel; a faithful and loving friend. Everything I see resulting from the world's view of romantic relationships is what I most despise—people getting hurt by betrayal and divorce, children being devastated by the destruction of their homes, individuals becoming more selfish and more hedonistic as they age.

If wisdom is known by her fruit, the Bible is the sweetest teaching that has ever been told.

Biblical love is a Christ-centered love that seeks to perfect holiness out of reverence for God (2 Corinthians 7:1). As we end this journey together, I ask you to pause and try to imagine the pleasure you give God by loving his son well. Your husband will quite likely, at times, take your love and devotion for granted. He may act in critical ways. He may be selfish and inconsiderate. But he's not the only one living in your home! An all-seeing God receives great pleasure when his daughters love his sons, and he showers his spiritual blessings in the form of a soul-filling intimacy that is unlike any other. The psalmist writes this:

> How wonderful, how beautiful,
>   when brothers and sisters get along!
> It's like costly anointing oil . . .
> It's like the dew on Mount Hermon . . .
> Yes, that's where GOD commands the blessing,
>   ordains eternal life.

Psalm 133 MSG

I know that relationships can be difficult and hurtful. I know that being married to a man who stumbles in many ways (James 3:2) can grow tiresome and be exhausting. But I also know that God is real, that his Son has made a mighty sacrifice for our sins, that his Holy Spirit will empower us, that his living Word will guide us, and that his promise of heavenly rewards is more secure and more certain than anything this world offers.

As you continue this life journey, seek the Lord for guidance on how to build the type of marriage he desires. Call on him to give you his wisdom in developing the sacred art of loving an imperfect partner so that your husband can become all that God wants him to be.

As you begin to influence your husband, you will see the Lord influence you as well—most importantly, he'll draw you ever closer to him.

ACKNOWLEDGMENTS

There are so many people to thank.

First, thank you to those who agreed to let your stories inspire others. Many of you chose to remain anonymous, so I'll respect your privacy. You know who you are, and I am deeply grateful for the courage it took to unfold your lives for the benefit of others.

Second, my "four therapists," who provided their expert analysis (and the specific, relevant education I lack in this regard) and helped shape this book accordingly: Dr. Melody Rhode, Leslie Vernick, Dr. Mitch Whitman, and Dr. Steve Wilke. Thank you for being so generous with your understanding and so patient with my lack of it.

Then to the readers. Donna Burgess, Cheryl Scruggs, Jo Franz, Lisa Fetters, Dina Horne, and Nicole Whitacre were so helpful for the first edition of this book. This new edition was greatly shaped by the additional comments of David and Megan Cox, Sheila Wray Gregoire, and additional comments from Dr. Melody Rhode and Leslie Vernick.

I especially want to thank Mary Kay Smith and Dr. Rebecca Wilke, who have both previewed several of my books. Thank you for loving me and this work in progress enough to speak the hard word when it needed to be spoken and for challenging me, consistently and persistently, to go deeper. You both are true friends.

None of the aforementioned may fully agree with all that is said in the book you now hold, but I believe everything is that much closer to the truth—and much better said—because of their service.

I also want to thank John Sloan at Zondervan, who had his hands full trying to redirect an initially scattered manuscript. My appreciation goes to Dirk Buursma, for his word management and encouragement, as well as to David Morris, Tom Dean, Brandon Henderson, Robin Barnett, and the entire Zondervan team.

Many thanks also to Curtis Yates and Mike Salisbury at Yates & Yates, and to Alli Sepulveda at Second Baptist Church in Houston.

My wife has been no less than a saint throughout this ordeal. She has read, reread, and listened to me think out loud more than any wife should ever have to endure over a lifetime. She has done far more than merely "influence" this man; God has used her to reshape him. I love you, Lisa.

NOTES

Introduction: God Hears and Sees

1. Leslie Vernick, *The Emotionally Destructive Marriage: How to Find Your Voice and Reclaim Your Hope* (Colorado Springs: WaterBrook, 2013).

Chapter 1: The Glory of God in a Woman

1. C. F. Keil and F. Delitzsch, *Commentary on the Old Testament: The Pentateuch* (Grand Rapids: Eerdmans, 1956), 103.
2. William Lane, *Mark* (New International Commentary on the New Testament; Grand Rapids: Eerdmans, 1974), 356–57.

Chapter 2: "Be Worthy of Me"

1. David McCullough, "Knowing History and Knowing Who We Are," *Imprimis* 34.4 (April 2005): 5, https://imprimis.hillsdale.edu/knowing -history-and-knowing-who-we-are (accessed May 30, 2017).
2. Cited in André Castelot, *Josephine* (New York: Harper & Row, 1967), 332.
3. Thanks to my friend Dina Horne for this great insight.

Chapter 3: The Beauty of God's Strength in a Woman

1. The term "functional fixedness" originated in psychology as a way of describing the tendency "to cling to set patterns and overlook possible new approaches" for problem solving ("What Is Functional Fixedness?" *Psychology Dictionary* online, http://psychologydictionary.org/functional-fixedness [accessed May 30, 2017]).
2. D. Elton Trueblood, *The Life We Prize* (New York: Harper & Brothers, 1951), 158.
3. Cited in Del Jones, "FedEx Chief Takes Cue from Leaders in History," *USA Today*, June 20, 2005, https://usatoday30.usatoday.com/money/companies/ management/2005-06-19-fedex-advice_x.htm (accessed May 30, 2017).

Chapter 4: Accepting a Man Where He Is

1. "The GQ Poll: The State of Man," *GQ* (December 2004), 224.
2. Lysa TerKeurst, *Capture His Heart: Becoming the Godly Wife Your Husband Desires* (Chicago: Moody, 2002), 12–13.
3. Dan Allender, *How Children Raise Parents: The Art of Listening to Your Family* (Colorado Springs: WaterBrook, 2003), 196.
4. Allender, *How Children Raise Parents*, 196.
5. Allender, *How Children Raise Parents*, 197.

Chapter 5: Asking God for Fresh Eyes

1. The speaker is Harry Belafonte, who told the story to Bono (see Michka Assayas, *Bono: In Conversation with Michka Assayas* [New York: Riverhead, 2005], 96).
2. Assayas, *Bono*, 96, emphasis added.
3. Assayas, *Bono*, 97.
4. Louann Brizendine, MD, *The Male Brain: A Breakthrough Understanding of How Men and Boys Think* (New York: Random House, 2010), xv.
5. Norma Smalley, "Differences Can Strengthen a Marriage," in *The Joy of a Promise Kept: The Powerful Role Wives Play* (Sisters, OR: Multnomah, 1996), 39.
6. Elyse Fitzpatrick, *Helper by Design: God's Perfect Plan for Women in Marriage* (Chicago: Moody, 2003), 54.
7. Fitzpatrick, *Helper by Design*, 55.
8. Patricia Palau, "Influencing Our World for Christ," in *The Joy of a Promise Kept*, 148.
9. Palau, "Influencing Our World," 149.
10. Palau, "Influencing Our World," 152.
11. Martie Stowell, "When He Doesn't Keep His Promises," in *The Joy of a Promise Kept*, 164–68.
12. Ruth Bell Graham, *It's My Turn* (Old Tappan, NJ: Revell, 1982), 74.
13. See Niall McCarthy, "What Percentage of U.S. Wives Earn More Than Their Husbands?" *Forbes*, November 19, 2015, www.forbes.com/sites/niallmccarthy/2015/11/19/what-percentage-of-us-wives-earn-more-than-their-husbands-infographic/#3b5fee32724a (accessed May 30, 2017).
14. Ginny Graves, "As Women Rise in Society, Many Still Don't Do 'Equal,'" *USA Today*, June 30, 2005, 13A.
15. Linda Dillow, *Creative Counterpart: Becoming the Woman, Wife, and Mother You've Longed to Be* (Nashville: Nelson, 2003), 178.
16. This account is from Eastern European folklore, which states that the attacking king—Konrad III—allowed the Duke of Bavaria and his men to live, so moved

was he by the wives' actions; see Ruthilde M. Kronberg, *Clever Folk: Tales of Wisdom, Wit, and Wonder* (Englewood, CO: Libraries Unlimited, 1993), 5–6.

Chapter 6: The Helper

1. Kelli B. Trujillo, "Complementarian Versus Egalitarian: What's the Correct View?" *Today's Christian Woman* (March 2014), www.todays christianwoman.com/articles/2014/march-week-4/complementarian -versus-egalitarian.html (accessed May 30, 2017).

2. Thomas à Kempis, *The Imitation of Christ*, trans. Aloysius Croft and Harold Bolton (London: Catholic Way, 2013), 97.

3. Quoted in Trujillo, "Complementarian Versus Egalitarian: What's the Correct View?"

4. Laura Doyle, *The Surrendered Wife: A Practical Guide to Finding Intimacy, Passion, and Peace with a Man* (New York: Fireside, 1999).

Chapter 7: Understanding the Male Mind

1. Louann Brizendine, MD, *The Male Brain: A Breakthrough Understanding of How Men and Boys Think* (New York: Random House, 2010), 2.

2. Brizendine, *Male Brain*, 2.

3. Michael Gurian, *What Could He Be Thinking? How a Man's Mind Really Works* (New York: St. Martin's, 2003), 12.

4. Brizendine, *Male Brain*, xvi.

5. See Gurian, *What Could He Be Thinking?* 15.

6. Gurian, *What Could He Be Thinking?* 16.

7. Cited in Gurian, *What Could He Be Thinking?* 86.

8. Gurian, *What Could He Be Thinking?* 82–84.

9. Gurian, *What Could He Be Thinking?* 475.

10. John Gottman, "From *The Seven Principles for Making Marriage Work*," in *The Book of Marriage: The Wisest Answers to the Toughest Questions*, ed. Dana Mack and David Blankenhorn (Grand Rapids: Eerdmans, 2001), 472.

11. Gottman, "From *The Seven Principles*," 473.

12. Cited in Shaunti Feldhahn, *For Women Only: What You Need to Know About the Inner Lives of Men* (Sisters, OR: Multnomah, 2004), 146.

13. Linda Weber, "Building a Strong Marriage," in *The Joy of a Promise Kept* (Sisters, OR: Multnomah, 1998), 97.

14. See Brizendine, *Male Brain*, 96.

15. See the discussion in Brizendine, *Male Brain*, 96–97.

16. Brizendine, *Male Brain*, xvi.

17. Brizendine, *Male Brain*, xvi.

18. Brizendine, *Male Brain*, 15.

19. Brizendine, *Male Brain*, 15–16.

20. Brizendine, *Male Brain*, 113.

Chapter 8: Ray and Jo: Taming the Temper, Part 1

1. Louann Brizendine, MD, *The Male Brain: A Breakthrough Understanding of How Men and Boys Think* (New York: Random House, 2010), 102.

2. Ed Welch, "How to Disarm an Angry Person," CCEF blog, March 30, 2010, www.ccef.org/resources/blog/how-disarm-angry-person (accessed May 30, 2017).

3. Welch, "How to Disarm an Angry Person."

4. Shaunti Feldhahn, *For Women Only: What You Need to Know About the Inner Lives of Men* (Sisters, OR: Multnomah, 2004), 24.

5. Feldhahn, *For Women Only*, 24.

6. Feldhahn, *For Women Only*, 25.

7. Thanks to Leslie Vernick for offering helpful suggestions for this paragraph.

8. Leslie Vernick, *The Emotionally Destructive Marriage: How to Find Your Voice and Reclaim Your Hope* (Colorado Springs: WaterBrook, 2013); Chip Ingram and Becca Johnson, *Overcoming Emotions That Destroy: Practical Help for Those Angry Feelings That Ruin Relationships* (Grand Rapids: Baker, 2009).

9. I'm indebted to Elton Trueblood for this insight.

Chapter 9: Taming the Temper, Part 2

1. Kevin DeYoung, *What Does the Bible Really Teach about Homosexuality?* (Wheaton, IL: Crossway, 2015), 94.

2. Quoted in Amy Patterson-Neubert, "Get Serious: Domestic Violence Is Not a Joke," *Purdue News*, October 16, 2003, www.purdue.edu/uns/html4ever/031016.Arriaga.violence.html (accessed May 30, 2017); see Ximena Arriaga, "Joking Violence Among Highly Committed Individuals," *Journal of Interpersonal Violence* 17.6 (June 2002): 591–610.

Chapter 11: Pure Passion

1. Louann Brizendine, MD, *The Male Brain: A Breakthrough Understanding of How Men and Boys Think* (New York: Random House, 2010), 4.

2. Brizendine, *Male Brain*, 69.

3. Quoted in Michael Callahan, "The Man Behind History's Most Iconic Movie Posters, from *Breakfast at Tiffany's* to James Bond," *Vanity Fair*, April 2017, www.vanityfair.com/style/2017/04/robert-mcginnis-movie-posters-illustrations (accessed May 30, 2017).

4. Cindy Crosby, "The Best Sex (Survey) Ever!" *Today's Christian Woman*, September 12, 2008, www.todayschristianwoman.com/articles/2008/september/best-sex-survey-ever.html (accessed May 30, 2017).

5. Michael Gurian, *What Could He Be Thinking? How a Man's Mind Really Works* (New York: St. Martin's, 2003), 109–10.

6. Gurian, *What Could He Be Thinking?* 113.

7. Shaunti Feldhahn, *For Women Only: What You Need to Know about the Inner Lives of Men* (Sisters, OR: Multnomah, 2004), 100.

8. Feldhahn, *For Women Only*, 100.

9. Feldhahn, *For Women Only*, 95.

10. Sheila Wray Gregoire, *The Good Girl's Guide to Great Sex* (Grand Rapids: Zondervan, 2012).

Chapter 12: The Problem of Porn

1. Dr. Fisher's comments are taken from a blog post he wrote titled "How to Treat a Porn Addiction," *To Love, Honor & Vacuum*, December 1, 2016, http://tolovehonorandvacuum.com/2016/12/treat-porn-addiction-psychologist-speaks (accessed May 30, 2017) and his follow-up remarks delivered to me personally. His wife's comments later in this section are based on her remarks in their online seminar on porn addiction, www.christiancrush.com/p/pornography-addiction-help.html (accessed May 30, 2017).

Chapter 14: John and Catherine: Finding Faith

1. Account and quotes taken from George and Karen Grant, *Best Friends: The Ordinary Relationships of Extraordinary People* (Nashville: Cumberland, 1998).

2. Grant and Grant, *Best Friends*, 113.

3. Charles W. Colson, *Born Again* (Old Tappan, NJ: Chosen, 1976).

Epilogue: Everlasting Beauty

1. Quoted in David McCullough, *John Adams* (New York: Simon & Schuster, 2001), 168.

2. McCullough, *John Adams*, 172.

3. McCullough, *John Adams*, 172.

4. McCullough, *John Adams*, 262.

5. McCullough, *John Adams*, 428–29.

6. McCullough, *John Adams*, 479.

7. McCullough, *John Adams*, 623.

8. McCullough, *John Adams*, 626.

A NOTE FROM GARY

Dear Readers,

Thank you so much for joining me on this journey. I hope you found it helpful. My sincere prayer is that you will have gained both significant insight into your husband's heart and mind and renewed spiritual fervor for God.

Some of you may be wondering, *What should I do now?* I have three suggestions. First, if you haven't read *Sacred Marriage*, I encourage you and your husband to do so, as this book provides the foundational thought for what you've just read. In addition to providing stories of how women have learned to draw nearer to their God as they learned to love their husbands, *Sacred Marriage* can introduce your husband to some of these same concepts in a context that will challenge *him*.

Second, consider reading *Devotions for a Sacred Marriage*. By reading one devotional entry a week (preferably with your spouse), and doing so faithfully for a year, you can begin to train your heart and mind to look at marriage through the perspective of how God is challenging you spiritually and personally. It takes time to retrain our minds to think biblically; I've worked hard to create a practical tool for just this purpose.

Finally, if you then want to take your marriage to the next level, consider reading *Cherish: The One Word That Changes Everything for Your Marriage*. This book explores practical ways to help couples not just love each other but cherish each other.

May God bless you as you seek to serve him by becoming the woman he created you to be, and may God continue to make your marriage a truly sacred, soul-shaping union that reflects Christ's love for the church.

The peace of Christ,
Gary Thomas

CONTACTING GARY

Although Gary enjoys hearing from readers, it is neither prudent nor possible for him to offer counsel via email, mail, Facebook, or other social media. Thanks for your understanding.

Website:
www.garythomas.com

Blog:
www.garythomas.com/blog

Twitter:
@garyLthomas

Facebook:
www.facebook.com/authorgarythomas

To book Gary for a speaking event, please contact him through his website or email alli@garythomas.com.

Sacred Marriage

What If God Designed Marriage to Make Us Holy More Than to Make Us Happy?

Gary Thomas

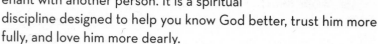

Your marriage is more than a sacred covenant with another person. It is a spiritual discipline designed to help you know God better, trust him more fully, and love him more dearly.

Sacred Marriage reveals how marriage trains us to love God and others well, how it exposes sin and makes us more aware of God's presence, how good marriages foster good prayer, how married sex feeds the spiritual life, and more.

The revised edition of *Sacred Marriage* takes into account the ways men's and women's roles have expanded since the book was first written. It has been streamlined to be a faster read without losing the depth that so many readers have valued.

Sacred Marriage uncovers the mystery of God's overarching purpose. This book may very well alter profoundly the contours of your marriage. It will most certainly change you. Because whether it is delightful or difficult, your marriage can become a doorway to a closer walk with God.

Available in stores and online!

Devotions for a Sacred Marriage

A Year of Weekly Devotions for Couples

Gary Thomas, bestselling author of Sacred Marriage

What if God designed marriage to make us holy more than to make us happy? By popular demand, the author of *Sacred Marriage* returns to the topic of how God uses marriage to expand our souls and make us holy.

With all new material, *Devotions for a Sacred Marriage* explores how God can reveal himself to you through your marriage and help you grow closer to him, as well as to your spouse. Fifty-two devotions encourage you to build your marriage around God's priorities.

From learning to live with a fellow sinner, to the process of two becoming one, to sharing our lives as brothers and sisters in Christ, *Devotions for a Sacred Marriage* challenges couples to embrace the profound and soul-stretching reality of Christian marriage.

Available in stores and online!

Sacred Marriage
Participant's Guide with DVD

What If God Designed Marriage to Make Us Holy More Than to Make Us Happy?

Gary Thomas with Kevin and Sherry Harney

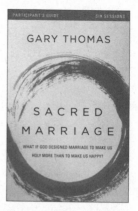

In this six-session small group Bible study, Gary Thomas invites you to see how God can use marriage as a discipline and a motivation to reflect more of the character of Jesus.

Your marriage is much more than a union between you and your spouse. It is a spiritual discipline ideally suited to help you know God more fully and intimately. *Sacred Marriage* shifts the focus from marital enrichment to spiritual enrichment in ways that can help you love your mate more. Whether it is delightful or difficult, your marriage can become a doorway to a closer walk with God.

Everything about your marriage—from the history you and your spouse create, to the love you share, to the forgiveness you both offer and seek—is filled with the capacity to help you grow in Christ's character.

In addition to life-changing insights, you'll find a wealth of discussion questions in this Participant's Guide that will spark meaningful conversation in your group, between you and your spouse, or to simply ponder by yourself. You'll also find self-assessments, activities, and highlights, all created to help you engage deeply and prayerfully with the content of this study.

Sessions include:
- God's Purpose for Marriage: More Than We Imagine
- The Refining Power of Marriage
- The God-Centered Spouse
- Sacred History
- Sexual Saints
- Marriage: The Love Laboratory

Cherish

The One Word That Changes Everything for Your Marriage

Gary Thomas, bestselling author of Sacred Marriage

Every man and woman wants to be cherished by their spouse. This book points to how a couple can make that happen.

When a husband and wife know they are cherished by their spouse, it brings out the best in both of them.

Bestselling author Gary Thomas believes that discovering how to better cherish your spouse has the power to infuse your relationship with new hope and promise. His earlier groundbreaking book, *Sacred Marriage*, changed the way husbands and wives thought aobut God's purpose for marriage. Now, he goes beyond love to explore how to create a *cherishing* marriage.

- Understand how you as a husband or wife can shape your mind and heart to treasure your spouse above all other men or women in the world.
- Learn how to remove the obstacles that keep you from holding your spouse in the highest regard.
- Discover the practical act of "showcasing" your spouse, which helps them thrive even as it increases your own affection for them.
- Husbands will be challenged to no longer make their wives feel "invisible," but rather honored, seen, and adored.
- Learn how to draw on God's empowering presence and truth to delight in your spouse as God delights in you.

Fill your relationship with new hope and promise. Unleash the power of cherish in your marriage.

Available in stores and online!

Cherish Study Guide with DVD

The One Word That Changes Everything for Your Marriage

Gary Thomas
with Beth Graybill

Millions of couples getting married have pledged to "love and to cherish, till death do us part." Most of us understand and get the love part ... but what does it mean to cherish our spouse? Why do we say it once at the wedding and then rarely even mention it again?

In this six-session video Bible study, Gary Thomas draws on personal stories and teachings from the Bible to show how cherishing can have a powerful effect on marriage. Learning to truly cherish each other turns marriage from an obligation into a delight and lifts marriage above a commitment to a precious priority. It is the melody that makes a marriage sing.

Many couples today survive by gritting their teeth and holding on. Or they find themselves just going through the motions in their relationship. But cherishing our spouse can reverse this pattern and can breathe light, hope, and new life into a marriage— even one marred by neglect and disrespect.

The *Cherish* Study Guide includes video discussion questions, Bible exploration, and personal study and reflection materials for use between sessions.

Sessions include:
- To Love and to Cherish
- Your Honor
- Taking Your Marriage to the Next Level
- Cherishing Your Unique Spouse
- This Is How Your Spouse Stumbles
- Keep on Cherishing